LITERARY
TITANS
REVISITED

LITERARY TITANS REVISITED

The Earle Toppings
Interviews with CanLit
Poets and Writers
of the Sixties

edited by
ANNE URBANCIC

DUNDURN
TORONTO

Printer: Webcom

Library and Archives Canada Cataloguing in Publication

Toppings, Earle, interviewer
    Literary titans revisited : the Earle Toppings interviews with CanLit poets and writers of the sixties / edited by Anne Urbancic.

Includes bibliographical references and index.
Issued in print and electronic formats.
ISBN 978-1-4597-3871-3 (softcover).--ISBN 978-1-4597-3872-0 (PDF).-- ISBN 978-1-4597-3873-7 (EPUB)

    1. Authors, Canadian (English)--Interviews. 2. Canadian literature
(English)--20th century--History and criticism. I. Urbancic, Anne, 1954-,
editor II. Title.

PS8117.T64 2017   C810.9'0054   C2017-902314-4
                                              C2017-902315-2

1   2   3   4   5   21   20   19   18   17

Conseil des Arts du Canada   Canada Council for the Arts   Canada   ONTARIO ARTS COUNCIL CONSEIL DES ARTS DE L'ONTARIO an Ontario government agency un organisme du gouvernement de l'Ontario

We acknowledge the support of the **Canada Council for the Arts**, which last year invested $153 million to bring the arts to Canadians throughout the country, and the **Ontario Arts Council** for our publishing program. We also acknowledge the financial support of the **Government of Ontario**, through the **Ontario Book Publishing Tax Credit** and the **Ontario Media Development Corporation**, and the **Government of Canada**.

Nous remercions le **Conseil des arts du Canada** de son soutien. L'an dernier, le Conseil a investi 153 millions de dollars pour mettre de l'art dans la vie des Canadiennes et des Canadiens de tout le pays.

— *J. Kirk Howard, President*

The publisher is not responsible for websites or their content unless they are owned by the publisher.

Printed and bound in Canada.

VISIT US AT

 dundurn.com | @dundurnpress |  dundurnpress | dundurnpress

Dundurn
3 Church Street, Suite 500
Toronto, Ontario, Canada
M5E 1M2

CONTENTS

INTRODUCTION

I magine the trepidation but also the excitement of a first-year student sent to the Victoria University Special Collections (or any archival facility, really) to choose an interesting subject whose letters, diaries, papers, artefacts, and ephemera could result in a fine final grade — if the student reads them and analyzes them appropriately. Where to start? How to organize all the information? And, finally, when to finish? Because as we all know, when we have discovered a treasure trove, we'd like the exploration to continue indefinitely.

This is what many of my students experience as they approach their major assignment in my first-year historiography and cultural memory course at Victoria College in the University of Toronto. I am always astonished by their discoveries, how carefully and thoughtfully they analyze and present their findings, and, most of all, how many of them are inspired to pursue more archival and primary source research as they continue their studies.

The historiography course is the genesis of the project that has turned into the little volume you are reading. It began with a young woman, Griffin Kelly, whose name will appear again later; the treasure box she examined contained papers, notes, and booklets but most significantly, a series of compact discs. Intrigued, she probed further and contacted the donor, Earle Toppings, who still resided in Toronto. He joined the class the day she presented her findings and then stayed to chat. Thanks to Earle Toppings, the end of the course was the beginning of our project.

What Griffin found on the compact discs were the interviews and readings of sixteen Canadian authors and poets. These sixteen are the pantheon of writers whose work heralded the birth of what is now affectionately called CanLit. As a genre, Canadian literature arrived late. Canada prides itself on its many excellent and exceptional authors and poets, but they had not often appeared on the world's literary stages until the second half of the twentieth century. Why? Many of the interviews you will read here will give you reasons to ponder and some insights. The interviewees acknowledged that, sadly, their works had been largely overlooked, except, perhaps, by an academic elite.

Nevertheless, as you read their interviews and poetry, you will soon discover that they are writers with universal appeal. They are uniquely Canadian but not narrowly academic. Their artistry meets all literary standards of excellence, and their themes speak to all of us. These sixteen writers were the powerhouses of literature in the 1960s and early 1970s. They provided the energy, the encouragement, and the inspiration for the fine poets and prose writers who have followed.

When former editor turned radio host and literary aficionado Earle Toppings chanced upon some unclaimed academic funds, he decided to record the voices of this pantheon. He used reel-to-reel tapes, which had become an obsolete medium years later when he tried to find a way to preserve them. The master tapes were no longer available. Undaunted, he found a technician, Dean Allen, who agreed to transfer the reel copies to compact discs. Even more happily for our project, Toppings donated the discs and relevant papers to Victoria University Special Collections where Griffin found them.

Transcribing the tapes ensured a new life for the authors Toppings captured on his tapes. These writers are all gone now, but in the pages of this book they remain fresh: perceptive, fascinating, sometimes almost prescient. Their words abound with acute observations and thoughtful reflections on their lives, on life in Canada, on Canada's life. It does not take long to realize the universality and timelessness of their work. Their writing explores themes that our society continues to grapple with today, almost half a century after they sat down with Dr. Toppings in a closet-size recording studio in downtown Toronto: the plight of the marginalized, the environment, the difficulties of finding one's self and place, the anxiety of getting it all wrong, the longing for love, the search for justice. Toppings expertly invites them to reveal the inner workings of their writing and their thoughts — not their "third divorce" as Toppings says in his own interview, but the fundamental elements that shaped their words, their sentences, their rhythms. Sixteen writers in frank conversation. Then, as a lagniappe, in his interview with the students, Toppings shares his own memories of the recording sessions to enrich our knowledge and thrill us with his interpretations of the writers and poets who sat opposite him at the recording table.

While the written page does not offer the timbre and cadences of their voices, it nonetheless brings back to us their conversations and readings that inform and delight. To revisit Gwendolyn McEwan's words in "The Compass," for example, is to envisage the shy exchange between the two writers on the same train: the eloquence of the young poet is meaningfully juxtaposed with the illiterate old man just learning to trace the letters of the alphabet, even though he, unschooled as he is, is the one who literally holds life's compass in his hand through his experiences. To read of Hugh Garner's difficult youth in his own parlance and contrast it with Mordecai Richler's contention that working at hard jobs would have made him more of a writer than having published a novel at age nineteen gives us pause to reflect on how our own selves are shaped by daily challenges. Raymond Souster evokes a cheeky but sympathetic smile with his image of two lovers in an amorous embrace, zipped up in a sleeping bag in front of City Hall. Is theirs a comment on restrictive social convention or an act of freedom? Earle Birney asks the same question in his poignant lines about the bear on the road to Delhi: the lumbering animal is taught to dance to earn small sums for his impoverished trainers. Are the trainers any freer than the bear? Miriam Waddington considers how her Jewish heritage affects how she sees the world; Irving Layton is also concerned with how being Jewish influences his poetry. In his self-recognition of being a father and a son, his poetry also reflects the interplay, sometimes gentle, sometimes gruff, of family. Eli Mandel presents a mythopoeic worldview, combining elements of myth and reality into a life lesson. Neither didactic nor pedantic, his lines evoke traces of tales told before recorded time, tales that continue to be relevant today. Dorothy Livesay describes how her own growth into personhood resembles the Canadian environment, and she envisages herself as the prairie wind or the silence of the vast country that envelops her. This metamorphosis is almost imperceptible to her as she engages in the act of creating poetry, and only later does she realize that her work marries nature and art. She does this in lines that imaginatively intertwine a Bartok concerto and a sunlit geranium brightening her windowsill.

Other writers also contemplate the influence of the Canadian land-scape on our collective psyche: what does *Canadian landscape* mean? How does it vary across the thousands of kilometres of this political entity that is Canada? How does it change over time? How does it feel to be part of it? Read the interviews of Morley Callaghan, Hugh MacLennan, and Margaret Laurence: all were established internationally before they gained the often grudging acknowledgement of Canadians. Nevertheless, they were all anxious to showcase the Canada they knew. In their words on tape, they celebrate their Canadian perspectives, as does F.R. Scott who delves into the promise of Canada's future with his invitation to give new names to the Canadian landscape. Why new names? For him the Canadian land is free, it is fresh; it is not burdened with the traditions, the histories, and the troubles of Europe; and therefore it deserves new, unencumbered names. Not so for Sinclair Ross, whose interview reveals an underlying but unmistakeable bitterness for not being read, not being understood, not being accepted. Al Purdy is not so harsh. For him it is true that Canada is not perfect, as he points out in his poignantly metaphorical verses about broken Indigenous art pieces that represent the plight of Canada's First Nations. His lines call for us to come to some understanding of who we are as Canadians and of how to accept the many generations that came before us, despite the brokenness. Just how many generations are needed before we understand our essential nature as Canadians? James Reaney suggests "1024 great great great great great great great great grandparents"; these are the generations that lead to the birth of one child.

The four undergraduate students who transcribed the tapes made a profound engagement with Canadian literature. The winners of Victoria College's first Northrop Frye Centre Undergraduate Research Award, they spent hours beyond their regular academic obligations researching, listening, typing, discussing, and, I'm quite certain, fretting over the final manuscript. Geoff Baillie, Amy Kalbun, Griffin Kelly, and Vipasha Shaikh are each responsible for four chapters of this book. They were helped immeasurably by Pratt Special Collections librarians Agatha Barc and Colin Deinhardt, who prepared training sessions for the specialized research demands and mentored the students throughout the project. With them, of course, was Earle Toppings, who patiently answered inquiries and himself agreed to an in-depth interview, moderated by Agatha Barc. His conversation with the students fills in many gaps, offers additional facts, and provides a comprehensive context for the complete project, both the original one and this written version.

From the first days of this project, we realized its significance as a personal history of the early years of CanLit. It is personal because it is told through the words of the poets and authors who nurtured Canadian literature into what it has become. It is a history because it records and preserves the nature and status of Canadian literature in the 1960s and early 1970s.

Perhaps the awareness that the writers display about their work and its place on the literary stage was prompted by the highly successful Canadian centennial celebration, especially Expo 67, the world exposition held in Montreal. Expo 67 marked a milestone moment when Canadians from sea to sea to sea began to take a new look at themselves and their society. And, despite tensions, they liked what they saw. That this present volume should celebrate Canada's sesquicentennial is a wonderful and appropriate coincidence. We see what they saw, and we like it very much.

Just a final note: as we worked we noticed that in many cases the poems read by our poets differed from their published versions. We have noted substantial discrepancies. We have chosen to respect the lines as read on the audiotapes.

MARGARET LAURENCE (1926–1987)

Margaret Laurence was a major western Canadian novelist and short-story writer, best known for chronicling life on the prairies from the perspectives of independent women. Born in 1926 in Neepawa, Manitoba, her early life was marked by tragedy. She lost her parents and grandmother in very quick succession as a child. These events introduced the concepts of mortality and impermanence into her life at a young age; these themes are carried throughout her writing. Laurence's stepmother, Margaret Simpson Wemyss, consistently supported Laurence's writing; she nurtured her daughter's interest in academia and encouraged her to make her passion a career. Laurence attended United College in Winnipeg and graduated in 1947. After she completed her studies, she worked as a reporter at the *Winnipeg Citizen* newspaper, a co-operative daily. In 1947 she married Jack Laurence, and together they moved to England, and then Ghana and Somaliland (now Somalia) for his career as an engineer.

Laurence's time in Africa gave her the push to write and a chance to express herself. Laurence wrote her first novel, *This Side Jordan*, in 1960, and then an account of their life in Somaliland, *The Prophet's Camel Bell*, in 1963. She was dedicated to social reform, an inclination arising from her own upbringing during the Great Depression. Her experience in Africa gave her direct contact with greater inequality. It furthered her interest in writing about the life of the individual, given her belief in the importance of recognizing and reflecting on personal experiences. She returned to Canada where she began writing what became her most popular novels: a series of interwoven stories about the fictional town of Manawaka, all of which are based on her hometown, Neepawa. The novels are characterized by their exploration of social themes and the presence of strong female characters, bold choices in Canadian literature at the time. These books, like *Bird in the House* (1970) and *A Jest of God* (1966), depict women as individuals, mothers, daughters, and professionals in situations so ordinary and every day that they are seldom remembered or valued. Her protagonists are identified by their strength, distinct sense of self, and independence. The semi-autobiographical elements of the novels gave Laurence the opportunity to reconcile with elements of her life, such as the passing of close family members. In addition, several Manawaka books feature the Tonnere family. The Tonneres are Métis who struggle with poverty, alcoholism, and discrimination by the rest of the town. Their isolation and plight is an accurate depiction of the Canadian treatment of Indigenous peoples.

Laurence's contributions to Canadian literature were recognized in 1972 when she was awarded the Order of Canada. She also won two Governor General's Awards for *Jest of God* and *The Diviners* (1974). Laurence described her works as an "act of hope," because they illuminate the history and life of the individual, attempts to reflect and recognize the value of each person. Margaret Laurence died in 1987.

References

Laurence, Margaret. *The Diviners*. Toronto: McClelland and Stewart, 1974.
———. *A Jest of God*. Toronto: McClelland and Stewart, 1966.
———. *This Side Jordan*. Toronto: McClelland and Stewart, 1960.
Nicholson, Colin. *Critical Approaches to the Fiction of Margaret Laurence*. Vancouver: UBC Press, 1990.
Thomas, Clara. *The Manawaka World of Margaret Laurence*. Toronto: McClelland and Stewart, 1975.

RECORDED ON APRIL 30, 1970

ET: "That peculiar voyage of exploration which constitutes a novel." Those are the words of Margaret Laurence. Margaret Laurence is with us, and I'd like to ask her first of all something about her background. That is, Margaret,

what foundation did you have for being a writer? Did you go to university or were you a dropout? Did you write for a newspaper?

ML: I wasn't a dropout. I don't think there were very many dropouts in my time. I grew up, you see, during the Depression and during the war in a small prairie town. Yes, I did go to university; it was really, extraordinarily difficult for my mother, who was a widow, to send me to university because no one had any money in those days and I wanted to go to university very much and went to what was then United College in Winnipeg. I worked on student newspapers and after I graduated, I worked on the old *Winnipeg Citizen*, which I now realize is not just Canada's only co-operative daily, but the English-speaking world has never apparently had a co-operative daily newspaper except the *Winnipeg Citizen*. Now it only lasted a year, but it was a great experience.

I think that what it did for me was to help me cut down the kind of purple prose that I had been writing at university and to learn, perhaps, a little more about a clean style. But it also taught one thing and that was I personally could not combine journalism with my own writing, because when you've been pounding a typewriter all day, and writing obituaries and news stories, there's no way you can go home at night and start working on a novel.

As far as what actually made me become a writer, I think I always was a writer. It seemed to me that from the time I was a very young kid, this was my natural mode of expressing myself. I used to tell stories, apparently, before I could write, and as soon as I learned to write at school, I used to write poetry and stories, and my mother used to read them and give me a kind of criticism of them … she was very good, as a matter of fact. She was my stepmother … my father had married my mother's sister a year after my own mother's death … and so, I was brought up by my stepmother and I loved her very dearly. And she was great on criticizing my stories because she was always very tactful and yet very honest. I can remember when I was about … I must have been about ten, twelve, and I wrote a play about the English aristocracy. Well, as you can well imagine what a prairie kid knew about the English aristocracy was minimal, and my mother gently suggested that it might be a good idea … some people thought it was a good idea … to write about what you knew.

ET: Were there certain events … it sounds as if there were, prairie town and all that — it was a very full life, for a very young girl — are there certain events that you remember vividly in your life that were dramatic and that somehow influenced your own art?

ML: I think this sounds like a very gloomy thing to say, but I think the things that probably influenced my writing to great extent were the number of deaths in the family. My mother had died when I was four, and my father died when I was ten or eleven, and a very beloved grandmother died about a year after that; and so it seems to me that there were a number of deaths in the family, and my childhood seems to be sort of signposted by these events. I don't know whether this actually made me want to write more; I think it probably did. I was a pretty solitary child, and these events must obviously have had a pretty deep impact; but many years later I found myself writing a series of autobiographical short stories, which have been collected in a book called *A Bird in the House*. These are the only autobiographical fiction I've ever written, but most of these stories are more or less as it happened to me as a child … and these deaths come in, at least the death of my grandmother and the death of my father … and it was only through writing those stories that I began to see how deeply I must have been affected by this as a kid.

ET: This is interesting because it is actually one of the things I was going to ask you. There is, in an amount of your writing, mention of funeral parlours, and there's almost a fear of death … or as if death is imminent … as if the angel of death is hovering over some of your stories.

ML: I think this is true probably, although I like to think that there is a great deal of humour in my writing, too. I think I have always got this kind of ambiguous attitude towards life, but I think you're right … there is a sort of sense of death. You see, most kids don't realize when they're very young that they themselves are going to die. I was never in the slightest doubt about it, because I think my mother and father dying and so on. And of course as far as the funeral parlour business is concerned, I think the reason for that coming in — this was at a very subconscious level I suppose — but my grandfather was an undertaker. Now, this was the old man who stalks through the short stories in *A Bird in the House*. He was Ontario Irish — they used to say in my family "famine-Irish but thank God Protestant" — and he had had to leave school when he was twelve, when his father died, to support his mother and two no-good brothers … and his brothers really were no good, too. I only knew one of them, who comes into the stories as Uncle Dan, and he really was a horse trader and a drunk … and he was one of the most charming and delightful men I have ever known. I used to just love him as a kid. He used to take me tobogganing. He always … whenever he bowled into town, his old navy serge overcoat … used to have a pocket full of humbugs [candies]. They were always covered with a kind of disgusting looking fluff, and he was a great guy and he used to sing stage Irish songs, and I have thought since how very unfair it was, really, that all of us loved him. None of us loved the old man but that it was the old man, my grandfather, who had actually supported his brother for years. When my grandfather went to Manitoba, which was in the late 1800s, he went out by steamer and he walked from Winnipeg to Portage la Prairie as a kid of about oh … I suppose seventeen or eighteen. He didn't have a nickel in his pockets. He was really, totally, a self-made man in that way. He was a genuine pioneer. He was a cabinetmaker, and he became later on an undertaker … which was very often done in those days, because, after all, the cabinetmakers made all coffins … and I think this is possibly one reason why the sort of funeral parlour thing comes in. Although by the time I came along, he was no longer in the undertaking business, but he had more or less forced one of his sons to go into the business, and my uncle had not really wanted to, I think. So perhaps, you know, part of this comes from there. But the thing that interests me about the old man at this distance ... because I'm sure that he had an enormous influence not only on my life and my character and everything, but on my writing as well ... and what happened when I wrote *A Bird in the House*, all those stories, was that when I began them I still actively disliked my grandfather although he'd been dead for many years. By the time I wrote the last story, I no longer detested him: in fact, in some kind of peculiar begrudging way, I knew that I loved him.

ET: Do you find that writing is a form of reconciliation, not with people you know necessarily but to some extent with oneself but also with the characters and situations you're writing about?

ML: Yes, it certainly is for me, anyway, and that's why that remark that you made in the beginning quotation from something I had said about a novel being "a voyage of discovery." Well, for me this is what it is, and it's partly, I think, a sort of attempt always on the part of a writer to come to terms with oneself, with one's past, with one's childhood experiences, and also with various emotional dilemmas of one's present life even. So that, although except in those autobiographical short stories, I've never written directly about myself; that is, all my fiction is fiction. The characters are not drawn from life; none of them are. Lots of people have asked me where Hagar came from, the old lady in *The Stone Angel*. Well, I don't know where she came from: she just suddenly presented herself to me, and after she'd been living in my mind for a few years, I felt as though she were beginning to tell me her life story. But I could see after I'd finished the book, that, in point of fact, what I had been doing, partly at least, was to try to explore, at a kind of depth level, my own ancestry, 'cause she was my grandfather's generation, my grandparents' generation, and she was of Scots Presbyterian background, which is my background, and she had all the stern virtues of the kind of people I came from, and this was both her strength and her tragedy.

ET: You're exploring a culture in a way: you're getting to know again, the people you lived among ... not specific people, not Minnie and Fred, but the types of people you knew.

ML: I think this is right and because of this, because of trying to come to some kind of terms with one's own background, what one is really trying to do, too, is to reconcile the warring elements within oneself because, of course, all of us are very ambiguous in our feelings about our families, about every aspect of life, and I think what one is really trying to do is to come to some kind of reconciliation with all of the various aspects of one's own character.

ET: Margaret, you've said that in your one book of non-fiction, *The Prophet's Camel Bell* — which I suppose one might call a travel book for want of a good definition — you've said that that's not really as true as your novels. You seem to feel the truth of what you have to say is conveyed in fiction. How do you explain that?

ML: Well, it seems to me that — just speaking personally; this is not true for all writers, but it's true for me, I think — I don't think I can tell as much of the truth, as much as my own truth, because after all there is no absolute truth. When I say "tell the truth," I mean as I see it ... and I don't think I can in non-fiction as well as I can in fiction, partly because I'm too inhibited. That is, one is talking about people who really exist and you really have to consider them. And in this particular instance, with *The Prophet's Camel Bell*, this was about our experiences in Somaliland, and I did find that it was extremely difficult, particularly with the Europeans whom I had not liked, and there were many. There was no way, really, that I was going to write a sort of scathing denunciation of them because after all, they were passing out of history ... they were like the dinosaurs ... that it would really be flogging a dead horse. But it was very difficult to write even about the people that I liked, because one has to consider people's privacy, you know, and so that where I am dealing with fictional characters, you're sort of totally free ... and this is a very exhilarating as well as painful process because you are totally free to put down anything about the character that seems relevant.

ET: Also, if you're writing as a journalist, or a researcher, you're talking about someone's truth. You're not talking about your truth, in the sense of your personal truth; you're trying to explain the truth of someone else, I would expect.

ML: Well, yes, you are, and of course to this extent you're never sure that you're interpreting correctly. You're never really sure of that with your fictional characters, but that's all you've got, you've got to try and interpret as correctly as you can. And I think this is one reason why the last four books of fiction — all of the books of fiction set in Canada — have been written in the first person. *The Fire-Dwellers* wasn't totally in the first person; there was a certain amount of third person narration because I wanted to get some slight sort of sense of distance with Stacey. Almost all of those four books are written in the first person, and I think this is because I feel very strongly that this is the way we view life. We can only view through one pair of eyes ... that's all we've got ... so that what I think I'm trying to do when I write in the first person and through the eyes of the chief character — what I'm really trying to do is to see life through their eyes, not necessarily my own and —

ET: And without being omniscient, without being some kind of God figure on the outside.

ML: Well, this is the whole point. This is exactly the reason why with the contemporary novel, so many people do write in the first person, because it just doesn't seem possible anymore to take the God's eye view. And I don't say this is the only way of writing: obviously many people still can write, and write extraordinarily well, in the third person. But some of us don't find this any longer very possible because, in fact, one is perceiving life only through one pair of eyes, as I say, and I think what I'm trying to do when I write in the first person is to sort of, for the time that I'm writing, almost take on the persona of that character. In other words, when I'm actually trying to get it down on paper, to become that character, which is a kind of sleight of hand. But you see, this is the whole thing that I feel about writing, that in a way what a writer's trying to do is be a magician of some kind.

ET: When you write a story or write a novel, what do you want it to do most of all?

ML: I think I'm concerned with character more than with anything else. What I would like to be able to do more than anything is to create characters that practically step off the printed page. I think this is partly because I didn't realize this for a long time, but I do realize it about myself now. I am really very much concerned about individuals because I think that in this present world, an individual is really losing value, is being depersonalized by this kind of society. I think this is appalling, and I think the only thing a writer can do is to try to create individual characters who will appear to the reader as real people, with real individual dilemmas. In other words, to try to make the reader feel the character's pain, that this particular person matters. I felt that very much about somebody like Hagar, who's ninety years old, and what can happen to her. Obviously, she's going to die, but it's the manner of her dying and the manner of her past life that matters. And I felt the same thing about Rachel in *A Jest of God*. She's a thirty-four-year old spinster schoolteacher in a small town and in a sense you can say well, she's an ordinary individual, she doesn't matter very much. I think she matters tremendously and I think that we ignore this kind of individual at our very great peril. I felt the same about Stacey in *The Fire-Dwellers*. And first when I began to write, I thought, *Good heavens, who's going to be interested in reading about a middle-aged woman with four children and you know ten pounds of excess fat, and all this sort of thing?*

ET: Because everybody's going to say she's ordinary.

ML: Because everybody's going to say she's ordinary. She is not ordinary, because nobody is, and I thought very much about that. I kept thinking of the remark that Willy Loman's wife made in Arthur Miller's play *Death of a Salesman*: "Attention must be paid." And I really do believe that; and I mean maybe that sounds corny, but this is my article of faith. Although I think this is a terrifying world that we live in, the act of writing itself is almost an act of faith, almost an act of hope. And in a profound sense it's a kind of celebration of life: it's really saying, at the heart of it, life is very much worth living and, for God's sake, let's make of it what we can.

ET: Do you think that your books can change things? Do you think they can change people? Do you think they can change the reader's way of looking at his life?

ML: I don't know. I don't think it's really given to a writer to know that. I think that it's sort of the same, perhaps, as with a teacher: that whatever effect your books may have had, you don't generally know. Sometimes, you get a kind of feedback where people will say to you what a particular book has meant to them. I remember one remark that a woman made to me not very long ago, which really touched me very much. She said that when she read *The Stone Angel*, it helped her very much to understand better her aged mother and she said: "But looking at it the other way around, Mother helped me to understand Hagar": which I thought was great because what it had communicated to her was the sense that Hagar was a real person, and this is what really matters to me.

ET: You've said, Margaret, that what you want to do — one of the chief things you want to do — is to convey what everybody knows but nobody says. What do you mean by that?

ML: Well, I think, for example, when I made that remark probably I was thinking of Stacey in *The Fire-Dwellers*. I think I must have been thinking of her. I can't exactly remember but it seemed to me that an awful lot of Stacey's life ... a lot of the dilemmas that she felt, a lot of the hang-ups that she had, a lot of the anguish that she felt toward her children and so on ... were things that a great many people must feel, but don't really talk about very much, perhaps don't even express to themselves as much as Stacey did, because she verbalized very extensively in her mind. And I think that I felt that this kind of person perceived quite a lot about herself, and that an awful lot of people must know these same things but didn't necessarily go around spouting about them, of course. This is where it's lovely to be a writer because you can go around talking about things that people don't talk about normally. This is kind of poetic licence, I suppose.

ET: And in your focusing so intensely on this character Stacey in *The Fire-Dwellers*, you show that, although she seems average, outwardly, really she has very deep and penetrated conflicts, concerns, hopes. She's also a person in our Canadian tradition, I think, who denies herself a great deal and continually disputes with herself, doesn't she? She's continually saying, "No, Stacey, you can't think that" ... it's not allowed that you could think negatively, of herself.

ML: Yes, she has got a great many conflicts and she tries to come to a kind of settlement of them. I don't think she really succeeds, although she does to some extent. But certainly she's always arguing with herself and even her discussions with God … her sort of monologues, where she's addressing God … she's really in a sense addressing herself. She's carrying on a conversation, an imaginary conversation with God, a god in whom she only half believes and also only half disbelieves … so she is a sort of mass of ambiguities. Personally, I feel great sympathy for her because I feel I am a mass of ambiguities, too, and I think almost everybody is.

ET: And this, as you say, is what people won't admit: they know it but they won't say it.

Something that is exactly the opposite of despair, lest I convey any sense of despair, is that these people do hang on so tightly and that they really have such an enormous amount of courage: Rachael, Stacey, Hagar. And perhaps one of the most obvious elements of hope in these books is that these people damn well don't give up.

ML: I think that's right. I feel very much about all of them that they really are survivors: they're not about to lie down and die before they have to. And I think this is a sort of very important aspect of life, really. I think it is a triumph in a sense just to survive with some kind of dignity and hopefully, some joy. I think of Stacey as almost Hagar's spiritual granddaughter, because at the very end of the book, she says something like, "Give me another forty years, Lord, and I may mutate into a matriarch." I was thinking of Hagar as I wrote that. But I think also, as well as dealing with the theme of survival, that in almost all my writing, I dealt also with the theme really of freedom, which I began writing about, I think, in the African books. At that time, it seemed to me with my first novel, *This Side Jordan*, that I was talking about freedom in terms of African independence but I was also thinking of it in terms of Nathaniel's inner freedom because the outer freedom, the outer independence, is never really enough. It's what goes on inside that matters as well, and Nathaniel had great hang-ups and difficulties in freeing himself from the sort of the dead hand of the past, as it were. It was only years later that I realized this particular dilemma of freeing oneself from the ancestral past without actually throwing the whole of the past overboard, that this was my dilemma, as well as Nathaniel's. It was a great many people's dilemma; it was not just an African one — it was a universal one if you like. And I think that the whole sort of theme of inner freedom is something that to some extent comes into all my writing because certainly in those three novels, *The Stone Angel*, *A Jest of God*, and *The Fire-Dwellers*, all these characters, in some way or other, are trying to reach some sort of inner freedom, which means that they can give and receive love, that they can experience joy, that they can really become more alive.

ET: Yes, these characters, then, are all in a process of growth.

ML: Oh, yes, very much, and I think this is something, that perhaps one could almost equate freedom, inner freedom, with growth in that way.

ET: And if we don't stop growing, there's still hope for us. You've lived and continue to live in a sense, Margaret, in three worlds — Africa, England, and Canada — and your writing can be marvellously varied from one continent to another. I'm especially fond of the stories in *The Tomorrow Tamer*, the African stories, partly because they bring me people I don't know. I know the prairie people, but I don't know the Africans and you bring them complete with colour and dialect and the way their minds work and the way they respond to white Europeans. Do you find that you are a different writer on different shores? For example, are you planning to write out of an English context?[1]

ML: I don't think I am. I think that England is full of good novelists, and let them deal with their own people. I would not. Even if I went back to Africa now, I don't think I'd write anything more out of Africa. I think that probably I will have to continue writing out of my own background. This is not to say that I might not write something that is set in England. I might, but I think that the chief characters would probably have to be people who had backgrounds that I knew extremely well, such as my own; because, after all, I think now that the thing that counts when writing a novel is that you really are making use of a great many details from the past that you didn't even know you knew. This is the sort of real, cultural strength. I don't think that what I wrote about Africa was totally false or phony. I really think that it did have some authenticity, and West African friends have told me that they think it does, too. But when I finished writing those stories, and that novel, I felt that I really had gone as far as I personally could go to get inside the minds and hearts of people of a totally different culture from my own. I knew that if I went on writing about Africa, I would really be writing about it in a sense as a tourist. And that's one reason why I wanted to return … and I mean return spiritually, mentally … and write out of my own background.

ET: Do you mean while you were in Africa you still wrote as a stranger, and you were writing about the intermingling of strangers and Indigenous people?

ML: I am not sure how true my portraits of Africans are; it's something I really can't know. I think some of them came across reasonably well, because I have got a fairly good ear for human speech.

ET: Well, there certainly is a truth in that we expect these people to be presented as a white Canadian sees them.

ML: Well, this is it, you see. The point is that I couldn't possibly write as an African. I couldn't write that deeply from the inside.

ET: And you're not trying to … you're not intending to.

ML: No! Because it was only years after I finished *This Side Jordan* and *The Tomorrow Tamer,* when I began to read a great deal of writing by Africans such as Chinua Achebe from Nigeria.[2] And I began to realize then how right I had been in stopping writing about Africa, because really only an African could write very deeply from the inside … and also only a Canadian born in a small prairie town could write about that very deeply from the inside, and that was my business. As Mordecai Richler[3] once said about his own background in Montreal, he said: "This was my time and my place, and I have set myself to get it exactly right."

ET: It's very heartening to people who read books to see that you've had so much acceptance in your own country, before many, many, many years have gone by. People like Morley Callaghan[4] were neglected for a long, long time in their own country except for programs and CBC. How do you feel about being a writer in this country? Can you stay in this country and survive as a writer, or do you have to go where writing has a higher value, in England for example?

ML: No, I could survive here as a writer better than I could ultimately in England. Actually, my books have continued to sell in Canada better than anywhere else. I certainly couldn't survive probably without American sales as well, but I think that I could probably survive as a writer on writing in this country far better than in England. For example, if my books had been published only in England, I would be starving. It isn't that my publishers don't want to give me as high an advance as they can, but there are thousands of novels published in England every year. There are more novels apparently in England in a year than in America, which is astonishing when you think of it. So that naturally, the individual writer does really very poorly unless their works are published elsewhere. I think at this point I could survive as a writer, and probably in every other way, too, better in Canada than anywhere else, and I want to come back and live here, and I will.

ET: Margaret Laurence, as a writer, what do you most want to be remembered for?

ML: I don't think that it's very realistic for a writer to expect to be remembered longer than about twenty-five years, if you're lucky. You know we're not really in it for the immortality stakes. I think it was Arthur Miller who expressed it very well: he said that if a writer was trying to write in order to become immortal, it was like trying to carve your name on a block of ice, out in the middle of the street on a hot July day … and I'm sure this is true. I don't think I will be remembered. If I'm remembered for a short time, I would like it to be probably for having created maybe even just one character that came alive.

Transcribed by Griffin Kelly

MORLEY CALLAGHAN (1903–1990)

Morley Callaghan is considered one of Canada's greatest writers because of his prolific writing career and association with the Lost Generation arts community. Callaghan was born in 1903 in Toronto and raised as a Roman Catholic. He attended St. Michael's College at the University of Toronto and went on to study law. After completing his education, Callaghan worked as a reporter for the *Toronto Star*, which he credits for teaching him clean, sparse prose. In the newsroom Callaghan met Ernest Hemingway, who helped him connect with the elite literary communities in New York and Paris. This led to the publication of Callaghan's first novel, *Strange Fugitive*, in 1928, considered the first Canadian urban novel. The story follows a gangster in 1920s prohibition-era Toronto. Callaghan's novel takes place in a neighbourhood called "The Ward," a slum area of the city characterized by high rates of crime, poverty, and drug use. Callaghan stated that his books, like *Such Is My Beloved* (1934) and *More Joy in Heaven* (1937), were all based on life in Toronto and Montreal. These expressions of the urban experience offered a contrasting vision of Canada from the traditional pastoral narrative. Callaghan was deeply committed to writing from an independent perspective, one untouched and uninfluenced by literary trends or other authors. He was concerned about the adoption of trends, as he felt that common themes in art or society would narrow the exchange of ideas. This was especially important for writers, who have a social responsibility to depict the human experience accurately. Such a reflection should not be diluted by trends. Consequently, Callaghan believed that an independent writing voice and style were crucial to success. He felt that each individual has their own private understanding of the world from which they draw personal dignity and strength to create a sense of independence and freedom. Callaghan was often critical of publishers who did not want to challenge audiences by sharing crucial distinctive voices.

The importance of the inner world is seen in his writing, through his exploration of private shame and humiliation that characters grapple with, such as the priest who aids prostitutes in *Such Is My Beloved*.

Callaghan's career was marked by his inclusion in the Parisian literary community of the late 1920s, but he was quick to differentiate himself from major figureheads of the time, like James Joyce. His close friendship with Hemingway ended abruptly after a boxing match in which Callaghan knocked out Hemingway while F. Scott Fitzgerald looked on. Callaghan reflects on this time in his memoir, *That Summer in Paris* (1963). After returning to Toronto, Callaghan worked as a radio broadcaster from the 1930s to the 1950s to support his young family. He returned to the literary scene in 1951 with *The Loved and the Lost*, for which he received a Governor General's Award. In 1982 he was given the Order of Canada. He died in 1990, leaving a legacy as one of Canada's most influential writers.

References

Callaghan, Morley. "Solzhenitsyn." *Tamarack Review* 55 (1970): 71–76.

———. *Such Is My Beloved.* Toronto: McClelland and Stewart, 1957.

———. *That Summer in Paris: Memories of Tangled Friendships with Hemingway, Fitzgerald, and Some Others.* New York: Coward-McCann, 1963.

Edwards, Justin D. "Strange Fugitive, Strange City: Reading Urban Space in Morley Callaghan's Toronto." *Studies in Canadian Literature* 23, no. 1 (1998): 213–27.

Snider, Norman. "Why Morley Callaghan Still Matters." *Globe and Mail*, October 25, 2008.

Vyhnak, Carola. "Morley Callaghan Both Loved and Lost in Toronto." *Toronto Star*, August 25, 2015.

Whalley, George, and Morley Callaghan. *Writing in Canada; Proceedings of the Canadian Writers' Conference, Queen's University, 28–31 July 1955.* Toronto: Macmillan of Canada, 1956.

ET: "I choose to think that the art of fiction is the greatest of all arts because the writer has for his material the ways of men and women in their relationship to each other. It is an art that has a providential quality. The writer in his pages is giving form to the stuff of life." That was written by Morley Callaghan. Mr. Callaghan is with us and I'd appreciate it if he'd comment a little further on that quotation of his.

MC: Well, that's put very well just as it is. I don't know if it needs any further comment, but the interesting thing about it is there's no mystification in that. If you, anybody, who has lived in this world, say beyond his boyhood, knows that his whole life simply consists of his relationships, it's all life is ... unless you get marooned on an island; then you die of loneliness. Soon as you're in a world, in any kind of society ... society, one's personal life ... everything lies in the relationships, whether you are going to reorganize society, reorganize family, everything lies in relationships.

Now, it so happens, you see, that in fiction, maybe it takes a writer some time to realize or wonder whether his work has any depth or if there's something dreadfully wrong with it. And if there is, you see, then he discovers that what you might call his characters somehow rather don't seem to create a recognizable layer of reality in the way they meet or mesh together and so on. And when the work is extraordinary, the characters in the book will have a kind of unquestioned relationship ... the relationships will seem to be almost inevitable, even when they're almost chance encounters. This is what will give verisimilitude to the thing ... why you'll say, "This is life!"

Take a Chekhovian play. Well, it seems to me that Chekhov, far more than Shakespeare, for example, knows that the beauty and the poetry and the drama and the whole aura that he's going to wrap the scene in, the whole mystery of life, will simply come out of getting people to come together and show them in certain relationships. You may say, "Shakespeare, doesn't he do this?" No, Shakespeare does it in scenes, that is, scenes that are going somewhere and are advancing his theme, and this is great, you know. I'm not trying to put Shakespeare down, but he would be advancing the theme to some powerful conclusion, whereas the great poignant moments in Chekhov seem to come in irrelevant scenes ... simply out of the relationship of the characters, because they are there; because within themselves, they have a kind of being, and these little sets of beings, call them characters, are brushing against each other all the time. And so the play is held together because the relationships are right; you see now that by the very nature of his work ... the artist, the fiction writer ... he's simply creating a basis of all societies. That is, he is dealing with the relationships of people. Then if you want to go on ... I use that word *providential*, I suppose, in a Christian sense ... but if you want to go on to the whole business of ethics, and morality, and even of religion ... you see that all comes out of man and his relationship with another man or another woman. The whole thing is there, in those relationships, you see, and whatever the man he is ... that is the artist, writer ... he'll show all this about himself in the way he handles those relationships. He's really giving you his view of life in the way he handles those relationships ... so to go jump beyond what you see, this is why it's providential. It takes on the artist, takes almost an aspect of providence, because the whole thing is in his hands.

ET: Mr. Callaghan, what are your thoughts on material? You were interested in what people do to each other, as you say, the way they relate to each other. What is your material, or what can you tell us about the material you work with?

MC: You can take the shabbiest piece of old material, this might be a little bit typical, but if your perception into that material is distinguished, if it's unique, if it's your own material, the story will be distinctive, and you'll get it printed. People will read that. I remember Sinclair Lewis,[1] when I was first starting to write ... the thing he said about writing, what he said about me — which was widely quoted at the time — was that he knew no one who found

the remarkable in the ordinary as I do. And he said that was great art; he said
that is the job of the artist. Tolstoy had this conviction, too, you know: find
the remarkable in the ordinary. Now, the way it is now, I see fashions, trends
change, and the current idea is to hit the reader so hard on the mouth, in the
eye, or something, shock him with material that is strange to him … so strange
to him that his jaw will fall slack. Well, that's all right; you do get a shock, and
other writers get pushed aside, but I don't think they last long. I'll give you an
idea of what I mean by an old story. Did you take to talking about movies?
Did you see *Midnight Cowboy*?[2] Now that's a very interesting piece. It's not
accidental that that movie did so well, because the story in it, the relationship
between those two men, the ridiculous imbecile and charming cowboy, you
know, and Dustin Hoffman. You see, actually, the relationship between those
two, which was what was holding the story together, was ancient; it's been
done so often by writers that most writers would be ashamed to ever have
touched the thing you see, two misfits, two lonely, down —

ET: *Of Mice and Men.*[3]

MC: Two beaten guys, yeah, and, finally, it ends up with one guy carrying one
guy off to Florida to have him die in the sunlight or something. Well, this is
Ladies' Home Journal or something. *Ladies' Home Journal* would be embarrassed
to do that story straight, but the important thing about the story, about the
movie, as far as the success, they dressed it up; there was fantasy, they put it in
a bed of fantasy, and then they had all the current things going for it: homo-
sexuality, sexuality, the perversion of 42nd Street, the absolute permissiveness
of society. All these things were just really window dressing. They made the
thing seem utterly new. This is great, and in it was this really beaten-up, moving, sentimental old story which Dustin Hoffman does so well. That was the
thing … this is what you can do with any kind of material. Your material might
be absolutely old, shabby, but if you see it freshly, this is all you want. That's art.

ET: What do you think, Mr. Callaghan, is the most important single skill or
attribute of the writer? What does a writer have to have?

MC: Boy, I don't know. I guess the two things he simply has to have: he has
to have an eye and an ear. If he hasn't got an eye and an ear he simply can't go

anywhere. The eye and the ear are probably more important than facility, because, well, dreadful, superficial hacks can have great facility. He may write very painfully, very laboriously, and almost clumsily; he may seem to be fumbling. But if the eye and the ear are unique, you see, he could be a very remarkable writer.

ET: When you write, then, do you feel that you're seeing something in your characters and in the way they relate to each other that other people don't see?

MC: No, I don't make as big a thing out of it as that. I just try very hard to have a thing grow in my head until it seems to add up to something that I think should be impressive, that moves me and I think has some universal application. It's something like a cake, I suppose, in an oven; this cake in your oven, and it's just cooking away there and suddenly gets to the point where you think, you know, this is it. A writer is always like an oven going on, always the whole series of little biscuits cooking in this oven, and sometimes, you know, you open the oven door and peek in, and some of the cakes have fallen. You remember probably … I don't know whether your mother used to do it … I remember my mother when she was making a cake, she'd put a straw in the cake to see if it was going to fall or something; well, that's what a writer is doing. He has a whole series of little biscuits in the oven. Sometimes he puts a straw in and the cake falls, you know, and he just forgets it. It doesn't grow beyond a certain point that — when you know you've got a story, when just suddenly, there it is. My style consists of having the right feeling … seeing the thing as I want to see it … then writing as rapidly as possible and trying to reject all literature along the way — if you can figure that out — anything that remotely resembles the literary touch or someone else's touch.

ET: What had put your back up about being part of literature?

MC: Because, you see, the job of a writer is to make literature, and now there's some very great men who have thought that writing must depend on literature, that writing is almost an evolutionary growth of literature, that all of literature relates, and that it is nothing to worry about if your work shows the influences of others. I figured this would happen automatically, that if there were influences in your mind, and on your eye and so on, and they would come out, just as you'd try to reject everything.

ET: When you speak about literature, do you think of literature as a subject that's studied in university or a critical discipline? Something that is rather apart from the writer because it's like a secondary industry that feeds on what he produces?

MC: No, I'm not speaking of literature of this respect. If you're going to, you should have the impulse … the impulse should be strong enough in you … and within the impulse would be this business of your eye and your ear … and that coupled with the urge you should have that should be strong enough to make you forget any influences there have been on you. If you ever came to a place where you stopped and said to yourself, "Now how would Conrad do this?"[4] or "How would Joyce do it?" That means that your compulsion at that point has broken down.

ET: Do you mean that it's your story, and you're doing your best to tell it your way?

MC: That's about all it amounts to. My story. This is the way I'd like to tell that story. In fact, this is the only way I think I could tell this story. And if you convince yourself that if you tell it right, it's a great story. That's all there is to it, really. This is my story, you see, this is the way I like telling stories. The trouble with my work is that it looks, right at the start, as if you know what this is all about, because it looks familiar, the way it's put down; it all looks as if this is going to be very familiar, and then you have to read on to realize that it's not familiar … you're entering another thing … but on the surface it's all familiar, and this has been the handicap.

ET: Is there something Oriental in your background or have you read Oriental philosophy? There's something very —

MC: This is very strange, and very perceptive you should say that because I'll tell you a little secret. When I was about nineteen or twenty in college, Arthur Waley's translation[5] of Chinese poems fascinated me and in an odd kind of way. I mean later on, Ezra Pound[6] also translated Chinese poems, like cantos and all that kind of stuff. I may have been relying on Waley's translation but the thing must be there. I was fascinated at the way these poems hung in the air. They had none of the stuff, the flourish, of European literature … they were just there. That is, the ones that I liked. There were others of a more formal order that you would say were definitely within a tradition. Maybe the ones I liked so much were also definitely within a tradition, I couldn't say; but the grander ones, which were obviously within a more florid Chinese tradition, they didn't appeal to me. I could sort of see that same thing in the European, but there was a whole order of poems in different periods where the poem just seemed to hang there … you know, be by itself … and this used to fascinate me, you know. You either got the impact of the thing or you didn't get it.

ET: And you didn't approach it by comparing it with anything else?

MC: No, you don't. It didn't pay to compare it with anything else. I wanted to get stories, or get novels so that they didn't fit into the technique of the novel. They should've fit into the technique, but that technique of the novel stuff … that's for writers about the novel. I wanted to write stories that shouldn't be demonstrating technique.

ET: Some people are concerned that you hadn't written about particularly Canadian themes, and you note yourself that you haven't written a book about John A. MacDonald or the Mounted Police. It seems to me, though, that you were perhaps our first international writer in the twenties. What do Canadian themes mean to you, or what does it mean to you to say that you are a Canadian novelist?

MC: Well, you see, this is all rather odd. *Strange Fugitive* was written right here in Toronto; and *Such Is My Beloved,* just lifted right off the streets of Toronto; and *More Joy in Heaven* is lifted right off the streets of Toronto. You never get more in this world … you won't get stuff written about Canadians, Canadian scenes of cities … more than you get in those books. Now it used to bother people that why did Americans, why did New York people, who have written a lot of stories in the *New Yorker,* why did they want to print these things of mine, not some of these other Canadians' things? Well, there is only one simple answer. You should know the answer without asking me: these were better. That's all there was to them. There was a notion prevailing that if you write … this was a dreadful thing we did … if you are a

Canadian, that you have a kind of very special quality about you so that it will only be published in Canada and will only be liked by other writers who can't get published anywhere else. This is stupid.

ET: I think, too, that some of these people are under the misapprehension that the theme has to serve some other purpose — history or geography or something.

MC: I was kidding about John A. MacDonald. That was in that speech I made because, when I was a boy I remember there was always somebody writing a Big Canadian Novel, and I used to note with some wonder that the CPR[7] didn't get in to it. Sir John A. did. And this all struck me as rather preposterous. I didn't know Sir John A. MacDonald; I had, at that time, nothing to do with the CPR. I didn't see the romance of Canada. And as far as Sir John A. MacDonald is concerned, there's a very interesting point involved here. One of the things I was smart enough to discover at the age of seventeen was that politics was a substitute for culture in this country. People could all talk politics and nothing else, and no one read anything but political documents. You weren't going to have a riot over the performance of a strange symphony or a book, but you might well have a political riot. This is all raw. This doesn't represent an advanced state of culture in any way. You look at your historians ... they're still doing it: they write the lives. A history is a history of the people, I suppose, or there's no use in calling it the history of the people. [Historians] don't deal with the history of the people at all; they just write about the manoeuvrings, the triumphs and successes of politicians who would all be long ago forgotten if the historians didn't keep dragging them in, and no one remembers the name of politicians.

ET: When students are directed to your books now, to find background on yourself, they're of course sent to look up *That Summer in Paris*, and your great book on ... I believe it was 1928 ... that you spent in France.

MC: 1929.

ET: Twenty-nine. Was that a particular golden period for you, and could you tell us something about what it did to you as a person?

MC: It wasn't a golden period for me. You must remember, I was astonishingly successful, and I had friends in Paris before I went there … correspondents … and when I went there, around the corner I was immediately known. And —

ET: People looked for writers then the way they look for movie stars now.

MC: Yes, that is exactly it, so I had friends right from the beginning. Then, the arrogance of a young man is very great. I didn't think, *I am here being influenced by remarkable men.* The charm of the [Latin] Quarter was that many of us thought we were all great, and, you know, we weren't being influenced by anybody particular. If anybody wanted to be influenced by me, I was there, and if there was anybody I wanted to be influenced by, there he was.

For example, a man like [James] Joyce. Joyce was doing something then that I definitely did not try and do, one of the reasons being that the world was full of people trying to do what Joyce did better. There seemed to be no percentage whatever in getting into that, and I remembered this when I wrote *The Loved and The Lost*, which is, I think, a pretty good book. I remember the *Canadian Forum* reviewed it and rather unfavourably. They had no more understanding of that book — rather pathetic. Anyway, one of the reviewers said that this was a real strange case. He said, here I had the advantage of knowing Joyce and I showed no influence of him whatever. Now, I would have thought … if you think there's doubt in that, you go back to 1952 and look up that *Forum* review, and I'm telling you that line is there … and if I'd been an editor of a magazine, I would have called that young professor in, or whoever he was, and I would've said, "Now look you big, thick-headed chump, it would be a distinction, you know, if you managed to write a book knowing Joyce and being in that circle without showing the influence of Joyce. This might make him very interesting, you see." This was a tribute, but people get so caught up in fashions, so caught up in trends, that the poor guy thought I ought to be showing the influence of James Joyce. Why? James Joyce wasn't showing the influence of me — true he was older and so on … but you know, this was my attitude around the [Latin] Quarter, and it was the attitude of most writers around there … they weren't going there to be influenced by —

ET: What you say is interesting, because it's exactly the kind of thing a professor would say: "Wait a minute, here now, where is the influence of Joyce? We want to see some influence of Joyce." But, nevertheless, was there a kind of stimulus, an encouragement?

MC: Yes, to a remarkable degree, and I'll tell you what the great thing, the really great thing was ... the great thing was that it was more important to be a great writer and be a fine writer than anything else on earth. Or a great painter ... to be great, you know, in your chosen field ... this was the world. This was the best there was in the world and that represented almost the highest aspiration of man, in that world of the [Latin] Quarter. So there were all these people pouring in from all over, particularly around August ... well, no, in the spring or late fall, people would come from all over ... and they came really just hoping to see these writers. Sitting around where the writers sat ... it was a very big thing, you see. To be a tycoon, a great business tycoon, that was great ... that gave you a lot of money, but no one was going to get excited about that.

ET: No prestige.

MC: No, no prestige. Helena Rubenstein[8] used to come over to the Quarter with her husband, Titus, and sit with us. They were friends of ours and so on, but her interests was she was a collector ... she collected ... a collection of paintings.

ET: So she talked art, not business.

MC: Yeah, and her husband you see, Titus, was an editor of the Black Mannequin Press he had over there. But it was the greatest thing in the world being a writer. I doubt whether in Toronto you could convince many people that the greatest thing in the world was to be a writer. Very funny, you know, that Royal Bank dinner[9] ...

ET: Oh, yes.

MC: This was a rather astonishing —

ET: When you got the fifty grand.

MC: Yeah, but I mean at the dinner itself ... you know, the sort of ... you almost could believe, you know, with people all standing up on their feet ... you could almost for a moment ... I almost for a moment had the astonishing feeling that it was important to be a writer. Now maybe ... maybe ... all of the money that has been coming my way has been making people feel this ... and that's rather sad ... but it was an astonishing thing, you know. I mean last year it was a Cardinal and this year a writer ... this is rather astonishing. It makes this a rather strange country, don't you think?

ET: I think it does really, and this country has a rather strange way of recognizing work it considers to be of value.

MC: It has indeed. Claude Bissell[10] wrote me a note and said ... you know the Arctic guy ... "Rather odd, but it melts very, very slowly, but it melts."

ET: Yes, I think it was a very genuine recognition, and I'm sure, too, that people are more aware of your books, and they're in reprints now that are readily available. As you were saying, the three great novels you did in the twenties and thirties are now selling very well in New Canadian Library paperbacks.

MC: Yeah.

ET: Mr. Callaghan, just in closing, I wonder if I can ask you, what you would most like to be remembered for?

MC: Oh dear, I don't know ... I would like to be remembered for my work. You mean which book? Oh heavens, I would not pick a book. It's like your books are your children. There are some books ... there's a book of mine, you see, you can't tell about these things ... there's a book called *It's Never Over*, and no one ever writes about that book. I never see anything about it. And, when [Edmund] Wilson[11] was writing about me, gathering, reading a lot ...

ET: The only thing we see about it now, is that it's very valuable now ... first editions.

MC: That's true, and he tried to get me to give it to him, and I looked around in the house and I saw I can't find it … and I remember he said to one of my sons, "I wonder if he understands that there are people over in this world who go to great lengths to have me read a book of theirs … now I can't even get him to give me this book." And then, Scott Fitzgerald[12] took a bitter crack at that book, and we'd had a fight so that didn't count. Scott referred to it as my "death house masterpiece" in which I had blown up completely. And Wilson, who was in Rome at the time, asked, "What is this death house masterpiece?" So, since I was a little wounded by the Fitzgerald business, I let him see the book. This is rather astonishing. He phoned me and he said that he started reading the book. He couldn't put it down … he sat reading it all night. He said, "Don't kid yourself about Scott." He said he knew how good a book that is, that was. What is this? That's a remarkable book. Now, this is a very funny thing, I never see the book referred to at all. It is maybe a good idea to get that in the New Canadian Library.

ET: *It's Never Over* was published, when, in '31?

MC: In — yeah, about that. It's an odd book.

ET: What does it do to you when you read it?

MC: I told you, I haven't read the book since I wrote it. I don't know what it does to me. I am willing to take Wilson's word for me that if he reads that book thirty-five years later and says, "This is a very remarkable thing. I couldn't put it down," then I'm perfectly willing to believe that, because I thought it was very remarkable when I wrote it. And I remember one of the New York reviewers said it was a new sensation in literature. So I won't promise to read the book, but I think I should get that book in the New Canadian Library.

ET: We can certainly hope that students can soon find a reprint of *It's Never Over* by Morley Callaghan.

MC: That was a nice way to end the thing with that story about Fitzgerald.

ET: That's a beautiful tape. That's great going.

Transcribed by Griffin Kelly

HUGH GARNER
(1913–1979)

Hugh Garner spoke his mind. On this, if nothing else, there was consensus. Notorious as an abrasive, obnoxious, maladroit malcontent (Stuewe xii–xiii), Garner gleefully castigated "stuffed shirts," "do-gooders" (1–2), "phoney-balonies and sob-sisters" (xii), declaring to Earle Toppings that he would never "ever be socially acceptable." Garner's self-installation as an outsider on the Canadian literary landscape was the source of his popular and critical acclaim (223), as his works were propelled, in the words of Doug Fetherling, by "the irregular heartbeat of the derelict" (2) and shot through with "the essential sadness of life" (8).

To understand Garner, it is vital first to understand the neighbourhood in which he was raised. Born in Batley, England, in 1913, Garner and his family moved to Toronto when he was six years old, shortly after which his father left his mother alone with their two young children. Garner's mother moved the family into the working-class Cabbagetown neighbourhood, so named for the vegetable gardens of its predominantly English, Scottish, and Irish residents. Garner later described this area — an immigrant enclave since the 1830s — as a medley of Victorian-era houses, some clean, others dilapidated, inhabited by "generally unskilled working people" who "believed in God, the Royal Family, the Conservative Party, and private enterprise" (Fetherling 17). Garner spent his childhood exploring the rabbit's warren of the Cabbagetown slum, swimming in the Don River, loitering on the corner of Broadview Avenue and Gerrard Street, and visiting the local library (Stuewe 14–16). These childhood experiences kick-started what biographer Paul Stuewe calls Garner's "ceaseless guerilla battle against those who presumed to know what was good for him" (20) and would later serve as one of his primary inspirational wellsprings.

Garner's diverse and checkered professional record was another fount of literary inspiration. Whether he was reporting for the *Toronto Star* or serving as a bicycle messenger, riding the rails or enrolling in the International Brigades during the Spanish Civil War, Garner's wealth of employment experiences enriched his writing: as he told Earle Toppings, "most of my stories are based on … things I've done; I've fictionalized stories around them." Indeed, once well established as an author, this broad swath of experience allowed Garner to engage in multiple literary spheres, including public relations director for *Liberty* and associate editor for *Saturday Night* in the 1950s. These practical insights formed "the flesh of his prose" (Fetherling 2) and the foundation of his literary gift: the ability to capture the crest and swell of working-class life in all its blemished majesty.

Despite his popularity, his receipt of the 1963 Governor General's Award for *Hugh Garner's Best Stories*, and the singularity of his voice in the Canadian canon, fame never clouded Garner's head, nor blunted his tongue. In his riotously intoxicated behaviour at the 1955 Canadian Writer's Conference at Queen's University (Stuewe 126–29), and his bold and unabashed declaration that the student population needed "more radicals such as Jesus Christ and Freud" (118–19), Garner continued to rail against "phoney-balonies and sob-sisters" (xii). Though his honesty and lack of social inhibition repelled critics, it invariably attracted readers. Nowhere was this more apparent than at Garner's funeral. Though the attendees included literary luminaries, such as Jack McClelland, Robert Weaver, and Doug Fetherling, there were also many ordinary individuals who came to honour Garner's life and work. Garner did not simply speak his own mind; he also spoke for those working-class, anonymous masses, whose lives he had captured in such vivid detail. He had been their mouthpiece, their representative, their interlocutor with the wider Canadian literary landscape. Hugh Garner spoke his mind and, in doing so, he spoke for the people.

References

"About." *Cabbagetown People.* Accessed September 2015. www.cabaggetown
    people.ca/about.

Fetherling, Doug. *Hugh Garner.* Toronto: Forum House, 1972.

Garner, Hugh. *One Damn Thing After Another.* Toronto: McGraw-Hill
    Ryerson, 1973.

Stuewe, Paul. *The Storms Below: The Turbulent Life and Times of Hugh Garner.*
    Toronto: James Lorimer, 1988.

RECORDED ON AUGUST 12, 1970

ET: "He is a sensible, blunt man who knows what real life is, and he gives it to us straight." Michael Hornyansky said that about novelist Hugh Garner. Mr. Garner is with us, and I'd like to ask him first, what are some of the things you've worked at, Hugh, that you think have given you raw material for writing?

HG: Almost everything. I think that a writer who goes only to school, only to college, is wasting his time. I think it's a waste of time for a writer to go to college. I mean, *Tom Brown's Schooldays* was written a long time ago,[1] and Scott Fitzgerald[2] wrote college novels and so, what else do they know? They don't know, for instance, what it's like to work eight hours a day on a shipping floor, or as a harvest hand, or delivering handbills, or whatever. And all, all the jobs I've ever had have contributed to my general knowledge. I mean, I don't have to research how to read a gas meter, for instance, you know, things of that nature, and I think that I've used most of these things, especially in my short stories. I've used them for a variety — a tremendous variety — of trades and so forth, of which I have an intimate knowledge.

ET: You did say that you did not become a writer to grow rich, famous, or socially acceptable.

HG: That's true also.

ET: Did you happen to become rich, famous, and socially acceptable by accident, having become a well-known writer?

HG: I have never become rich, socially acceptable, or what's the other one?

ET: Or famous. Well, you have become famous.

HG: Perhaps a little bit of ... a little bit of that fame ... but rich or socially acceptable, no. I don't think I'll ever be socially acceptable.

ET: Hugh Garner, could you tell us about your early days as a writer? This is a story that I always enjoy hearing myself. When you finally made the decision [to write]. You've given the impression that you're a somewhat impulsive person: if you decide to do something, you'll do it by three o'clock that afternoon ... you'll change your way of living ... bang, you're set to accomplish it. And when you really decided that you would put your life on the line, how did you go about becoming a writer?

HG: Well, first of all, in 1936, just out of pure nonsense, I wrote a piece called "Cabbagetown," a small piece ... just a very small piece ... and I had no typewriter ... I printed it. I don't write, incidentally; I print with a pen ... even letters and so forth. I sent it in to the *Canadian Forum* magazine, and I believe that Northrop Frye or someone was the editor ... I'm not quite sure. Anyhow, whoever it was, they bought the piece, which rather surprised me and surprised all the neighbours and so forth. And of course I got nothing for it but a three-month subscription, or something, but I did that. Then I went to the Spanish Civil War and when I came back, I did another piece called "Christmas Eve in Cabbagetown," the same way ... sent it to *Canadian Forum*, and they accepted that. This would be in 1938.

Then, I did nothing at all about writing throughout the war years until 1946. Then, I started to be a writer. I was discharged in October of 1945, and I was just spending all of my money on beer and so forth, my war service gratuities, and having a lot of fun at it, I mean ... not running it down. But then, my wife and children were up here and we were living with my mother up in the east end of Toronto, and the house got rather crowded because my brother came back from overseas, and so my wife and children went back to the family farm on the Gaspé. I was left here, by myself, and I took a room up on St. Joseph Street, which is a street running off Yonge Street — Toronto's main street — sort of a crummy rooming house neighbourhood. And, on New Year's Day of 1946, I decided that I was going to set myself down and write a book. I went down to Kresge's [department store], I bought myself some paper, I bought myself a fountain pen — in those days there were no ballpoints, I don't think — I bought a fountain pen, and the one thing I didn't buy, which I should've, was an eraser. And I signed up for a veteran's course, a DVA[3] course, in co-operative management, about which I had about as much interest as I have in nuclear physics. But it paid the rent. I received money while I was taking this course.

ET: Was this a course in retailing?

HG: At that time, the farmers of Ontario had set up farmers' co-operatives, consumer co-operatives, or producer co-operatives. For instance, they would sell their chicken mash and so forth through a co-operative system. And we were ostensibly being trained to manage these places. It was really a gimmick and a come-on, but you know, it was rather interesting what war veterans took up ... you know ballet dancing and ukulele playing and all sorts of nonsense ... and I happened to take this because it gave, as I said, gave me this income, of which I sent some to my wife. It paid my rent in this rooming house and kept me out of the pool halls and beer parlours during the day. And I wrote in the evenings.

And I sat down, and I started, page one of *Cabbagetown*. The course lasted three months; I wrote the book in three months. I was elected class valedictorian. I didn't drink during this period; I was quite overweight from drinking beer for the last four or five years ... I took off almost forty pounds, consciously. I wrote a chapter a night, and on weekends I corrected the chapters of the previous week. I was voted class valedictorian. I went out of the course and the book was written. I went out and got drunk and told them to stuff their course, told the teacher to go to hell, was kicked out of the class: the valedictorian was kicked out and that was the end of ... of both *Cabbagetown* and my scholastic career.

ET: And eventually it was published in paperback, I believe?

HG: Yes, it was published by William Collins — there's a lot more to it before that. Macmillan turned it down, and there was a young lady working for Macmillan then called [Peggy] Blackstock,[4] who is now in New York, and she was the only one who really encouraged me. And I rewrote it twice for Macmillan, and they turned it down each time. Finally she said to me "Why don't you take it upstairs to Collins?" Collins at that time rented a floor in the Macmillan building. So I took it up to Macmillan — er, up to Collins — and there again was turned down, rewritten, and turned down again.

Before this, I'd hired ... through a newspaper ad ... a woman typist, a housewife who was doing freelance typing to help her husband pay the down payment on a bungalow or something ... and she had typed it on onionskin paper, which was disastrous, you know. I paid her sixty-five dollars for it, knowing that it was useless, but at least now I had a typewritten copy of the thing. Impossible to give to an editor to read ... he was reading five pages down, you know.

So then, I rented a typewriter ... in those days, you could rent them for five dollars a month. And I retyped the whole thing myself. And all this went on and on and on until I said to myself, "To heck with it." At that time I was working as a clerk in an oil company, and they were getting a little sick of me around Collins. There were two fellas there, Robin Ross Taylor and Charles Sweeney. Both of them happened to be naval veterans, the same as I was. And they said to me, "Have you a book about the navy?" And I said, "Yes, as a matter of fact, I have!"

ET: Happen to have one ...

HG: Yes, I had three-quarters of a book. I didn't know what to call it ... *Landlubber Lying Down Below*, something like that ... and I had three-quarters of it written. And so they said, have you a book about the navy — I said yes — and I went home and wrote the last quarter of the book on the weekend. I took it in on a Tuesday, they bought it on the Friday, and they gave me an advance of five-hundred dollars, and I was in business as a professional writer. That's how it all began.

ET: And subsequently *Cabbagetown* was published.

HG: *Cabbagetown* was then published by Collins as a paperback, as a very chopped-up version of the original, yes.

ET: And finally, just in recent years, published by Ryerson in a hard cover, the complete version.

HG: The complete one, yes. Luckily, I kept one complete manuscript, and that's the one that Ryerson published in 1968.

ET: Hugh, could you describe what Cabbagetown was like to you when you were a boy? Could you tell us some of the sights and sounds, and some of the oddities, and some of the funny things you remember from that part of Toronto, which has changed, I should imagine, quite a lot in the interim. I remember you told me one time it was "the largest Anglo-Saxon slum in North America."

HG: Yeah, that's true. Someone the other day interviewing me asked me where I'd got that quote, and I said, "I didn't get it from anywhere, I made it up, it's my own quote!" And it's true we have Negro slums, French Canadian slums … I mean, Saint Henri in Montreal and so forth … we have Mexican slums, we have Indian slums … all sorts of slums … but this happened to be Anglo-Saxons. We were the establishment! You know, we were the lowest of the low, and yet we were the people that immigrants think of as being the people who run the country. And that's exactly what Cabbagetown was at that time.

ET: You were the top guys in a slum.

HG: Yeah, we were the top guys — I mean, we were Scotchmen and Englishmen, you know, and you can't beat them in the establishment. And yet we were the poor. And so it was an oddity in that respect. Most of the families were first- and second-generation immigrants from England,

Scotland — working-class immigrants — and we were poor, there's no getting away from it. As to your original question ... what did I find about it, and so forth ... slums are fine for kids. Whenever I hear bleeding hearts talking about kids who never saw a cow, I feel like going and punching them right in the mouth. In the first place, every kid has seen a cow, even if you've only seen them at the Canadian National Exhibition ... but some kids don't care if they ever see a cow! There's places to play ... there's more places for a slum kid to play than any kid out in suburbia. It's the kids in suburbia who go crazy lurking over green lawns. In the slums you have lumberyards to climb, piles of lumber; you have railway tracks; you have boxcars to climb on. We had swimming and so forth, you know. If we wanted a sort of country atmosphere, we just had to walk up the Don River: the Don Valley at that time, before it was filled with freeways, was a wild jungle, you know ... and slum kids, I feel no sorrow for slum kids. I think they have a wonderful time. I feel a lot more sorrow for the kids out in Don Mills.[5]

ET: And then, Hugh, your life during the Depression, was, well, to us, I suppose it would seem ... looking back ... a colourful time, because we haven't really participated in quite the same way. I believe you even rode the rods during the Depression.

HG: Oh, yes, all over.

ET: What does that mean for kids who haven't heard the term?

HG: *Riding the rods* means — well, actually it was an anachronism even then — riding the rods meant the brake-rods under old-time boxcars ... and the hobo used to lay planks across these brake rods and lie upon them, you see. But in my days as a hobo, the boxcars had been changed ... there were no such thing as rods ... and we used to ride the tops or inside the empty cars if we could get in. And the whole of North America, it seems to me, was on the bum: all the young people, we'd travel freely from, well, let's say from Quebec City to Los Angeles. I travelled all over the United States, down into Mexico, and just the same as the kids today. I notice today, downtown, you see kids with packs on their backs. They tell me out west —

ET: And they touch you for a quarter, just like in the old days.

HG: Yeah, of course. Yes, but these are middle-class kids, you know.

ET: Their old man's a doctor.

HG: Yes, they've bummed out of society. The only difference is that we did it more for necessity. But it was the same thing ... it was the youthful urge to travel and to get away from the home atmosphere. You see, Earle, when you are a slum dweller, and you're living at home, you're poor. But when you're away from home and on the bum, you're broke. Now, there's a tremendous difference between being broke and being poor, and I suppose that was the reason I did it, anyway. I never felt poor when I was away from home. I felt broke, and I was sleeping on the ground and sleeping in boxcars and this and that, and eating in Salvation Army hostels and so forth, but it was an adventure. It was much better than sitting around the house wondering if I could get a job at eight dollars a week pushing a cart, you know.

ET: So in a way it was a profitable decision ... when you were eventually going to be a writer ... you were using your time to a lot better advantage really, as you say, than you would have been pushing a cart for eight dollars a week.

HG: Yeah. Yeah.

ET: Did you ever get your head broken? Did you ever meet any hostility as you travelled around the continent?

HG: Yes, indeed. Never had my head broken, but last year I remember my wife and I were out in California, and we drove through Bakersfield — it's on the main line of the Southern Pacific between Los Angeles and San Francisco — and I remember a time when a Japanese kid and I were hanging on to the side ladder of the boxcar of the freight train going sixty miles an hour and a brakeman [was] stamping on our hands. And first the Jap kid and then myself switching hands while this guy tried to knock us off, and it would've been sheer death, you know ... and so we had things like that. And I was kicked out of towns, ordered out of towns by town marshals ... things of that nature.

ET: There are people that you met in these encounters. First in a slum as a small boy, then in the Depression, and in the Spanish Civil War ... I suppose characters you'll never forget, and faces and talk that eventually got into your books in some form.

HG: Yes, indeed, almost everything did or a lot of things. I shouldn't put it that way. Perhaps a better way is that a lot of things in my books are those things. I can remember, for instance, sitting around a fire, a hobo fire, in what we used to call a jungle. A jungle to a hobo is any place along a riverbank where he can make a fire and boil up his tea and so forth. Somewhere near, I think it was Transcona, Manitoba, and a young fellow — I believe he was from Windsor, Ontario — singing the "Sweetheart of Sigma Chi," and I've never heard it sung as beautifully before or since. And those little vignettes still come to me, and I've used a lot of them in my stories and books, and they're sort of wonderful. They're part of my life, I ... I enjoy them very much.

ET: When we come to the topic of Canadian themes, you've, I think, in a way, written more graphically Canadian than a good many fiction writers ... stories, for example, such as "One Mile of Ice" or "The Magnet" or "Hunky" about Ontario tobacco farmers and immigrants, or "One, Two, Three Little Indians" about Canadian Indians' desperate plight in the white society that's against them. Did you have any deliberate sense of trying to portray what was happening in Canada, or did this just happen to be where your roots were?

HG: I've written, for instance, two short stories about the tobacco farms. I worked —

ET: You worked on them.

HG: I worked, yes, priming tobacco in 1939, and it's a rather dramatic locale. It's something that other writers have ignored. Strangely enough, other writers cannot write — most Canadian writers with their university backgrounds and their nice cotton-batten lives, cannot write about some things ... and I'm the only one I know who's written a short story, for instance, about a factory, which was called "$E = MC^2$," about a farm implement company in which I've also worked. And so I've used all of these things to write, not to be consciously different but because I know these things so intimately. When "E = MC²" was read by an actor on the air one time, he was amazed that I knew so much about using gauges and things like that. But I was an inspector in the punch-press department of this joint, and you know, carrying a gauge and calipers was just the same as a plumber carrying a wrench; I just knew it, and you can't fake that stuff. A person who comes out of a university and tries to write about a factory worker is just butting his head against a wall, there's no factory worker in the world that wouldn't spot him as a phony.

But it was all done unconsciously … it wasn't done to sort of write a pattern about various Canadian phenomena or various Canadian milieus, or anything of that nature; it just happened that I happened to know things. For instance, you tell me about the short story there, "One Mile of Ice." This happened to be the Restigouche River, which is the borderline between Quebec and New Brunswick, and I happened to cross it one night with my brother-in-law in the wintertime when there were holes in the ice and so forth. We were going to the liquor store, as a matter of fact. I'd cross … you know, like little Levi … jumping ice floe to ice floe to a liquor store. And the story is based just on that thing. This bitter cold … it was terrifically cold … and the bitter wind … and I just imagined from that what would happen to a couple of men in a horse and cutter going across, and the horse and cutter going in a hole, and the terrific freezing and so forth … and I remember the editor of *Holiday*, who turned the story down, writing me about it and saying that his feet were cold when he finished reading it. But most of my stories are based on things that I've done but I've fictionalized stories around them … you know what I mean?

ET: The feeling I had when I read "One Mile of Ice" — nobody could ever say this was not a Canadian story … nobody could say it was not set in Canada. You fought in the Spanish Civil War, and you've said, "It's one of the nice things I did."

HG: Yeah, yeah, I think that I've done very few nice things in my life, but —

ET: I think you're being pretty hard on yourself.

HG: No, really I haven't. I've been a pretty selfish person, I think. Well, just an ordinary selfish … we're all pretty selfish.

ET: We all are.

HG: You know, we'll give to the blood bank or something and then pat ourselves on the back until we give ourselves pneumonia … but I think that fighting in the Spanish War was one of the decent things I did. It's one of the things I've never regretted doing, and, as Hemingway said, it was a good war. And it *was* a good war. We lost it, and we were defeated by superior arms, and by international diplomacy and so forth … but the fellows who fought there to me were a conglomerate of people from possibly twenty or thirty nations, everywhere from Chile to Japan, in the International Brigades. And they were quite a bunch of guys. I mean, you know, we were all — most of us were kids, and just looking back on that sort of brings a tear to my eye when I think of the kids who died at the age of nineteen or twenty for a cause that was lost before they even got there, let's put it that way. And they were nice guys; most of them were communists, and a lot of them were plain adventurers … and a lot of them were people who belonged to socialist groups, anarchist groups, and all sorts of groups of the Left … but we were tied together with an esprit de corps which has never been duplicated since. There's never been an International Brigade since; and I say International Brigade although it should be plural, because there were five brigades, and —

ET: Completely voluntary.

HG: All voluntary, yeah, and … no … that was a nice thing. I'm glad I did it.

ET: Did you have a great feeling of ideology at the time? Did you feel that this was a stand against the spread of fascism in the world?

HG: No, but I had a great feeling of … what shall I call it? It's not love … a great feeling that the people of Spain deserved help. That the elected government, the democratic people of Spain, deserved the help of the world. I felt that very deeply. I was never so involved in my life. World War Two to me was just, you know, it was a thing you went and did, but I never regained that sense of dedication … and this is the first time I've ever said this, I was dedicated to the cause of the people of Spain … and you know, it's a funny thing to be that way about a foreign nation and so forth, but I felt that way and I've never felt that way since. I don't feel that way today, for instance, about the Viet Cong — although I'm on their side in the Indo-China War — but … dedication. That's the first time I've ever put it that way, but it's true. And, I'm a little ashamed of voicing it, you know. It's not Hugh Garner, but it's true, nevertheless.

ET: Hugh Garner, what would you most like to be remembered for?

HG: I think that right now, with a lot of my stories being used in high-school textbooks — and a great many of them are — there's hardly a month goes by that I don't receive requests for stories for high-school texts, including American texts. I think that the fact that I'm getting through to another generation, the fact that I'm sort of being born again in another generation through my work … which is pure accident … is very gratifying to me. And I think that that's probably the thing that I like most. Now, what would I like to be remembered for? I think I'd like to be remembered for an honest man, a guy who has told guys to stuff it when he couldn't afford to. I've told guys to stuff it when I was on relief. I mean, this isn't a new thing now that I have clout. I did it when I didn't, and I think that's probably my best trait. And I'd like to be remembered as an honest guy who wrote honestly about ordinary subjects and brought ordinary people to life for the reading public.

Transcribed by Amy Kalbun

HUGH MACLENNAN
(1907–1990)

H ugh MacLennan was born in Cape Breton, Nova Scotia, and moved to Halifax as a child. He studied at Dalhousie University and was a Rhodes scholar at Oxford before enrolling as a Ph.D. student in classics at Princeton. MacLennan told Earle Toppings in the interview that despite all his upper-middle-class education, the only job he could find after his Ph.D. was at Lower Canada College as a high-school teacher. A professor in his later years, he wrote a series of noted novels that won Governor General's Awards.

MacLennan conceptualized his stories in relation to place, especially his hometown, and the feelings of rootlessness he continuously felt while away. In talking to Toppings, he revealed his first novel was rejected by twenty-one publishers. One of the editors had commented in the manuscript: "Who is this writer? Is he British, American? It is hard to tell." This was an epiphany for MacLennan who understood from this that all good writing had to be tied to a place and that he had to go back to his roots in particular.

Such an attitude seemed to have a dual purpose: he tried to develop a sense of home in his works and reveal that home to the reader. MacLennan insists that he had to make Canada known, and thus his novels explore every facet of the Canadian character as a way of showing the country to the reader. For example, *Barometer Rising* (1941), MacLennan's first novel, is centred on the tragic explosion in 1917 in Halifax Harbour, a tragedy that was only surpassed as a wartime incident by the Pearl Harbor explosion that occurred in 1941 during the Second World War. MacLennan uses this historical event as his centerpiece to explore Canadian identity and how it manifests itself as a duality of British and American culture (Morpurgo par. 4–5).

As mentioned by J.E. Morpurgo, the creation of a Canadian literary canon through a focus such as MacLennan's has its pitfalls. The critic notes how earlier Canadian writers using this tradition all seemed to have similar traits, including the fact that their families had been in Canada generation after generation (par. 2).

Making Canada known to a wide audience encompassed more authors than MacLennan, of course. Time and time again, Canadian writers choose to portray Canadian character through their own unique perspectives. Judging from MacLennan and his particular oeuvre, this approach enhanced his pages and allowed him to become an expert verbal portraitist. His characters come alive in their strengths and foibles. In novels such as *Two Solitudes* (1945), he captures exquisitely how fraught with anxiety and doubt is the "Canadian-ness" of the postwar period. Yet his careful attention to the human elements of his characters ensures that they are recognized on a universal level and beyond the time frame of the novel.

References

"MacLennan, Hugh." In *Benét's Reader's Encyclopedia of American Literature*, edited by George B. Perkins, Barbara Perkins, and Phillip Leininger, 661. New York: HarperCollins, 1991.

Morpurgo, J.E. "Hugh MacLennan: Overview." In *Reference Guide to English Literature*, 2nd ed., edited by D.L. Kirkpatrick. Chicago: St. James Press, 1991.

RECORDED ON SEPTEMBER 15, 1970

ET: "Canadian writers are hungry writers. They are writers who have had to work exceedingly hard in order to live. They are writers who write not just for money but because the excitement of discovering Canada compels them to write." Those words were written by Hugh MacLennan. Mr. MacLennan is with us, and I'd like to ask him if he would comment further on the excitement of discovering Canada. Mr. MacLennan, is this still what you are doing primarily in a novel?

HM: For that point of view now, I feel I've discovered it as much as I am going to. When I began writing, this really was an unknown country to itself and far more so to the rest of the world. Now, Bruce Hutchison wrote this famous book called _The Unknown Country_[1] roughly a little bit after I had the same idea myself; I mean, I'm not saying he got the title from me because I know he didn't, but that was the situation then. And any form of literature depends upon recognitions, otherwise you can't make a dramatic scene. If nobody knows what anything is like in Canada in the social scene, you could write a very primitive novel, but we were beyond the age of primitive novels then; it was impossible even if you wished to do it. You could write a poem, yes, but even the poets had the same difficulty. It was necessary to make Canada visible; it was necessary to make it tangible, to be able really to write of it and out of it and it was quite a story as to how I finally learned that. It took me eight years.

ET: Would you tell us about the process of learning to write a novel?

HM: Yes, this I can certainly tell you from the standpoint of Canada. You see, I was born in Cape Breton Island. My voice, as you hear, is a Gaelic voice so my people had been in Cape Breton Island for 150 years. I grew up in Halifax, and I never crossed the frontier of Nova Scotia even into New Brunswick until I'd been four years in England, all over Europe, and over half of the United States. Therefore, I never thought of myself as a Canadian until one day in the States with a junkyard car when I was a graduate student. It couldn't climb hills; it was always breaking down. I had gone out to Chicago to see a girl who later was my first wife — she died about thirteen years ago — and the car, it had such trouble getting over the Pennsylvania

Mountains that my future father-in-law told me to return via the water route. In other words, it took me into Ontario — this was the Depression — and I reached the old King's Highway and went around and then came back via Niagara Falls. Filled up this old seven-passenger Studebaker that I had bought for about seven dollars with about six hitchhikers who were all unemployed then, and we had a wonderful time, and, by God, I was home in Ontario. This stuck in my mind somewhat but not well enough.

I wrote one novel, which I set partly — mostly about bootleggers — in Nova Scotia and the States; another one I began in Austria, mixed up with the Austrian revolt, which paved the way for fascism in Europe, and mixed up that a bit with the United States. That book I worked very hard on. The manuscript's now in the McGill Library. My friend and colleague [Eli Kluge?] has read it and said it was fairly interesting, but I can't really remember it myself. It went through twenty-one publishers in New York, all of whom rejected it, and the last one made the comment that really showed me where I stood. It was Longmans Green and it was a woman. She said — she sent this to my agent, because she didn't know where I came from, my New York agent — "I think this man could become a good novelist but there's something lacking here. We don't know who he is. He doesn't write like an American, that's for certain. He doesn't write like an Englishman. Who is he?" And then suddenly it hit me right between the eyes that every work of fiction, no matter how international and universal it is in its scope, is profoundly and deeply rooted in the community out of which the writer grew. He gets his overtones … it's such an intimate form … his overtones, his values, these are built into him without him knowing it. And I'm not talking here about this everlasting modern word *problem*. I only use the word *problem* for technical problems … that's what they are. But I suddenly remembered what Aristotle had written, that "all drama depends on the familiar" because it depends upon recognitions. I'll give you an example. Just about that time, Lillian Smith, an American writer, had written a book called *Strange Fruit*[2] … it was quite famous. She grabbed the readers everywhere all over the world with the very first sentence, which showed you that a black girl was in love with a white man on a hot summer night in a small town in Alabama. Dynamite lies underneath that. Then, the idea shot into my mind that if an English Canadian in Montreal were in love with a French Canadian girl, who would know outside of Quebec? It wouldn't be anything like as bad as in the [U.S.]

South, but it was bad enough, or it was then. Then I realized that every element of Canada had to be really explored, including the landscape. Our climate is a rational climate. Waldo Frank,[3] after reading *Two Solitudes* ... he was a very well-known American writer then ... said it reminded him of a Russian novel: quite a number of writers and American critics have pointed that out. Of course, Canada is intimately varied. I've come from the Atlantic Coast; I've lived in French Canada; I've been all over the country and up in the North now. So there's been a constant discovery, and I have found a common denominator here.

ET: Mr. MacLennan, what are some of the events that have shaped you as a writer?

HM: Well, that's a very good question to ask any writer because I think a writer can seldom know that for certain. I'll give you an example of Hemingway — it's quite clear that his sharp and traumatic experience in the war when he was barely eighteen, on the Italian front when he was wounded and nearly killed by a mortar shell and had about five hundred hunks of old iron in him, and was then machine-gunned when he was carrying a dying soldier on his back ... that had an enormous influence on Hemingway's work, on his world view and his obsession with war and violence. But there was another influence that was probably greater on Hemingway, and I think Edmund Wilson[4] said this to me once, that was his father's suicide. That gave him the dread that one day he would do it himself, and he finally did.

For myself, I would have to list a number of events far less personally dramatic than that. One was the outbreak of the war of 1914. My memory began ... my coherent memory began just about then. And that was also when we moved from Cape Breton to Halifax. My father was also enlisted in the medical corps and went overseas in 1915. Halifax is the only North American city in memory, in living memory, that has had any experience of war. It obsessed us when we were there as children. I could, to this day, list the names and tonnage and general armament of every capital ship in the British and German navies ... I could do it. It's not a very valuable thing to know, but this was sort of built-in because the convoys were always coming and going. Halifax was jammed with sailors and soldiers and then came the explosion on top of everything else. And when the atom bomb went off in

Hiroshima, it was announced that this was a bigger explosion than the one over Halifax, which had been the worst prior to that.

Other obvious events, like coming down … really I suppose, I was a clansman at seven from Cape Breton … to an Anglo-Saxon city like Halifax, a city, too, which had the usual Canadian divisions, but they made peace with it … Catholic and Protestant, Irish and the rest of them. Such little Canadian touches as the fact that the Halifax Irish were always the first at the recruiting stations, and when I asked an Irish monsignor many years later why that was so, he said, "Well, you think we're like the Boston Irish." And then there was going to Oxford as a Rhodes Scholar, and travelling around Europe, a totally new world, as a poor student who could live on nothing. And then there was not being able to get a job in 1932 on the account of the Depression when I got out of Oxford, and then going to Princeton for a Ph.D. and finding how utterly different the United States was … far more foreign to me in many ways than Germany. Another was aiming for an academic career in the classics at the very moment when they were largely being abandoned. And therefore the first teaching job I could get after all this load-up of education was twenty-five bucks a week in Montreal in a school and a subsequent lifetime, really, in Quebec. Another was marrying an American girl of a very great strength of character and talent when I was rich enough to be able to promise her eighteen hundred dollars a year. And another, to be perfectly frank, was living with that same person, not really too long later, for ten years as rheumatic fever gradually destroyed her. Which made me realize that some of the things that are deepest and most common in human experiences are not caused necessarily by a character.

If you apply this to writing … I had a discussion, I remember, with the [now] late Theodore Spencer, who was a Boylston Professor of English at Harvard,[5] saying this question of illness brings in the matter of the human spirit … it brings in the matter of injustice and justice. Cosmic, you might say. And I suppose as a result of that experience — though the character was not my wife, Dorothy — came that book *The Watch That Ends the Night*. Now, I'm going to continue with this because your question is terribly fruitful. Any commitment to writing — such as I have had and many other writers have had — I am now convinced, must have a deeper source than environment or any simple chain of events. With me, this began in the form of what Lewis Mumford[6] calls an apparition. I was sixteen years old … it was a night of wind and tumbling clouds about a full moon, and a lonely shore outside of Halifax. And suddenly the whole world I lived in seemed like a moving invisible fragment of millions of other worlds, a multitude of unknown worlds inside of myself. Now, that's badly described, you cannot describe an apparition — you can simply say it had an impact. That has to be made concrete later. And maybe Paul in the light on the road to Damascus is one of those classic examples, perhaps the most famous one in history.

I always sensed without knowing it, what scientists have proved only recently, that all of us have a genetic inheritance formed hundreds of thousands of years ago, an instinct that, combined with another mysterious agent discovered only last year, [which] Freud called "memory traces on the subconsciousness." You don't know what they are, but they are there. Now, recorded history may be fascinating and awe-inspiring, but it is only a fragment of time, and we don't know anything much about recorded history beyond the Egyptians ... that's only yesterday. That is small compared to the hundreds of millennia after man grew his big brain and travelled all over the world and survived the Ice Ages. Some poets and writers and artists, usually without knowing it, seem to be in tune with the few scattered fragments of this unknown past. And I think in some of them, strange fish are exploded to the surface from this abyss. You can mention a few. The first one that occurs to me is Sophocles, Oedipus, or perhaps even more noteworthy, Captain Ahab and Moby Dick. Whoever wrote the first verses of Genesis, you know, trying to describe the Creation, must have relied on some such unknown knowledge, for only recently geographers and oceanographers, with all their accurate scientific instruments, have not entirely obliterated the symbolic and poetic truth of the first chapter of Genesis. Now this may be all guesswork ... it's nothing I can prove.

ET: Mr. MacLennan, you speak of an apparition, and you compare it with Paul on the road to Damascus.[7] Now, do you mean that this was a great flash of enlightenment and, along with it was there some sense of vocation?

HM: A sense of vocation, yes, to understand it. To understand where I was. Search for identity is really what you'd say today. This is where it's encouraged me in the line of work I've taken because I've been very, very steadily and heavily criticized, particularly in the academies, for concentrating on Canada and what they call the "Canadian identity" and so forth, and why I'm not a cosmopolitan writer. I say, well, try and see ... and see what you get. But I could now say we now know definitely — the anthropologists and biologists have proved this ... the studying of all species — that the first need of any species, or any individual within the species, or any tribe within the species, is a sense of identity. The second is a sense of stimulation. And the third, way down the list, is security. We've been taught exactly the opposite for the last forty years. And that's why students are certainly in revolt, because they're claiming an identity and they haven't got it. Dr. Spock[8] was wrong.

ET: Have you encountered any barrier of non-interest in your years of writing? There's a line you have again in *Two Solitudes,* something about Canada being tongue-tied because it worried that others would not be interested in what it had to say. Have you found Canada interested in what you have to say?

HM: I have found a wonderful response on the whole from the Canadian readers. In the days when the books were reviewed by newspapermen, on the whole, they didn't have any high critical knowledge, or anything like this ... neither again were they highfalutin. They took this, quite rightly, as Kip Fadiman[9] once said to me, as news. He said a good reviewer takes a good book as good news. If a famous writer writes a bad book, that's news, too.

ET: So if a newspaperman reviews it, he looks for an angle.

HM: Often did, but often didn't. However, that was perhaps unsophisticated. But the general public, yes, I've found a very, very strong response in Canada. The academic and the highly educated person, particularly connected with literature, was in a curious colonial position for many years here. He had made the grade in Oxford and Harvard or Cambridge and he came back. He would feel embarrassed if he went there and said, "Have you got any Canadian writers?" "Oh, no, we haven't got any because, after all, who are we going to put up to people who are famous?" For example if you had said, seven or eight years ago ... and I'll give you a concrete example ... Leonard Cohen, I used to know pretty well ... and Leonard came to me and he said, "You know, I've got an idea of reciting poetry in nightclubs," which, he said, "I'm starting." I said I thought it was a wonderful idea. Now in the days when everybody was talking about Bob Dylan and the rest of them, and you'd say, "We've got the best folksinger right here in Canada," they'd say, "Are you nuts? How much money is he making?" Well, look at Leonard now. Now, that was exactly the same attitude that they had in places from their own position ... they had made exactly their own establishment. It's just like our old establishment that I used to observe in Halifax, and later, even worse in Montreal. I remember somebody from the old *crème de la crème sieurs* of Montreal saying, he said: "See plays here? Why, we see our plays in London and New York." Robertson Davies once made a gorgeous line ... one of the most civilized and wittiest writers in the world, you know, but he had the misfortune of being born in Ontario ... and when he wrote a play ... I think the novel was hilarious, he is a master of language ... it was a flop here, naturally.[10] He wrote this, he said, "No Toronto audience is going to laugh at a joke in a comedy seen on a Toronto stage, unless there they have a gilt-edge guarantee that an audience in London or New York has laughed at it previously." Well, we're getting over that at last. Thank God we're over that at last!

ET: Mr. MacLennan, you've said, "It has never been so hard to write a serious novel the public will accept. Not only is it more difficult than ever to make a fictional character credible, it is harder still to make him seem interesting and important. So far as the public for novels is concerned, its threshold of boredom is the lowest it has ever been."

HM: In the 1920s the novel was both realistic and dramatic, and at times romantic. It was dealing with great social questions. It was dealing with a war and with poverty and the Depression and so forth. It then began to falter immediately after the Second World War. Whenever any kind of art form becomes too easy to make money out of, then it is in trouble. Jonathan Cape, the famous English publisher,[11] came over to America to tell Doubleday [Publishers] ... he told me this ... that, "You are wrong to regard publishing as an industry and to talk about selling novels by the carload. You'll sell them by copies." Suddenly the public turned away from them, and contemporary novelists were groping around because we've undergone a fantastic social revolution. All manner of classes and social groups are being intermingled today. Frontier lines are getting very hard to determine and there is a certain competition, I suppose, for the reader's time. There's tremendous competition with television today ... not that that, I think, is a fundamental competitor to the novel. The main thing is to get something coherent; you cannot write about anti-heroes all the time. And if any art form cannot create an acceptable character who is in traditional form a king ... you know, Shakespeare's ... a great man or a woman ... of really great merit ... it has now quite truly come down in the United States to practically nothing but pornography. Now, this is not going to last. It can't.

ET: Because it becomes exhausting.

HM: There's nothing in it! I mean, there's nothing in pornography! I went with a newspaperman in Montreal around to half a dozen cinemas there looking at this stuff just for about five minutes ... all the same ... and all you saw in the film, you know, was the bald-headed row. I mean you didn't see any young people around. They find this excruciatingly dull.

ET: The young people don't have to have it symbolically. They can have a more interesting experience in reality.

HM: Exactly, and they're clean about it.

ET: What for you is the most important skill or gift of a writer?

HM: Oh, gosh. I think, though, that's easy enough, I can answer that. Tenacity and taking pains, and never being satisfied ... if that's a gift.

ET: It has then, I gather, a great deal to do with the working through the book and the working out of it.

HM: That's right. And it has to do with certain mysterious things. I have felt that one book really was given to me: that was *The Watch That Ends the Night*. I think that *Barometer Rising* ... I've never been able to understand why people still read it. I suppose it has a certain freshness ... it's an easy story, you know, something of a formula story that was plotted, that one, though the characters still hold it.

ET: Something *Barometer Rising* has is a very real richness of description and the feel of Halifax.

HM: Oh, yes, it did.

ET: I've only been in Halifax one weekend so I know nothing about it.

HM: Yes, it had that, it had that, because this was the one place that I knew best and this was a pioneer job. Nobody took that … except a few people in Canada … seriously when that book came out. I can tell you this about it: I finished that book the night of the fire raid on London, and if anybody had told me that in 1963 it would be published in Germany and sell about one hundred and fifty thousand copies in hardback in Germany, I wouldn't have cared about that … just were we going to lose the war? But Edmund Wilson thought it was a wonderful book. I shouldn't downgrade it at all. I suppose in a way it was a struggle but anything that rests on something that comes so much out of an atmosphere from when you were young — and your first book — can often be easier than a second one.

ET: It seems to me this is something the novel can still do in a period when we are floundering to try to find vessels to contain the experiences we're involved in. A novel can be profoundly moving if it's something that the writer, and that writer only, knew in a particularly deep way.

HM: Yes, that's true and it doesn't matter when, but he's got to be, somehow or other, in tune — and I insist on this — he's got to be in tune with his time … he's got to be true to this. Thus, however boring — it's the only word for it — large sections of Dostoevsky may be … where they're involved in Russian situations and social situations in Russia … and that goes for *Anna Karenina* and Tolstoy, too … that was necessary for both of them then. Those books are stupendous right now … *David Copperfield*[12] is very readable right now, and Galsworthy has certainly proved to mankind that … after they'd thrown him on the junk heap … the critics have for forty years, as he was a dirty word at the university.[13] But as the saying goes, a hundred million Russians can't be wrong. He was true for his time, you see.

ET: And on the BBC and on the CBC television is the proof. Eugene O'Neill said that the playwright either writes for the theatre of his time or he doesn't write for the theatre at all.[14]

HM: He's correct. He has to, otherwise he can't get shown ... you could put it that way with the theatre; that's a pretty expensive operation.

ET: How would you compare your fictional world and the real world? Are they one and the same? Are there differences? For example, Hemingway said, "If it's a good story, it's truer than if it really happened."

HM: Yes, that was perfectly true. I'm sure he never heard Aristotle said the same thing. Yes, it is true. I'm not going to get into the metaphysics there and semantics. You'll see what I mean ... let's keep out of that. But our capacity to perceive is very limited, and the job of artists of all kinds is to make order out of chaos. And that means distilling what is there — I've sometimes compared it to a distillery — a multitude of things ... artist's selection. That goes back again to a Greek by the name of Empedocles,[15] but it depends on what you select. Art is also rejection, to get rid of all trappings, to boil it down as much as you can to essentials. Journalism, of course, is not art though it can be made so ... it can be. There are some people who've done it. Rebecca West has written journalism that's art.[16] Every now and then it comes off.

ET: In your novels, in the selection of pieces of life that you put in them, and especially with your social concerns and political concerns, you are obviously then using the novel partly to channel a tension or something you think is enormously important and may be missed otherwise.

HM: It depends really on the book. I suppose more people in Canada, though not recently, have read my *Two Solitudes* than [have] read anything else I've written ... and this was natural because pedagogues said it deals with what they used to — so help me — call the Quebec Problem ... it was the Canadian Problem. And it had to be, to some extent. But that isn't the reason why anybody still reads that book. It's not the reason why it went into eight languages. Four days after I mailed the manuscript of that, the [now] late Senator Bouchard,[17] who had been the most powerful politician in Quebec — he'd been anticlerical — was, with a single oblique word by Cardinal Villeneuve,[18] finished … not as a senator in Ottawa … but he was ejected from all his offices in Quebec. Completely ostracized. Later, he wrote me, wondering how on Earth I could have written *Two Solitudes* so rapidly because he took it for granted that what happened was that I had had him in mind with this thing with Athanase Tallard.[19] That was a human story, a father and son situation which are always mixed up in this. My concept of politics, to quote myself elsewhere, is that all politics begins in the nursery. And that is why it retains such a nursery quality.

ET: And what you are writing about, as you say, is not the Quebec Problem but a problem of the human spirit.

HM: That was all I was writing about there. That book started out in a dream in which I saw two people. One emerged to me as being obviously … as he had reddish hair … a big man; the other a short, stocky man. They were in a quarrel with each other, shouting at the top of their voices at each other. And suddenly a voice said, "They're both stone deaf."

ET: Hugh MacLennan, as a writer, what do you most want to be remembered for?

HM: Well, I really don' t think of it very much. I think any writer would say for the general validity of what the French would call his oeuvre, his body of works. Speaking solely as a writer, it's bound to be very uneven. But really perhaps to be remembered for his oeuvre. I don't say that I will be, or anything like this. Many people are remembered for only one or two books. Many people only read one or two of Shakespeare's plays. I think it's perhaps a part of a whole in that way.

Transcribed by Vipasha Shaikh

MORDECAI RICHLER (1931–2001)

T he books and essays of this Montreal writer have enjoyed tremendous popularity both in Canada and across the world, as he became one of Canada's most formative literary icons and a definitive part of the Canadian literary canon. Many of his books focus on the theme of Jewish identity and other universal human themes, such as the father-son relationship. Critic Sam Sacks notes stories such as *The Apprenticeship of Duddy Kravitz* focus on the father-son relationship while also mocking the Jewish world of business. The genius of Richler, according to Sacks, comes from the fact that Richler's characters never learn, thus demonstrating one of the biggest flaws of human character (par. 1). This is perhaps best demonstrated in *Barney's Version*, in which the protagonist, Barney, never gains redemption for his past failures as a husband and father after he starts to show signs of Alzheimer's disease.

While he criticized Canadian identity, or lack thereof, Richler was nevertheless a writer of place. He set many of his novels in the Montreal he knew growing up. However, there remains a sense of rootlessness in his works. This is likely because he spent a significant portion of his writing career outside of Canada, as he lived in Europe from 1959 to 1972.

In this interview with Earle Toppings, Richler's emphasis on place and being oriented in space was evident when he talked about his limited life experience, unlike others who drew deeply on their personal backgrounds and used these as fundamental elements of their works. On the other hand, Richler criticized other Canadian writers who were afraid they would not be successful in the United States because they are too Canadian. After all, Richler contended, a novel set in Montreal could gain the same kind of reception as one set in Pittsburgh. He encountered this personally as a Canadian writer writing about Canada in American publications such as the *New Yorker* (Steyn pars. 6–11).

One gets the impression that Richler was critical and skeptical of all that surrounded him, including attitudes toward Canadian nationalism and other people's perceptions of him. Nonetheless, he was a writer with a keen eye for detail who understood how the world operated. This likely was born of his experience as a member of the Jewish minority that had a unique perspective on the Canadian landscape. Despite his begrudging and curmudgeonly acceptance of his own place in Canada, he remains one of this country's most remarkable talents.

References

Niven, Alastair. "Mordecai Richler: Overview." In *Reference Guide to English Literature*, 2nd ed., edited by D.L. Kirkpatrick. Chicago: St. James Press, 1991.

Sacks, Sam. "Richler Man, Poor Man: A Second Life for the Works of the Neglected Canadian-Jewish Novelist." *Commentary*, April 1, 2011. www.commentarymagazine.com/articles/richler-man-poor-man.

Steyn, Mark. "Mordecai Richler, 1931–2001." In *Contemporary Literary Criticism*, vol. 185, edited by Tom Burns and Jeffrey W. Hunter. Detroit: Gale, 2004.

RECORDED ON SEPTEMBER 18, 1970

ET: "Too often, I think it is we writers who are the fumbling, misfit, but unmistakably lovable heroes of our very own fictions. Triumphant in our vengeful imaginations as we never were in reality. Only a few contemporaries live up to be what I once took to be the novelist's primary moral responsibility — which is to be the loser's advocate." Those words are by Mordecai Richler. Mordecai Richler is with us. I'd like to ask him if he would comment a bit further on what he calls the primary moral responsibility of the writer, which is, as he says, to be the loser's advocate. Do you still feel the same way?

MR: Fundamentally, yes, but could I begin by explaining a little more fully what I meant by novelists becoming the unmistakably lovable heroes of their very own fictions? This is true of some really first-rate novelists of our time, like Herzog, but Herzog is the continuing story of Saul Bellow.[1] It works for Bellow but I think it's a dead-end road in the American novel, which also leads us into people like George Plimpton,[2] who write sort of fact novels, in which they are the heroes of their own adventures, either a baseball pitcher or a paper tiger. And then again, we have [Norman] Podhoretz[3] writing autobiography in the form of an old Balzac novel really, *Making It*, which tells you about a boy coming from the provinces to the big city and making good. And the largest ego of all must be [Norman] Mailer[4] who has begun to write about himself in third person and in his latest book about the moon landing. He calls himself Aquarius. He celebrates himself. Now, I think, it's too self-regarding and not the primary function of the novel to have greater admiration of people, less modish, more classical. It's like Brian Moore[5] who tells us what it's like to be an old maid and goes into the detail of essentially mean lives: the unhappy oppressed provincial schoolteacher, the bookkeeper, people who don't lead sensational lives but who measure them out, as we know, in coffee cups and, and lead lives of quiet desperation. I think the novelist does so to examine these lives in depth.

ET: I'd like to ask you also about something that Northrop Frye said, which was, I think, that contemporary literature tends to be ironic in its general attitude, and I think it is more concerned with trying to define the dangers of the world, more concerned with envisaging the world that we want to get away from, rather than the ideal. Is this part of your own experience with writing?

MR: Well, within every satirist, and I write a certain amount of satirical fiction, there is an embittered idealist. And the more one unleashes one's angers with contemporary corruptions, it's because it has departed so far from the ideal life. And so, there are moral judgments made in all these books and it's not frivolous, frivolity, to be funny about these things.

ET: Mr. Richler, could you tell us about your early experience in preparing yourself to become a writer, for example, back in 1949, in St. George Williams University in Montreal?[6]

MR: Well, there's a certain amount of brashness involved and conceit. I wanted to become a writer and I just thought, well, you sit down and write, and then you become a writer. Had I known as much as I know now, I may not have had that nerve because it *is* an act of nerve. I left, and went to Paris, which seemed a romantic thing to do, and wrote there because I thought nobody … being nineteen at the time … could write in a country as dull as Canada. And of course, the deeper I've gone into my own experience, my own writing, the more tightly or intricately involved I am with Canada and with my Canadian experience. I think certain doors of perception close after twenty, so that writers continue to mine the experiences they had before they became self-conscious and cunning about their experience. Once you become a writer, you seem to function on two levels — things happen to you and things are useful to you at the same time.

ET: So you keep on filing them as they happen.

MR: That's right. I think we develop a cunning about experience and, doors are closed, things don't reach you as deeply as they did in a time when you didn't think that way.

ET: And you didn't ever plan to use it in any kind of art.

MR: That's right, so one keeps dredging that experience up and there is a certain amount of … [George] Orwell[7] has mentioned this and other people … of vengeance connected with writing and one does, on the coarsest level, get even with the world for the slight imaginary paranoia, or real, that you've suffered.

ET: I rather got the impression in reading what you were saying about your period in 1949, when you were nineteen years old, that you felt if you stayed in Canada, something damaging would happen to you as a writer, or that you might never become a writer at all.

MR: Well, I was a romantic kid and I thought, somehow, if I went to Paris and sat in the same cafés as celebrated writers had sat in, I'd absorb something by osmosis. I make light of it now, but I wouldn't disown it; it was a romantic feeling I had. Canada then was not what it is now. Its standards were really picayune; the kind of people who were reviewing books or writing about books were embarrassing; the kind of books that were coming out were embarrassing. If one were, I guess, really ambitious as I was, it would have proved nothing to be published here or to be accepted here. Now that, mind you, was twenty years ago and I do think things have improved enormously, and that Montreal and Toronto are both pleasant cities to live in. I could live here quite happily, and were I twenty now, I doubt that I'd leave.

ET: Did you feel twenty years ago that the standards were too soft?

MR: Yes, and there's a danger the second time around that right now this country is shaking with nationalist feeling, some of it good, some of it bad. Now, I'm fundamentally for this and I would like this country not to fragment or become part of the United States. But the dark underside of this kind of nationalism is pushing Canadian writing too far, or painting or whatever, in the yearning to have a culture of our own. We can, and in the past, have made too much of writers not good enough. This works another way: when one visits Toronto or Montreal, there's still a number of writers who feel they're not known in New York and London because there's some conspiracy, international conspiracy, against Canada. Well, the truth is, no one gives a damn one way or another, and if you've written a good novel set in Pittsburgh or Montreal, they're equally acceptable, probably Montreal is inherently more interesting. There's no built-in prejudice against Canadian writers abroad. These are the dangers of nationalism anyway or some of the attendant dangers.

ET: You have said that you have emerged from the ghetto twice. I wonder if you could comment on your migrations between here and England.

MR: Well, that's related to the nationalist feeling, which is double-edged, I think, in that Canadians are touchy about people who have left. But there is a dichotomy of feeling. They both seem to take pleasure in someone leaving and making a reputation abroad, but at the same time, they feel that you've deserted the ship somehow, or you've become too smart for your own good.

ET: Do you think they tend to find that you're one of the men who says Canada is only a few acres of snow?[8]

MR: Well, I don't know. I guess there's some people who think I knock everything Canadian, which is not true. I've also been confronted by people who think there are editors in New York and London offering me bundles of cash to write derisive pieces about Canada. Now, the truth is, editors in New York and London would like me to write about anything but Canada, one way or another, because they don't feel there's that much interest. I'm interested, so I insist: "Well, I'll go to Israel for you, or I'll go do something else, but I would like to write this piece about Canada first." Unfortunately, there is not that much interest in Canada.

ET: You say that you are a satirist; do you think it's simply your satiric spirit that they don't accept; they expect you to be loyal-hearted?

MR: No, no. There have been two strands to my fiction. I've written several novels of character with certain satirical content, let's say *Duddy Kravitz*. Then after that, I became somewhat satiated with the novel of character, not as a reader but as a writer, and went off into satire. And I wrote a novel called *The Incomparable Atuk*, which is my first attempt at satire, in a book-length venture. And with *Cocksure*, I went as far as I could go with satire. And then, I've spent years trying to fuse these two strands, the novel of character and my satirical bent, into one long complex work, which is what I've just finished now. Whether it is successful or not is another question.

ET: The title of the novel that you just finished?

MR: Oh, that's *St. Urbain's Horseman*,[9] which I've been working on and off for five years and have had rough times with.

ET: You obviously have a commitment or you wouldn't allow yourself to spend five years on a book. How do you manage to keep yourself alive in the meantime?

MR: Ah, well, I don't sell very well, most serious novelists don't. But I am published in several countries and as one acquires a reputation, books are reprinted and there's a continuing small sale. But I don't live off my fiction, very few people do — I wish I could. I write film from time to time. I haven't really done a film for about four years, but I will be doing one now. And I do a certain amount of journalism. I do journalism for two reasons: one, I cannot go from novel to novel ...

ET: It's a matter of exhaustion.

MR: Just a failure of the powers of invention. I mean, I just can't do that. And I choose the kind of journalism that takes me into situations or areas I've not been to. I've travelled on the road with wrestlers for a week; I spent a week in an advertising company; I've gone out west for two weeks. This involves another problem: the longer you are a writer (and I've been writing for twenty years), the more removed you are from society in general, no matter what you do. Increasingly, your friends are other writers or directors or critics. You lose touch with certain realities and it's very frightening. I also began to write very early, unlike other writers who are friends of mine, let's say Brian Moore, who had a series of very unpleasant jobs between the ages of twenty and thirty and known those sort of discontents and can write about them. I can't draw on that in that I have been writing and have been published ever since I was twenty. I now regret, in retrospect, that I was published so early. Five more years knocking around, and, let's say, having had to do jobs I hated, would serve me much better now than that first novel does.

ET: So in choosing experiences, or in choosing journalistic assignments, I suppose you try to select something that will contribute —

MR: Yes, ultimately, yes.

ET: — to your most important work, which is writing novels.

MR: Yes. As a case in point might be, I went to Israel and I spent five weeks there actually for *Maclean's* [Magazine] about six years ago, and only in my last novel — this is *St. Urbain's Horseman* — there is a chapter set in Israel. I couldn't afford to go to Israel and spend a month there, and I wouldn't have had such varied experience had I not gone for a magazine and been able to move all over the country and talk to people. So, you do hope that years later it will filter through and can be used in fiction. Graham Greene — now I'm not comparing myself to Graham Greene,[10] but he's someone who had done that for years. He used to go, he wrote marvellous travel books, like *Journey Without Maps* and others, and then later, wrote a novel *A Burnt-Out Case* set in Africa, and then wrote a book about Mexico — now what was that called? — the Mexican travel book? I'm not sure, but the dentist sitting on the pier turns up in *The Power and the Glory*, which was probably his best novel and a very fine novel indeed.

ET: Film is touted as a prime competitor with the novel, and people who bemoan the passing of the novel say it's been partly killed by film and television. You've written for films. How does film writing contribute to or mitigate against your writing?

MR: It depends on the degree of one's commitment. I am not deeply committed to film, unlike my journalism. Again, I have also done journalism for magazines that paid very little for commentary, like *Encounter*, *Commentary*, and the *New Yorker*; but I've written films for money that I needed, and my commitment was no larger than that, except that I didn't want to embarrass myself along the way. But there's a younger generation of writers — I'm thirty-nine — young men in their twenties, that have a much deeper commitment than I ever had, and think they can do their real work in film. I can't, even under the best circumstances because, one, it's a group activity. A novelist is a loner, you go into your room, you're there all day, it's all yours. I'm sorry to digress, but I just finished this long novel — I turned it in to the publisher; now the jacket may be good or bad, the binding may fall apart, but all these are peripheral problems, they're not relevant. It's all mine and ultimately what counts is what I wrote. Once you're involved in film, you're part of a kind of jazz group and you're one other factor: there's the director, the actors, there's the budget, there's weather conditions, there's all manners of conditions and it doesn't suit me really.

ET: These young people you speak of, who have a more intense belief in film, perhaps, are they also in the driver's seat in that they are both directors and writers?

MR: No, very few of them can do both, if you can do both. I guess the great example is [Federico] Fellini, who actually made a marvellous film called *I vitelloni*,[11] really a first novel on film, which has the classic ending of the young man leaving the provincial town. And it is an astonishingly good film. Now, Fellini can make his own rules. But there are very few young men capable of doing both well. It's difficult enough to do either job well. There is a degree of ignorance involved in this, in that they are not — as much as one can generalize — a very well-read generation, and they have a confidence born of ignorance — and what they think is new was really old hat in the novel forty years ago. And had they bothered to read as late as James Joyce, they've done nothing new since. And so their confidence is washed on waves of ignorance to some extent.

ET: And you think this may affect the lasting quality of some of the work they do?

MR: Well, yes, because in film, unlike the novel, there are new masterpieces almost once a month, maybe more often, and two years later, we view them with embarrassment and giggle that we ever thought they were really that important. Take something years ago: *A Brief Encounter*[12] was once considered a great film, but if you saw *A Brief Encounter* on TV now, you'd just wonder how this could ever have been taken as more than a trifle, a middle-brow trifle. Also as there is so much technology involved in film, unlike the novel, you are able to do more with cameras this year than you could even do last year. And so, last year's film looks very old-fashioned. Which is not to say there aren't a number of film classics that triumph over these styles and modish attitudes.

ET: This may be an enormous advantage the novel has, as you imply, that it doesn't have any visual encumbrance; therefore, it doesn't date in the same way. The style doesn't, at least; the images that play in the reader's mind can still be partly his own.

MR: That's right, and the other side of it though, to be fair, is that we've all been influenced by film. All the novelists, and storytelling, even the most ostensibly inchoate kind of modern storytelling, has been influenced by the film, and the cutting of films because, when we were kids, we were brought up on film stories, and this was the first we knew of how to tell a story. So I think any novelist who's even forty-five today has been influenced to some extent by film. But I don't mean he's written a novel trying to make it into a film, or to sell to films, but he's been profoundly influenced in the way he tells his story, and the quickness of it, the kind of cutting that's used in novels, which owes something to film technique.

ET: You've been talking about differences in generations between yours and a generation younger again. You said something interesting when you were reviewing a book by George Plimpton, *Paper Lion*.[13] Referring to your generation and Plimpton's, you said, "One day I fear we will be put down as a trivial, peripheral bunch." I wondered if you thought that your generation was a trivial one, not a lost generation.

MR: Rather too much has been made of nostalgia, I think, or we have made too much of nostalgia and of the trash we were raised on, of *Fibber McGee and Molly*[14] and comic books and baseball players. It's charming and we all enjoyed it, but so what.

ET: You mean, we had shoddy gods?

MR: Yeah, yeah. And now we look back on it with nostalgia. Rather than talking, we exchange old bubble-gum cards, it seems to me. Now the generation before us, I mean think of people like George Orwell and Arthur Koestler[15] and others who define themselves against real issues, in relation to the Depression, the Spanish Civil War, to the Moscow Trials. They were very often wrong, but nevertheless their commitment was to humanity in a larger way, whereas ours is to good times and pleasure.

ET: Do you see any change in this? Do you see any change in the kind of subject matter writers are tackling, or the kinds of voices they're using?

MR: Well, the voices and attitudes towards experience are always changing, which is why the novel really will never die, I think. But fundamentally, all writing is about the same thing: it's about dying, about that brief flicker of time we have here, and the frustrations that creates. There are differences in style and attitudes and technique; there are experimental ways of writing and traditional ways, but really, when you get down to the crux, it's about death.

ET: How do you feel, yourself, about a book you've done, and you know yourself that it is a very good book, and even a profound book, such as *The Apprenticeship of Duddy Kravitz* or *Son of a Smaller Hero*? Is this a kind of death for you, in that it's complete? It's something you've done so well that there's a kind of finality about it?

MR: Well, no. First of all, I have a way of unburdening myself of what I've written. I think that's true of most writers I've spoken to certainly, in that once you finish the book it's gone. I can hardly remember most of the things that are in those books. And you become obsessed by something else. When occasionally, very rarely, in fact, I do look back at something, it's with uneasiness and embarrassment, usually. I don't mean there aren't things that please me, but nothing pleases me sufficiently so that I wouldn't want to try something better, and I think I can do it better next time.

ET: Is this just part of your evolution? You think that you've moved beyond what you were doing at that time?

MR: I hope so, otherwise there would be little reason for continuing.

ET: People whose work is weighed in some kind of public marketplace are often strangely defined. Do you find that your public image has been twisted by mass media and the people who write about you?

MR: Well, I'm most unaware; I don't know what my public image is, honestly. All that really matters, whether my public image is a good or bad one, or sympathetic or unsympathetic, is immaterial. All that matters are the books. Whatever somebody thinks of me, one way or another, is of no importance, unless they are friends of mine or enemies, if you like. But I'm not a performer or an entertainer, and all I send out into the marketplace are my books. The rest doesn't matter.

ET: So that you yourself are rather anonymous, working in your study —

MR: Yeah, and so it should be. I don't believe in the writer as a personality or as a performer. I think something terrible has happened to Norman Mailer, who is the most talented man, who has become his own most perfect work of art. The same is true of Allan Ginsberg.[16] He is the work of art, not what he writes.

ET: And you feel that he can't now retreat from this position, he has to go on being a public performer?

MR: He has accepted some kind of comic role in American experience, and it's sad, I think, and diminishing.

ET: What are some of the events you think that most shaped you as a writer?

MR: I wouldn't know about events —

ET: Experiences —

MR: Well, naturally, the fact that I am Jewish is enormously important, and I come out of a certain tradition. And the fact that I am Canadian, and it's the tensions between the two that make whatever, I guess, is interesting in my writing. Seems like one heritage, the Canadian — if you like, the Presbyterian heritage — says endure, endure, and the more unpleasant life is, the better it is for you; whereas Jewish tradition says enjoy, enjoy, and take your pleasures while you can, to some extent. So there are conflicts and tensions.

ET: You've said also that both your heritages may tend to feel that you've gone off to assimilationist fleshpots and that you have left your religious roots and your national roots for grander things, perhaps.

MR: Well, no, no. To a non-Jew, obviously, I couldn't be a more thoroughly Jewish writer, I think. Now, the Jewish community, those in the Jewish community who are fifty to sixty now, have a very involved relationship with their writers in America, in that they are still unsure of what's being written and of the critical things that are being said and should one do this; if it were written in Yiddish it would be okay; but for the Gentiles, they are unaware of the general tradition. If you take Sinclair Lewis's[17] early novels, which are very critical of American Protestant preachers and the middle class experience in the west: he could do this without being anti-Protestant, or anti-American. But for a Jewish writer, to write critically about the Jewish middle class is to be open to the charge of anti-Semitism among middle-class Jews. It would probably be more accurate to accuse me of being anti-Gentile in my writings, for mockery of certain Gentile values.

ET: When I read your books, I was amazed by the balance you hold, in that you are able to see into both religious traditions, both Jewish and Christian, and to find comic things in each or ridiculous things in each, beautiful things in each, without becoming a hard partisan on either side. I wonder if some of your readers don't realize that you're actually thinking and living beneath some of the surface things that you're satirizing, in other words, that there are many deep concerns that probably they're not giving you credit for.

MR: Well, yes. I feel that at times, yes. None of my more intelligent critics, however, because obviously even writing about it is an act of love, I would think, really. I mean, I'm putting my life into all this. I can't be doing it for profit.

ET: Mr. Richler, what for you, is the most important skill or gift of a writer?

MR: Well, to begin with, there's the fundamental thing over which you have no control: whether you're talented or not. Beyond that, it's hard work. I think Dorothy Parker[18] once said, "It's 10 percent talent and 90 percent holding your ass to a chair." It is hard work and you have to keep at it. I don't write only when I feel inspired, or moved to; when I'm on a novel, I work every day. There are days when I get absolutely nothing done, and I can sit around my office reading magazines or look at the sports. But I go up, as a discipline, every day and I try. In that day, it seems to me, you earn the bonuses of the good days. And then between books, I float around and drink and see friends and laze about. But once you're on a book, you have to work at it, or I do anyway.

ET: What's been the most important to you in mastering the English language? That, of course, is the basic implement with which you have to work, and a pretty difficult one.

MR: Well, I don't know. You have to have an instinct for words of some kind, an ear for how people talk. And, if you haven't, there is nothing anyone can do for you. I would not say I was a great image-maker, as some novelists are. I think, for instance, the most stylistic and fluent is John Updike.[19] I lack that facility.

ET: Sometimes it's an excessive facility, too.

MR: Yeah, it can be, but I do admire his skill with words. And I think Anthony Burgess[20] is another; he has enormous skill of that kind. I read a lot, not when I'm working on a novel. In fact, having just finished a novel, there is a stack of novels in the corner of my office which I will now be able to read, because if you're reading a very good writer, it tends to make vibrations or ripples in your own work, and also you think, *Well, someone's just written about that*, and it inhibits you. But between novels, I do read a lot.

ET: You read, then, something besides fiction, perhaps.

MR: Yes, I do read a lot of non-fiction.

ET: Is this biography?

MR: Well, I've just read a book about the Victorian underworld, about the rookeries of London, and con men, and it really is quite a marvellous book by a man called Chesney.[21] I read a certain amount of biography and literary history and also odd things — like books on the stock market and sports. In a novelist's mind, you must accumulate an enormous amount of trivia and know about all sorts of things that you needn't know if you're a poet. Then you're really expressing your own feelings and that's sufficient.

ET: As a writer, what would you most like to be remembered for?

MR: Well, when all is done, I would like to have written one book that will last and that would satisfy me. I mean, that's a great demand to make when I say that would satisfy me, but that's what I would like to do.

Transcribed by Vipasha Shaikh

SINCLAIR ROSS
(1908–1996)

Novelist and short-story writer Sinclair Ross spent most of his life on the Canadian prairies: first in Saskatchewan, where he was born and grew up, and afterward in Winnipeg. His connection to the rural landscapes of western Canada is evident in his best-known novel, *As For Me and My House*. The novel deals with a husband and wife, both aspiring artists, living in the fictional prairie town Horizon during the Great Depression. Their artistic ambitions run up against the harsh economic and social realities of their time and place.

Though he was quick to deny the comparison, the affinities between Ross's life and the life of the novel's protagonist, Philip, are hard to ignore. Philip spends his spare time sketching and painting, but he is kept from his passion by his professional occupation: preaching a gospel he doesn't believe in to a congregation he feels contempt for. Throughout Ross's life, writing remained an avocation rather than a vocation; lacking the confidence or financial means to pursue life as a professional writer, he worked at the Royal Bank of Canada from age sixteen until retirement, interrupted only to serve in the Canadian Army for four years during the Second World War.

In his interview with Mr. Toppings, Ross looked back on his career with the bitterness of someone whose aspirations have been warped by a social environment unsympathetic to his artistic nature. Finding himself at odds with the puritanical milieu of his upbringing, Ross left the prairies for Montreal in 1946, and apart from attending his mother's funeral in 1957, would never set foot there again. After his retirement in 1968 from

the Royal Bank, he left Canada to spend the seventies in Greece and Spain, eventually returning to Montreal in 1980.

A fundamental difference distinguishes Ross from his protagonist, Philip: where the latter surrendered his artistic talents to a false existence as a preacher, Ross continued, despite his lack of success, to publish novels all his life. Ross got the idea for *As For Me and My House* when he was similarly courted by a local minister into joining the clergy, but he opted out of a religious life to become a different kind of moralist, one devoted to seeking out the truth at the heart of life through his writing.

Now considered a modern classic of Canadian literature, *As For Me and My House* was a failure upon its release in 1941. It might have been that the Canadian literary scene was still too embryonic during the 1940s, or that federal subsidies didn't exist yet for publishing houses, or perhaps that nearly two decades were needed before Canada could appreciate its prairie mythology. Whatever the cause, the novel failed to attract the attention of literary scholars or reach a large audience until it was reprinted in 1957 by McClelland and Stewart Publishers. After that, it went on to become a staple of Canadian high-school and university syllabi, reaching a level of popularity and acclaim that Ross's other novels, *Whir of Gold* (1970), *The Well* (1958), and *Sawbones Memorial* (1974), failed to achieve.

Sinclair Ross received the Order of Canada in 1992. He died in 1996 in a nursing home in Vancouver.

RECORDED ON NOVEMBER 12, 1970

ET: "The most important body of fiction written about the Canadian West. In Sinclair Ross we may, through indifference and neglect, have permitted a fine artist to perish." Those two lines were written by novelist Edward McCourt in 1949.[1] Sinclair Ross is with us, and I'd like to ask him if we in Canada have allowed us to perish.

SR: Well, writers and artists are often neglected, and I don't think that the Canadian public should be rapped over the knuckles too hard because they didn't respond with more enthusiasm to *As For Me and My House.* I'm inclined to put it the other way and say that the trouble is I didn't make the sufficient impact. In fairness to myself, however, probably my failure to make the impact is because I am a western Canadian. Western Canada is a little apart from the rest of the world and probably the rest of the world isn't particularly interested in it. For instance, I remember reading once that Pearl Buck[2] said — I'm not sure the exact words, but the gist of it is something like this. She said, "A writer should be very careful in the choice of his birth place." And of course she wasn't being funny when she said that. She was born in China, grew up in China, and when she started writing, apparently for a long time, all her stories came back, and sometimes she would get a note from an editor: "We like the story, it's well-written etcetera, but we're not interested in China." Well, I think that's true … that literary decisions in the English language are made in New York and London and, to some extent, in Toronto, and I don't think they're particularly interested in Saskatchewan.

ET: There is, though, something universal in what you've written in that it has relation, surely, to times of drought, anxiety, poverty, and hardship in almost any nation of the earth. I'm wondering, too, if *As For Me and My House,* your best-known book, which was published in 1941, if it was, like many good books, a bit ahead of its time, in that the vogue for the thirties and the vogue of Depression studies did not come until a great deal later. For example, it's only now that it's become fashionable to do mixed-media kits on the 1930s.

SR: Yes, yes. When *As For Me and My House* came out, of course, it fell flat on its face. And it was out of print from about '42, I think, until it came out in the New Canadian Library in 1958. Speaking of neglect, probably if it had come out earlier in that edition, and Canadians had become more aware of it, I might have been encouraged, because by that time, the years had gone on, and it was much more difficult to break away from what I was doing to become what you might call a professional writer ... to make my living as a writer.

ET: It's hard to send a book on into the world and find that there is no response. I can see that that could be disheartening. Could you tell us a bit about what moved you to write *As For Me and My House*? Why did you feel motivated to write that book, which is a book about the Dust Bowl period in the thirties in Saskatchewan?

SR: That's something I'd never thought about.

ET: Had it been something that had been in your mind and in your soul for a long time?

SR: Probably, but it's a long time ago, and when you do these things, you don't keep notes. And it would be pretty hard to go back and trace the development of it. Just speaking of *As For Me and My House*, where the idea for the story came from was: I was living in a small town, and a United Church minister, he thought that I might make a better minister than I would a banker. So he made the suggestion, which was made to Philip: "Would you like to go in the Church?" And of course, I said no. It didn't tempt me at all, but ... and probably this is what they mean by having a writer's mind ... I started thinking, *Well, supposing somebody did accept that offer, and then he finds himself trapped.*

ET: And it got you started on —

SR: That was the idea. The United Church minister was a kind fellow who meant well but he wasn't a very good judge of human nature, of human character.

ET: You were working in a bank on the prairies.

SR: That's right, yes.

ET: What are some of the vivid experiences you had then? What do you feel really formed your roots and background in Saskatchewan?

SR: Well, just that I lived there all my life. I mean it was the life I knew. I didn't know any other life. It never occurred to me at that time of writing anything else. This was my background and the people I knew.

ET: What themes and ideas have continued to interest you?

SR: Well, of course, man's struggle with the land and the elements — that's the most obvious thing. One other theme, which isn't very apparent so far in what I've done, is that I'm interested in crime. Not the actual crime, but the mind, the criminal mentality, and the motivation for the crime. In a book I did called *The Well*,[3] I dabbled at that, and I wasn't able to do what I wanted to do. I failed, and that's why it isn't a very good book.

ET: If you're interested in a criminal's motivation or in the psychological distortion that makes him a criminal, do you feel that you are able to get insight into it as you write a book, as you write a character?

SR: Well, I try to, but that is where I failed in *The Well*, because I didn't succeed. I wanted the character to be a fairly sympathetic character, and I wanted to get inside him and follow him right through to carrying out a crime, to carrying out a murder, and I couldn't do it.

ET: Do you have some kind of basic intuition about the criminal mind, as you put it? Do you feel that the criminal is just any one of us, only he happens to be the one who commits the crime?

SR: Probably. It's a mystery. It puzzles me. I don't pretend to know the answers. And you ask if I have intuition. I don't know. Probably I haven't. But it fascinates me.

ET: Have you continued exploring criminality in your new book, called *A Whir of Gold*?[4]

SR: Yes, yes. I try, but whether I come up with the right answers or not, I don't know. The chief character takes part in a very stupid crime, and he puzzles himself over why he did it. And he makes plausible suggestions — probably they're not right. As I see it, it's a self-destructive urge and he himself is not aware of this. I'm hoping that, while *he* isn't aware of it, that the reader will be.

ET: Mr. Ross, why do you write? What do you really want to accomplish? Is it basically something for yourself?

SR: Well, you know, that's another question that, I don't know, that I never ask myself. I don't know whether writers *do* ask themselves. I suppose it goes back to "Look!" You know when we see something, and we're with somebody we say, "Look!" You're walking around the road, and you round the corner and there's a beautiful scene before you, or maybe a garden or an animal or something, and you say, "Look!" It isn't necessary because the other fellow has good eyes, too; he can see it. But we seem to have that urge, and if there's no one to whom we can say it, probably we feel just a little bit disappointed. I think that's the beginning of all writing. Things impress you and you have this urge that ... well, you feel it; this sounds a bit pompous, but you feel it so intensely that you must get it said and so you write it. I think probably that's the basic urge behind all writing.

ET: So that someone else can see it as well as you.

SR: That's right, yes. You have something to communicate. I suppose it's a form of conceit and arrogance. You feel that the way I feel it, that's the right way, and I must communicate the way I feel it.

ET: Do you have any opinions on commercialism? There's a line in your book, Philip's work in *As For Me and My House*, to the effect, "Instead of trying to make his story popular and saleable, he pushed it on somberly the way he felt it ought to go." Now, Philip, of course had made his living in the church, which he disliked and wished to leave. He was a frustrated artist who couldn't buy the free time to paint. And secondly, I'm wondering is there a parallel with yourself in that you spent much of your life in a bank, with little time to write.

SR: No, there's not really a parallel. It's not the same. I worked in a bank to make my living, but there was nothing disgraceful or shameful about that. Many people who want to become artists and writers, at one time in their life, they worked in an office or a factory or all sorts of jobs. But it's perfectly all right. But with Philip, he was in the church making his living, and he was preaching a gospel which he didn't believe. So, in other words, he was a hypocrite. That *was* something to be ashamed of. And that is the key of course *to* Philip, because he was big enough, honest enough, to look at himself squarely in the eye and say, "You're a heel, you're a hypocrite," and that takes some courage to do that. He never tried to rationalize, he never said, "Well, if I don't do the job, somebody else will. Maybe I'm doing just as well as the next fellow." He was too honest for that. But he wasn't big enough to do something about the trap he was in. He never got out.

ET: You don't feel, then, that having spent your life in a bank has hindered your writing or prevented you from writing?

SR: Ah, well, yes, probably it has, because you've only so much time, you've only so many hours a day. But I mean the parallel … there's not the parallel. Philip was ashamed of what he was doing, while I was never ashamed of working in a bank. It was just my way of making a living. So that's what I mean … there's not the parallel.

ET: I'm interested in the conflict between the simple and the complex. For example, Roy Daniells,[5] Canadian literary scholar, in introducing *As For Me and My House* said, "Simplicity is the keynote of Ross's artistic achievement," and concerning the stories, he said, "These brief narratives of pioneer settlers, their burdened wives, and imaginative, isolated children move the emotions as do few of our recent and more complex studies of character." I rather take issue with what he says about complex studies because I think that you have written characters infinitely more complex than he seems to be giving you credit for. For example, there's nothing simple at all about the Bentleys,[6] I don't think, about their personalities.

SR: Well, again, that's something … I never thought of it in terms of simple or complex. I was just trying to reveal these people and, yes, probably they were complex. Philip is complex. But I never thought of it in terms of simple or complex.

ET: There are many conflicting wants and aspirations, I think, impeding all the time, especially with Philip and with his wife, too.

SR: Yes, probably the characters in the short stories are more simple because their needs are more simple, and their urges and drives. But, it's a little difficult to say just what is simple and what is complex.

ET: Would you comment on some of the characters that are in all of your stories, such as the land, and some of the more ghostly elements, such as feelings of loneliness and striving for survival, the hard training of the hard-work ethic and puritanism? It seems to me that there's a real flavour of what it's like to live on the prairie, and to be part of that people, in your stories.

SR: Well, if that comes through, that is just because probably I wrote honestly of the life that I knew. This is the background I knew. For instance, you speak of puritanism. I'm sure that is correct, but I never thought of it as puritanism. The word *puritanism* never crossed my mind. I wrote about these people and that's what they were. For instance, you have a colour film on a camera and you snap a girl with a blue dress. Well, you get both the girl and the blue dress. You describe people … you get the people plus their religious beliefs, plus their moral attitudes. You can't separate them. So there was nothing conscious or deliberate about that when I did it. It was just describing the people, and what they are came through. It's the same way if you're writing about Canadians. You don't set out to write a Canadian novel, but if you write about Canadians, you've got a Canadian novel.

ET: When you write, you start with what you see. You start with the visual, and when you see these people, as you say, you see them in their entirety, and it doesn't strike you that they are necessarily fundamentalists or puritans or hidebound.

SR: No, but again, that's something you don't think about, and where you start on a story … it's that needle under the skin where you get the shot of something which grows and becomes your story. It's pretty hard to pin down because you don't take notes, as I say, at the time, and then by the time you do look at it, it's grown considerably. The actual beginning you probably don't pay any attention to. I've often tried to run down a story. For instance, "One's a Heifer": all I can remember of that is that I was out on horseback and a woman waved to me, and when I got to the door she said they had lost two calves. And she asked me if I've seen them, and she said, "One's a heifer and the other ain't." Well, that's a long way from a story, but that's what must have stayed in my mind.

ET: Do you find that you have many other givens that way? Either you hear a phrase, or you hear something memorable, and then you have to write about it sometime, even if it's much later?

SR: I don't think it works that way with me. I think probably something happens and then it becomes embedded in my mind, as it were, and then later I come back to it. But at the time I don't say, "Well, this is something I must write about." I think it grows and then reaches the stage where, well, it may be somewhat urgent. But that's later on. It may be months later or years later.

ET: What literary influences have you felt in your life? What books do you like to read? What authors have moved you?

SR: Oh, I've read all over the place. I've always read a great deal. I don't know of any that have influenced me. I suppose they have but I'm not aware of any particular influence. For one thing, when I started writing over thirty years ago, there wasn't very much western Canadian literature *to* influence me. But as a youngster I read [Walter] Scott[7] and [Charles] Dickens,[8] all sorts of things … [Joseph] Conrad[9] at one time … [Thomas] Hardy.[10] Probably Hardy, if anyone influenced me, probably Hardy … and a book like *Return of the Native* might've. But I'm not aware of the influence.

ET: What do you like to read now? Do you read current American and English fiction? Do you read biography? Do you read history?

SR: Everything, everything — whatever. I have no reading patterns, but I read a great deal, oh, yes.

ET: Are you part of some kind of fast-moving literary scene? And do you write reviews for fashionable journals? Do you lunch with book people all the time? Or do you live rather more by yourself, doing your own thinking?

SR: No, I know very few literary people. I'm completely out of the swim, as it were. And, of course, now that I'm living in Europe, I don't know anybody at all.

ET: Do you think this is for you a positive feature?

SR: Well, again, that's something I never think much about because, as I say, I have always lived apart and that's part of life now. If I knew more literary people, they might be stimulating. I don't know.

ET: But then also you come back to what you have to work with, which really is your own mind and your own senses. And that's still what you have to train and —

SR: That is the important thing, yes. Other writers, as I say, might be stimulating but you can't feed off them … they can only stimulate you. If you listen to them talking and knowing what they're doing, you might have a little spurt of rivalry sometimes that you might feel, "Well, I can do this, too." I don't know because as I say, I'm out of the swim.

ET: There *is* a good deal of rivalry and that's probably a healthy thing to stay out of. Probably a great waste of time. Could you sketch in, chronologically, a bit of your life story?

SR: I was in several small towns in Saskatchewan working in the bank, and then I went to Winnipeg when I was about — oh, I would be about twenty-two or twenty-three, and then I stayed there for about twelve or fourteen years, then I was four years in the Army, and then I was about twenty years in Montreal. And I've been retired for two and a half years now. At the present time, I'm living in Greece, but I don't expect to be there much longer.

ET: I see. What encouraged you to go to Greece?

SR: Health was the principal reason. I have a sort of arthritis, and I feel much better in a warm, dry climate.

ET: Is there a stimulus for your work in Greece that you wouldn't have found in Montreal?

SR: No, I don't think so. The only thing is living in a foreign country makes you more aware of yourself as a Canadian. You have a sense of Canadian identity, which probably you wouldn't have here. But whether that will make any difference in what I write, I don't know.

ET: Yes, it may make you recall. Are you able to see Canadian things and aspects of Canadian memories in a sharper way than you would if you were right on this soil?

SR: Probably, I'm not sure. As I say, I don't stop to think about these things but I think these do have an effect on you, on your subconscious.

ET: Mr. Ross, could you tell us about your new book, *A Whir of Gold*? When did you begin writing it? Something about the basic structure of the book and the impulse you had in writing it?

SR: Well, I started — oh, a great many years ago to write. I wrote a long short story, and nothing happened. It was an awkward length; it was too long for a short story and not even a novella length. I forgot about it. In a way I forgot about it, but one character in particular always stayed with me. Well, finally I got around to thinking that I could expand it and make a novel of it. And I spent quite a time working on the novel because there was one version which didn't go and then I finally have made another version. But it's Saskatchewan. One of the principal characters is an out-of-work musician in Montreal and the other is a girl from Nova Scotia. Speaking of my interest in the criminal mind — he takes part in a very stupid crime.

ET: Is this part of your thinking about crime, that it's a kind of lapse of the moment or a kind of stupid choice that one makes that could have been avoided?

SR: In this case, I think it's a self-destructive urge. He wanted to be a musician, and he became a popular musician instead of a serious musician. It was a logical choice to make, because at his age, and with his lack of background and training, it would have been impossible for him to become the musician he wanted to be. So it was a very sensible choice to take up popular music. But he, within himself, always felt guilty. Again, there was the guilt of the puritan conscience, I suppose … although again, I never thought it was the puritan conscience, because he'd had a fairly strict upbringing and then he'd broken with that. Well, he tries to analyze himself — why he took part in this crime — and he never hits the nail on the head, but I'm hoping the reader will see the reason for it, which is self-destructive. He feels guilty and from that flows this urge, not exactly to destroy himself, not suicide … he doesn't go that far … but it is self-destructive.

ET: A very strong feature in your books and stories is human survival. And one quotation from Margaret Laurence, who wrote the introduction to your collection of stories is, "In counterpoint to desolation runs the theme of renewal. Tomorrow it may rain. The next spring will ultimately come. Despite the somber tone of the dark themes of Sinclair Ross's short stories, man emerges as a creature who can survive, and survive with some remaining dignity against both outer and inner odds which are almost impossible."[11] Would you comment on this quality of survival?

SR: Well, survival is important to all of us. It's basic. Probably, in a story about the land in conflict with nature, it stands out in relief. But the problem of survival is just as acute for a man in an office or a factory. No matter what your job is, it's still survival. But it's probably more dramatic when you see man fighting against nature, against the land. Survival for rural people is a matter of holding their own against nature, against the elements. Survival for people in a city is more often a matter of holding their own against the neighbours. Now, I don't know whether this has any effect on the nature, on the character, of the people. It seems to me if we followed it through that it might be. This is just speculation. If your enemy is the land and the seasons, it seems to me it gives you more room to have faith in human nature, in the basic good in your fellow man; whereas if your enemy *is* your neighbour, well, you may become more wary and suspicious. I don't know whether that's true or not, but it's something to think about.

ET: Did you find this in your personal life, that survival was an important theme in your own life?

SR: No, I've never thought of it. I don't think we do *think* of it as survival, but it's an instinct and one way or another we *all* are struggling for that. It's part of life. Only in the case of a man on the land, it is thrown up in relief so that you see it and are aware that it is a struggle for survival.

ET: Allied with that is the hard-work ethic, and this is something you've said yourself about some of your people: "They were compelled not by labour, but by the spirit of labour, a spirit that pervaded their lives and brought with idleness a sense of guilt."

SR: Yes, I think that's probably true. I don't know whether it would be true of the people in Saskatchewan today, because this was written of people thirty and thirty-five years ago. But I think it certainly *was* true of them. Probably they've changed, yes.

ET: Yes. They really hated even to have Sunday an idle day.

SR: That's right, yes. I think there was a feeling of guilt if they rested, yes.

ET: I think you are a writer who has really an ethical position against selling out. This is very strong in the character of Philip in *As For Me and My House.* Have you, in your own work, striven not to make it commercial, not to make it popular, or not to make it saleable but to let the writing go the way you think it should go, even if it means it doesn't have a great audience?

SR: Well, I suppose I have. I feel that the story should be done a certain way, and I do it that way. At the same time, probably if I *could* write the other type of story, I *would*, but I don't think I can. I'm not adaptable enough for it. Because often what you might call light fiction, I don't think we should turn up our nose at it. It calls for great skill sometimes. It isn't everybody that can do it. You say, "Oh well, there's nothing to it; it's of no importance." But still, it calls for great skill to turn it out because everybody can't turn out a popular bestseller which is of no importance. Otherwise, we all would be doing it.

ET: Mr. Ross, what books have you not written yet? Or stories that you would like to write or that you are planning to write?

SR: Well, I have another novel about Saskatchewan coming up. I think it's coming up. I haven't done any work on it, but I have it pretty well completed in my mind. I know what's going to be in it, and I know what it's going to be about. That's the next thing I want to do.[12]

ET: Are you superstitious about talking about a book before it's written? Do you think that if you talk about it you won't write it?

SR: Not superstitious, but I think that you dissipate the urgency if you talk about it. I think it's wise not to talk about it.

ET: Have you found it possible to go ahead, to still have a stimulus to write, and to still derive satisfaction from writing, although your books don't sell in very large quantities?

SR: I suppose it's a compulsion. I always scribble and I suppose I — yes, I suppose it is a compulsion. I can't help it. I'm always getting something in my mind ... that I *should* write it down and I *want* to write it down, even though it does seem hopeless sometimes and all along it has often seemed hopeless. But I'll likely keep on scribbling.

ET: In what ways does it seem hopeless?

SR: Well, I have written so little and I've had such little success that I suppose that has had its effect on me. But I'm not too optimistic about the future, about *my* future as a writer.

ET: I think it was Scott Fitzgerald[13] who said that nothing fails like success, and it's really a great North American lesson. And sometimes not to succeed in the cheap, popular term of success is perhaps a blessing. I think there are much deeper ways to succeed. In other words, if the story really means something deep, and lasting, and personal to the reader, I think that's the greatest success that you could have. But you will probably never hear from the reader.

SR: That's right. That's right.

ET: There won't be any way that he can get in touch with you in Athens, Greece, or Montreal, Quebec. And what is a marvellous feature about writing, I think, is that it is preserved … it's on the record. People can go back to it. It may not be well received … no notice may be taken in 1941 … but 1971 might be the big year, they might begin to rediscover your books. Mr. Ross, as a writer, what do you most want to be remembered for?

SR: Oh, that's something else I never want to think about, because that would mean thinking about when you're dead, and I never go that far. But to answer your question: I suppose I would like people to say, if they talked about me after I'm dead, "Well, what he wrote was well written." And I would like to think that the people in my books were human and that they rang true. Oh, I'm wanting quite a lot now. And probably that I had said something revealing about human nature, human conflict, human predicament. That's enough.

Transcribed by Geoff Baillie

DOROTHY LIVESAY
(1909–1996)

"Is the reality more important than the imagined? Does it last longer ...? Somehow the advantage seems to be with the imagination, for there, there is no end ... there are no finalities" (Livesay, *Right Hand Left Hand* 23–26). So wrote Dorothy Livesay in her diary, on April 20, 1928. Livesay's life and work can be conceived as a perpetual oscillation between various polarities: imagination and reality, literary lyricism and activism, her bourgeois upbringing and her Marxist tendencies. She existed in an interstitial space between these dichotomies, drawing them together in her life and work and creating poetry that was both striking and significant.

Livesay was raised in a world full of literature: she was born on October 12, 1909, to JFB Livesay — the first general manager of the Canadian Press — and poet, journalist, and translator Florence Randall Livesay. Livesay's friend Jean ("Jim") Watts described their house as "a mad place, but full of books," where Livesay "spent her whole youth reading" (Lawson 45–46). Only later, Jim noted, did Livesay develop an interest in social issues. After enrolling in the University of Toronto to study modern languages, Livesay studied abroad at the University of Marseilles during her third year, where she became involved with the French communist movement. Her writing became increasingly politicized as she shifted away from her earlier lyrical style. Upon returning to Canada in 1932, she enrolled in a diploma course offered by the University of Toronto's School of Social Work. While working as a caseworker in Montreal, New Jersey, and Vancouver, she also engaged with leftist artist organizations, such as the Progressives Art Club and Vancouver's *New Frontier*. Indeed, her

Governor General Award–winning works, *Day and Night* and *Poems for the People*, were blatantly Marxist and anti-authoritarian, despite an interwar political climate hostile to leftism. Even after renouncing communism in the 1940s, Livesay remained socio-politically engaged, writing for CBC Radio beginning in the 1930s, and later, from 1959 to 1963, working for UNESCO in Paris and Zambia.

Livesay also advocated for a more active role for women in both literature and society. She recalled how her father had introduced her to canonical female writers such as Jane Austen, the Bronte sisters, and Katherine Mansfield, "creative women who dared to live by their own standards" (Livesay, *Right Hand Left Hand* 121–22). Livesay followed their example, not only through her writing, both poetic and journalistic, but also through her socio-political involvement and her teaching. Though many in the early to mid-twentieth century considered it almost absurd for a married woman to pursue a career in teaching, writing, or social work, Livesay forged her own independent career path, condemning the fact that "in theory [men and women] were free and equal" while "in practice, our right hand was tied to the kitchen sink" (124).

One of Livesay's most important contributions to the Canadian literary landscape was *Contemporary Verse*, a poetry magazine she founded in 1941 alongside Floris McLaren, Anne Marriot, and Doris Ferne. This magazine aimed to give voice to unknown writers experimenting with new verse forms and exploring socio-political themes. As McLaren later commented, "most of the books of poetry published in Canada since 1941 have ... their roots in *Contemporary Verse*" (Livesay, *Journey With My Selves* 164). Livesay also founded *Contemporary Verse 2* in 1975, to create "a lively discussion on the art of poetry" where *Contemporary Verse* had left off (*CV2*). Indeed, this was Livesay's aim and achievement throughout her multi-decade, multi-faceted career. Her work reflected and reinforced some of the most significant literary and socio-political shifts in the twentieth-century Canadian cultural landscape, endowing Canada with a literary legacy for which "there is no end ... there are no finalities" (Livesay, *Right Hand Left Hand* 23–26).

References

"About." *Contemporary Verse 2.* Accessed January 10, 2016. www. contemporaryverse2.ca/en/about.

Lawson, Jean. "Interview with 'Jim' Lawson." In *Right Hand Left Hand* by Dorothy Livesay. Erin, ON: Press Porcépic, 1977.

Livesay, Dorothy. *The Documentaries.* Toronto: Ryerson Press, 1968.

———. *Journey With My Selves.* Vancouver: Douglas and McIntyre, 1991.

———. *Right Hand Left Hand.* Erin, ON: Press Porcépic, 1977.

———. *Selected Poems of Dorothy Livesay.* Toronto: Ryerson Press, 1957.

———. *The Unquiet Bed.* Toronto: Ryerson Press, 1967.

Thompson, Lee Briscoe. *Dorothy Livesay.* Boston: Twayne, 1987.

Toppings, Earle. "Notes on Dorothy Livesay." 1969. Earle Toppings fonds, 2015.06, box 1, file 5. E.J. Pratt Library, Victoria University, University of Toronto.

Whalley, George, ed. *Writing in Canada: Proceedings of the Canadian Writer's Conference, Queen's University, 28–31 July 1955.* Toronto: Macmillan of Canada, 1956.

Zenari, Vivian. "Dorothy Livesay." *Athabasca University.* Last modified February 12, 2015. http://canadian-writers.athabascau.ca/english/ writers/dlivesay/dlivesay.php.

RECORDED ON JUNE 16, 1969

This is Dorothy Livesay. Behind all poetry is song; what Ezra Pound[1] called melopoeia, melody. And sometimes it's very hard to write a poem without hearing, in your mind, the music behind it. I do not know how it is with other poets, but as far as I am concerned, I am always hearing this other beat behind the ordinary spoken language. And I'm always hearing the melody.

Perhaps this consciousness developed in me quite early because, of course, we had no radio or television in those pre-World War One days, but we did have a piano. While my mother played nursery rhymes, or songs like "Little Brown Jug," my sister and I sang the words. During and after the war, Ukrainian immigrant girls came successively to Winnipeg. They lived

with us and acted as mother's help until they knew enough English to get a better job. And they sang rollicking or melancholy ballads in Ukrainian, songs which so interested my mother that she began strumming them on the piano, and asking for their story. Soon, she was learning to read Ukrainian herself, so as to translate the folk songs into English.

And thus it was that as a small child I felt words as being linked with music. In my mind, my poem was a tune, and I began to make up tunes before I found the words for them. Always I loved to hear poems read aloud but soon became independent of my mother's voice, and I'd take Robert Louis Stevenson's *A Child's Garden of Verses*, or perhaps some Irish ballads, and say them over to myself. By the time I was ten, I was trying to write a few such verses myself; and by the time I was thirteen, they began to flow easily and freely, so that a day wasn't a day unless I found a song in it. Here's one like that, written at that time — or when I was in my teens:

SUCH SILENCE

Some silence that is with beauty swept
With beauty swept all clean:
Some silence that is by summer kept,
By summer kept all green …

Give me such silence in a little wood
Where grass and quiet sun
Shall make no sound where I have run
Nor where my feet have stood.

At that young time, it never worried me that I could not sing beautifully nor keep my voice true. When alone in the garden or the woods, I just let go and sang. In the same way, I accompanied myself in a dance, my body moving and swinging as I sang. In the teens, however, my real problems began to come to the fore. To dance, the most primitive creative expression. But what happens if you're born clumsy? I wrote about that much later in the poem "Ballad of Me." It begins this way:

> Misbegotten
> born clumsy
> bursting feet first
> then topsy turvy
> falling downstairs:
> the fear of
> joy of
> falling.

> *Butterfingers*
> father called it
> throwing the balls
> which catch as catch can
> I couldn't.

> Was it the eyes' fault
> seeing the tennis net
> in two places?
> the ball flying, falling
> space-time team-up?

> What happened was:
> the world, chuckling sideways
> tossed me off
> left me wildly
> treading air
> to catch up.

When I was a child in wartime Winnipeg, there were no ballet classes and no one had heard of modern dance, a style that might well have suited my temperament. But in winter, when the wind waged its battles around the frame house, I trembled; and outside, I whirled with the snowflakes. Perhaps it was the memory of that kind of a beginning that made me later write the poem called "Signature." It's about being born in Winnipeg; it's also about my roots and my family name "Livesay," which has been recorded on an old tombstone in England. And this is the way the tombstone describes how the name should be: "Livesay the name God them gave; and now lives, aye, indeed they have." The poem then follows, "Signature":

> Born by a whim
> This time
> On a blowing plain
> I am as wind
> Playing high sky
> With a name —
> Winnipeg!
>
> So prairie gave breath:
> Child head, anemone
> Raised from the winter grass
> Pushing the mauve-veined cup
> Upward to world all sky
> Peopled with cloud.
>
> Ages before
> These violet veins
> Fingered their mauve
> Through England's green;
> These crocus eyes
> Glowed in stone
> On a poplar row
> Sturdy with Normandy;
> Or a sea-wall —
> War's peep-hole.

And longer than summers
Of conquering blood
Were my feet running
In a Roman wood
And my hair bound
In a vestal hood.

Stretched on the solitary sand
Of Egypt, I lay asunder:
Till the lover came,
The flowering night
Shaped me a name
And the earth shook under.

Now, when I waken here,
Earthbound
Strapped to the sound
Of a Winnipeg wind;
I dream of the next step
On into time —
Casting off skin,
Bones, veins, and eyes,
Flower without root,
Dancer without feet —
Gone in a cone of spiralled air,
And I only wind
Sucked to the sun's fire!

The prairie gave breath; I grew and died:
Alive on this air, these Lives abide.

I would now like to read a couple of poems which express what might be called my imagist mood. My mother, when I was in my teens — late teens — in Toronto, subscribed to the magazine *Poetry: Chicago*, and at that time, poets were beginning to break free from the old rhythms and meters, and concern themselves with the objects seen, rather in the manner of Chinese or Japanese poetry. And so, some of those early imagist poets, like Amy Lowell, and Vachel Lindsay, Carl Sandburg, were ones I enjoyed, and perhaps, quite unconsciously, began to imitate.[2]

GREEN RAIN

I remember long veils of green rain
Feathered like the shawl of my grandmother —
Green from the half-green of the spring trees
Waving in the valley.

I remember the road
Like the one which leads to my grandmother's house,
A warm house, with green carpets,
Geraniums, a trilling canary
And shining horsehair chairs;
And the silence, full of the rains falling
Was like my grandmother's parlour
Alive with herself and her voice rising and falling,
Rain and wind intermingled.

I remember that on that day
I was thinking only of my love
And of my love's house.
But now I remember the day
As I remember my grandmother.
I remember the rain as the feathery fringe of her shawl.

It seems evident now that the free verse poems were all solitary — myself talking to the wind — whereas the more structured lyrics envisage a partner. Through my twenties and experimentation with sex, it was simply this search for the perfect dancing partner. I had read Havelock Ellis's *The Dance of Life*,[3] and I believed in the consummation of body, of two bodies into one, the merging of self into self.

As a result of that, I wrote quite a series of short love poems which are in my selected poems *Selected Poems*. I might just read just one brief one from that period.

SONG FOR SOLOMON
One day's sorrow
Is not much
When there's grief
Still to touch:

But one day's sorrow
Drops a stone
That plunges deep
Through flesh, through bone.

After that lyrical period, I was plunged into the world. At the Sorbonne in Paris, where I was doing postgraduate work in French and Italian, I came against the whole problem of unemployment when nations are arming themselves, and the whole development in politics of the Hitler movement. When I returned to Canada, the results of that period of social orientation began to appear in my poetry, in the socially committed poems such as "The Outrider" and "Day and Night" — an attempt at narrative poetry, which hadn't all been published — celebrating the events of the Spanish Civil War. E.J. Pratt[4] gave me a great lift when he printed "Day and Night" in the first issue of the *Canadian Poetry Magazine* in 1936. Mine must have been the first Canadian poem to ignore maple leaves and concern itself with the desperate condition of people caught in a technological revolution. Here, the dance became ironic, and the poem begins "one step forward, two steps back, shove the lever, push it back."

I won't read all of "Day and Night" because it's quite long. But I will read one poem from that period, which was about Spain, about the Spanish poet Lorca, Federico García Lorca, who, it was said, was always singing with the people and for the people, his ballads to encourage them towards freedom.[5] He was eventually shot, and at that time, we believed he was shot by

Franco's men.[6] There are various different versions to the story, now that history has settled down. I'll find this poem in just a moment … ah, here we are, "Lorca." I was walking through Stanley Park in Vancouver, and I was very much in love with that kind of country, forest, and sea, and cliffside, and this happened at the time I heard of Lorca's death.

When veins congeal
And gesture is confounded
When pucker frowns no more
And voice's door
Is shut forever

On such a night
My bed will shrink
To single size
Sheets go cold
The heart hammer
With life-loud clamour
While someone covers up the eyes.

Ears are given
To hear the silence driven in
Nailed down.
And we descend now down from heaven
Into earth's mould, down.

While you —
You hold the light
Unbroken.

When you lived
Day shone from your face
Now the sun rays search
And find no answering torch.

If you were living now
This cliffside tree
With its embracing bough
Would speak to me.

If you were speaking now
The waves below
Would be the organ stops
For breath to blow.

And if your rigid head
Flung back its hair
Gulls in a sickle flight
Would circle there.

You make the flight
Unshaken.

You are alive!
O grass flash emerald sight
Dash of dog for ball
And skipping rope's bright blink
Lashing the light!

High in cloud
The sunset fruits are basketed
And fountains curl their plumes
On statue stone.

In secret thicket mould
Lovers defend their hold
Old couples hearing whisperings
Touch in a handclasp, quivering.
For you sang out aloud
Arching the silent wood
To stretch itself, tiptoe,
Above the crowd …

You hold the word
Unspoken.

You breathe.　You be!
Bare, stripped light
Time's fragment flagged
Against the dark.

You dance.　Explode
Unchallenged through the door
As bullets burst
Long deaths ago, your heart.

And song outsoars
The bomber's range
Serene with wind-
Maneuvered cloud.

Light flight and word
The unassailed, the token!

From 1939 to 1946, I wrote some fifty poems, many of them still unpublished. Right after the war, I went to England for the *Toronto Star* and recorded my responses to the postwar world, its hopes and doubts. On my return, encouraged by Malcolm Lowry,[7] I wrote my most thoroughly documented public poem, "Call My People Home." Yet I feel that this poem for radio managed to combine a sense of personal poignancy and alienation with a sense of social purpose. Many of the dance routines in this poem are perhaps simple to the point of being banal, but I insist that the nursery rhyme and ballad pattern are essential elements in poetry, not to be ignored. I suppose all my life I've fought against obscurantism. For me, the true intellectual is a simple person, who knows how to be close to nature and to ordinary people.

I'd like to choose a section from "Call My People Home" to read. It's quite a long half-hour poem for radio, describing the characters and people and events of the evacuation of the Japanese people from the west coast of Canada into the interior and into the east. This evacuation took place during World War Two because it was feared that the Japanese fishermen were spying. I believe, at the end of the event, it was proven that they were entirely loyal to Canada. However, they were scattered far. And one of the stories I read about in the Japanese newspaper was by a young girl who was taken, separated from her father who was sent to an interior camp for men only. And she was put into a hostel in Vancouver with her mother. The hostel actually was on the Vancouver Exhibition grounds, and it had been a stable for prize horses. I have her writing a letter to her lover. This is called "The Letter."

I wonder where in the inner country
On what train shooting between two mountains
You fly tonight, Susumu?
When I explain to you how it is here
You will understand, perhaps,
Why I've not been able to tell my mother
About you and me.

It is this: she's continually frightened —
Never having lived so, in a horse stall before.
My bunk is above hers, and all night I lie rigid
For fear to disturb her; but she is disturbed.
She has hung her pink petticoat from my bunk rail
Down over her head to be private; but nothing is private.
Hundreds of strangers lie breathing around us
Wakeful, or coughing; or in sleep tossing;
Hundreds of strangers pressing upon us
Like horses tethered, tied to a manger.

My mother lies wakeful with her eyes staring.
I cannot see her, but I know. She is thinking:
This is a nightmare. She is back in her home

Embroidering blossoms on a silk kimono
Talking to me of Yosh (the boy I mentioned,
The one I grew up with). She is making plans
To visit the go-between; to bake for a wedding.

My mother cannot believe her dream is over,
That she lies in a manger with her hands tethered.
So you'll understand now, Susumu:
I have not been able to tell my mother.
It is hard for me to believe, myself,
How you said the words, how you spoke of a garden
Where my name, MARIKO, would be written in
        flowers....
I wonder where in the inner country
On what train far from this animal silence
This thick night stifling my heart, my nostrils —
Where like a rocket shooting between two planets
Have you flown, Susumu? Have you gone?

But as we know, the Japanese people took their great evacuation with
extreme fortitude and resolution, and even with philosophy. And perhaps
now they're happy in a sense that they're scattered all over Canada and didn't
remain in a kind of ghetto in Vancouver.

Here is one of the final poems, by a student. And I feel it perhaps
describes the philosophical resignation of some of them.

THE PHILOSOPHER
To be alone is grace; to see it clear
Without rancor; to let the past be
And the future become. Rarely to remember
The painful needles turning in the flesh.

(I had looked out of the schoolroom window
And could not see the design, held dear

Of the shaken maples; nor the rain, searing and stinging
The burning rain in the eye.

I could not see, nor hear my name called:
Tatsuo, the Pythagoras theorem!
I could not think till the ruler rapped
On the desk, and my mind snapped.

The schoolroom faded, I could not hold
A book in my hand.
It was the not knowing; the must be gone
Yet the continual fear of going.

Yes, to remember is to go back; to take
The path along the dyke, the lands of my uncle
Stretching away from the river —
The dykeside where we played

Under his fruit trees, canopied with apples,
Falling asleep under a hedgerow of roses
To the gull's shrill chatter and the tide's recurrent
Whisper in the marshland that was home....)

To be alone is grace; to see it clear
Without rancor; to let the past be
And the future become. Especially to remember
The habit of grace chosen, accepted.[8]

The poem ends with a musical, ballad-type, little song, "Chorus of Niseis" — these are the young people.

Home, we discover, is where life is:
Not Manitoba's wheat

Ontario's walled cities
Nor a B.C. fishing fleet.

Home is something more than harbour —
Than father, mother, sons;
Home is the white face leaning over your shoulder
As well as the darker ones.

Home is labour, with the hand and heart,
The hard doing, and the rest when done;
A rougher ocean than we knew, a tougher earth,
A more magnetic sun.[9]

Perhaps I'll turn now to one poem from the middle period of my writing, called "Bartok and the Geranium." This is a poem that has been in a lot of anthologies, and I have even heard professors commenting on it, and saying that it is a contrast between nature and art. Well, I didn't know anything about that when I wrote it. I'd been teaching a class of housewives at night, teaching a class on creative writing, and I'd given them an exercise to do. I said I want you to find two images that are quite different from your everyday life — might be a baby tossing an apple, or a dog running after a ball, or ashes falling from the furnace as you shake it. I want you to try and combine those two images to create a tension, present a picture, something in the way a Japanese haiku does. Well, then the next day I lay at home in the dining room, after my rest, having sent my children to school, and I was listening to a CBC concert, and they were playing a piece of music I had never heard before, a concerto by Bela Bartok, a violin concerto. And in my window, in the sunlight, was a red geranium. As I lay there, I thought to myself, "Well, I've given my class an assignment to do to make a poem … I should be able to do one, too." And there it was, the geranium and the music of the violin. So there and then, I wrote "Bartok and the Geranium."

She lifts her green umbrellas
Towards the pane

Seeking her fill of sunlight
Or of rain;
Whatever falls
She has no commentary
Accepts, extends,
Blows out her furbelows,
Her bustling boughs;

And all the while he whirls
Explodes in space,
Never content with this small room:
Not even can he be
Confined to sky
But must speed high
From galaxy to galaxy,
Wrench from the stars their momentary calm,
Stir music on the moon.

She's daylight;
He is dark.
She's heaven's held breath
He storms and crackles
Spits with hell's own spark.

Yet in this room this moment now
These together breathe and be:
She, essence of serenity,
He in a mad intensity
Soars beyond sight
Then hurls, lost Lucifer,
From heaven's height.
And when he's done, he's out:

She leans a lip against the glass
And preens herself in light.

Well, what does it mean? I didn't know at the time. I just wanted to create the picture. But of course I can see now that there is an element of nature versus art in it, and also there is a contrast between the male and the female principal.

Here's a very different sort of poem, an experience I had when living alone in a cabin on Vancouver Island:

THE RAT

Every night I talked to him
(but he paid no attention)
— Go away
leave me alone
I want to sleep
sometimes I even said please

When this didn't work
I tried tantrums
banging and screaming I hurled myself
into his corner
he would be quiet for a small while
alert, listening
but as I was falling asleep
he would start all over again
gnawing and cracking his jaws
demolishing barriers

In the end I had no reserves left
save one —
yes, poison

Not actually POISON
the label said
just a merciful
leukemia
a gasp of air at the end
a mad dash for water ...

I found him, two days afterwards
he hadn't quite reached the lake
unslaked

and he wasn't a rat   but
a squirrel.

Between 1960 and 1963 I had the opportunity to work first in Paris
with UNESCO and then to go and teach English in northern Rhodesia, the
country that since got its independence and is called Zambia. The president
of that country I knew and talked with several times at the college where I
was, and in Lusaka. I have a little poem about him that I call "The Leader"
that's in a part of this longer poem called "Zambia."

Heaven lets down a rope
whereon I swing
the clapper of a bell
on sounding sky

and all below
they cluster with uplifted faces
black on white
and sway like flowers
to my wild clanging

whether sun burns me
or moon rivets with steely eye
I shall ring on
till flowers are black mouths
and the stones bleed my song.

"The Prophetess." This poem comes from the experience in Africa. Once
Kaunda[10] had been declared president of the Republic, he had to face the

problem of organizing and unifying his country. But there was a sect called the Lumpa sect which was rather anti-government, even though it was their own black government. This sect was anarchistic, something as the Doukhobors[11] have been. They didn't wish to participate in war, they didn't wish to participate in schooling their children. They believed that they had had a special revelation from God, that they were the true Christians, and that a woman, Alice Lenshina, was their leader.[12] She had an experience, apparently, the anthropologists have shown. She went out into the woods to gather mushrooms, and these mushrooms were of the kind, I believe, which do create visions. This is the story, then, of Alice Lenshina, and I call it "The Prophetess."

When the rains began,
trees shuddered and were green
the earth heaved
fingers of grass pierced the crust
lilies exploded, anemones
blew into being
out in the fields mushrooms
swelled
as women, belly-swollen.

You were with child then, Regina
and like the others
set out to gather mushrooms
when the hard hills had lowered heads
to graze
when the wild fig trees offered shade.

Walking slowly, surely,
eyes to earth
sensitive only
to the earth
you moved off the path
circled round hills
into green shadow

umbrella trees:
>no one saw you.

>No one saw you.
>No one knew what had happened.
>Mulenga, your husband, wondered:
>he reported you "lost" to the Boma[13]
>but no one went searching.

One day
two days
three — was it three days?
on that day the women returning from hoeing
saw you walking through the gardens
towards the village.

>*Mulenga! Mulenga!*
>*Our sister is back, Lenchina!*

At first you sat silent, rapt
the child ripe within you
stirring
you sat on the ground, beside
a small flame
stirring the millet.

>*Call the elders*, you said

And Mulenga brought them
to sit in the circle
to hear you speak:

>*Before you, my people*
>*I come as one naked, buried.*
>*For I who am living before you*
>*was dead*

and I who died once
died three times.

Pulled from the well of darkness
by their words clanging
clanging in my head
I reached for the rim of light
only to totter
and fall again

But again I was drawn[14]
and how I struggled
to hold on fast,
to listen, to stare
till the waters fell away
and I was hauled out safe
into dry air.

Look at me, look at me!
I am as one naked, buried,
for I who am living now
was dead, three times.

Ai   Ai   the people answered
cried out and marvelled
moved closer.

Not a white man's God I saw
lifting me up from death,
each time,
not a white man hammered with nails
on a wooden cross:
but a Lord incredibly shining,
a sheath of light
and my eyes trembled at the brightness
when I heard a voice crying:

Lenchina, Lenchina, you cannot die
your time is not yet come
there's work to do

And he pressed a Book against my forehead
and showed me the songs I must sing
to rouse you, my people.

Ai   Ai   How the people cry out now
as the fire flickers
as the night falls sudden and definite
darkening the faces.
Not by a white man's God
need we be saved
but by the resurrection of a woman
an African mother
Ai   Ai

The drums beat
tentative   questioning
the drums come out of hiding
now strong ones   bold ones
the drums beat louder and louder
for you, Lenchina
standing by the fire now
short and stumpy
rooted as a tree
a tree singing the new hosannah!

Lumpa   (in the highest)

lumpa   the drums beat
lumpa   lumpa
lumpa   lumpa   lumpa

Transcribed by Amy Kalbun

GWENDOLYN MACEWEN (1941–1987)

Gwendolyn MacEwen was a Toronto poet and author during the counterculture revolution of the 1960s. Her poetry is characterized by dark, violent, fantasy-laden imagery, and themes of magic and Middle Eastern mythology. MacEwen was born on September 1, 1941, in the west end of Toronto. Her parents, Elsie and Alick McEwen (MacEwen changed the spelling of her name in her youth as an act of independence), dealt with alcoholism and mental health issues that forced MacEwen and her sister to live with their uncle and aunt along with several foster children. Elsie spent years in mental institutions because of manic depression and multiple suicide attempts. MacEwen's father turned to alcohol in reaction to Elsie's condition but maintained a career as a natural landscape photographer and teacher at the Ontario Visual Arts School. His creativity was a point of inspiration for MacEwen's writing career, as was her tumultuous childhood. MacEwen's first poem was published in 1958 in the *Canadian Forum*, and in September 1959, she dropped out of high school to write fulltime. The new, dynamic arts community in Toronto during this time was centred on social spaces, like the Bohemian Embassy, and publishers, like House of Anansi, that offered support to MacEwen and other young writers, including Margaret Atwood and Michael Ondaatje.

MacEwen was interested in the ancient history of the Middle East, which she expresses in her poetry volumes, such as *A Breakfast for Barbarians* (1966) and *The Rising Fire* (1963). She learned to speak Hebrew and travelled alone to Egypt in 1966. MacEwen was also fascinated by magic and space travel. Her book *Julian the Magician* is based on her relationship with painter

Bob Mallory, who also explored fantasy and myth in his art. MacEwen wrote many poems about the first trips into space made by American and Russian astronauts, such as "Moon Landing, 1969," and the collection *The Armies of the Moon* (1972). The ancient world, magic, and other planets all offered a form of escape to MacEwen from her painful childhood and the reality of life in Toronto. She understood Canada to be "so quaint, so naive, so hopeless," because of her fascination with ancient Middle Eastern history, but her poetry demonstrates her vision of the urban landscape as violent and threatening. MacEwan describes cities as "apocalyptic" and "filthy kingdoms." Her work is unique in its exploration of the Canadian urban landscape, and although it is influenced by fantasy, it is a reflection of a city in a period of cultural growth and reconstruction.

Her contribution to the Canadian literary canon was recognized with two Governor General's Awards, one for *The Shadowmakers* (1969) and the other for *Afterworlds* (1987). MacEwen's need for escape eventually overtook her life; she isolated herself and became obsessed with privacy. She developed issues with alcoholism, succumbing to resulting health problems in 1987. She left a lasting impact on Canadian poetry with her bold, fantastic visions of other worlds.

References

MacEwen, Gwendolyn. *A Breakfast for Barbarians*. Toronto: Ryerson, 1966.

———. *Earth-light: Selected Poetry of Gwendolyn MacEwen, 1963–1982*. Toronto: General Publishing, 1982.

———. *The Poetry of Gwendolyn MacEwen: The Early Years*. Ed. by Barry Callaghan and Margaret Atwood. Toronto: Exile Editions, 1993.

———. *The Poetry of Gwendolyn MacEwen: The Later Years*. Ed. by Barry Callaghan and Margaret Atwood. Toronto: Exile Editions, 1994.

Sullivan, Rosemary. *Shadow Maker: The Life of Gwendolyn MacEwen*. Toronto: HarperCollins Canada, 1995.

RECORDED ON AUGUST 28, 1969

This is Gwendolyn MacEwen, reading some poems from earlier and later collections. I'd like to begin by reading a poem that was first published in *The Rising Fire* by Contact Press: it's called "Skulls and Drums."

you talked about sound, not
footstep sound, shiphorn, nightcry,
                                    but
strings collecting, silver
and catgut, violas riding
the waves of May like soft ships,
                                        yes
and anchoring senses,
the range, the register,
the index
            in the ear; the long
measure from the drums of our skulls
to the heart (and its particular tempo);
the music anchored there, gathered
in.

you will hear me now, I think,
while my skin still gathers tones of the sun in,
while we ride the bars, the slow passages
of these first minutes;

while the taut drums of our skulls
open
and all sounds enter
and the pores of our skin like slow valves open.

we will hear each other now, I think,
while nothing is known, while sound
and statement in the ear

leave all alternatives;
                    our skulls like drums,
                    like tonal caves
                    echo, enclose.

while the ribs of our bodies are great hulls
and the separate ships of our senses
for a minute

anchor.

for a minute in the same harbour

anchor.

The following poems will be from *A Breakfast for Barbarians*, published in 1966 by Ryerson Press. This is a book of celebration, of appetite and hunger, a sort of affirmation of the world, as this title poem should describe.

A BREAKFAST FOR BARBARIANS
my friends, my sweet barbarians,
there is that hunger which is not for food —
but an eye at the navel turns the appetite
round
with visions of some fabulous sandwich,
the brain's golden breakfast
                    eaten with beasts
                    with books on plates

let us make an anthology of recipes,
let us edit for breakfast
our most unspeakable appetites —
let us pool spoons, knives
and all cutlery in a cosmic cuisine,

let us answer hunger
with boiled chimera
and apocalyptic tea,
an arcane salad of spiced bibles,
tossed dictionaries —

> (O my barbarians
> we will consume our mysteries)

and can we, can we slake the gaping eye of our desires?
we will sit around our hewn wood table
until our hair is long and our eyes are feeble,
eating, my people, O my insatiates,
eating until we are no more able
to jack up the jaws any longer —

to no more complain of the soul's vulgar cavities,
to gaze at each other over the rust-heap of cutlery,
drinking a coffee that takes an eternity —
till, bursting, bleary,
we laugh, barbarians, and rock the universe —
and exclaim to each other over the table
over the table of bones and scrap metal
over the gigantic junk-heaped table:

by God that was a meal

For me the city has two separate aspects: one aspect is grim and the other is quite beautiful. This poem is called "The Children Are Laughing."

It is monday and the children are laughing
The children are laughing; they believe they are princes
They wear no shoes; they believe they are princes
And their filthy kingdom heaves up behind them

The filthy city heaves up behind them
They are older than I am, their feet are shoeless
They have lived a thousand years; the children are laughing
The children are laughing and their death is upon them

I have cried in the city (the children are laughing)
I have worn many colours (the children are laughing)
They are older than I am, their death is upon them
I will wear no shoes when the princes are dying

But I also find the city very beautiful, and I don't feel that the machine or the technological world is my enemy. I think that whatever man constructs must be beautiful if it is a true projection of himself.

THE METALLIC ANATOMY
Civilization means that I am hardened at the knees
Yet welded delicate — my mind a sickle, a crescent tool
   Strikes a shrill metallic key —
Some days I am simply a long scream
   Sculptured in metal, incredible.

Some tensile art, precise with joy
Breaks my lines, keens me
   To a tense and resonant thing,
And the vats of boiling gold in my brain
   Harden to shrill and intricate shapes.
Now I tell you Fall on your knees
   Before the quivering girders of your city,
Fall on your beautiful precise knees
   Beneath me in the black streets;
This is not poetry, but clean greed —

There is a sculpture which must be made.
O citizen pose for this image of the city.

This next poem was written way back in the dark ages when Yuri Gagarin[1] made the first space flight.

THE ASTRONAUTS

now his orbit exceeds three,
exceeds me, my narrow turning,
his body has become a zodiac of bone,
its own myth, a personal cosmology —

I would say he orbits himself only,
his own body,
making his flesh supreme
within its sensual belts —
(but I know there is more than this
I know there is more,
nor can dwindle down those outward galaxies
to internal atoms anymore)

now, Yuri, your orbits
stress my gravity,
the kinetics of your flesh
escapes these lines,
(and you, Valentina,[2] Russian Valentine,
female, dialectical, I imagine you
pivoting over the polar caps,
ferris-wheel woman, queen of hemispheres,
moving through the complex vacuum of a dream)

you flyers, where you are,
God does not need to be,
you have gashed the white void of His memory,
and orbits of verbs describe strange poetries —

I would kneel down under them, those orbits,
those huge and humming wheels,

while rockets rehearse a countdown
in the graded spaces of the spine,
then launched, arise to puncture
the positive zeros of the cosmos and the mind.

The following poem was written after I watched the performance of a young escape artist at the CNE[3] some years ago. I was struck by the beautiful, lyrical way he got out of the ropes and chains, and began to wonder if perhaps his performance wasn't a clearer demonstration of the fight for personal freedom than any poem could be.

Manzini: Escape Artist[4]

now there are no bonds except the flesh; listen —
there was this boy, Manzini, stubborn with
gut stood with black tights and a turquoise
leaf across his sex

and smirking while the big
brute tied his neck arms legs, Manzini
naked waist up and white with sweat

struggled. Silent, delinquent, he
was suddenly all teeth and knee, straining for slack
and excellent with sweat, inwardly
wondering if Houdini[5] would take as long
as he; fighting time and the drenched
muscular ropes, as though his tendons were worn
on the outside —

as though his own guts were the ropes
encircling him; it was beautiful; it was thursday; listen —
there was this boy, Manzini

finally free, slid as snake from
his own sweet agonized skin, to throw his entrails
white upon the floor
with a cry of victory —

now there are no bonds except the flesh,
but listen, it was thursday, there was this boy,
Manzini —

The only criticism I've ever had about a lot of modern poetry is that it tends to be an exploration of pain, a kind of dwelling on one's own wounds and scars. For me, poetry should also heal. It should seal up some of the wounds that life opens. This next poem is called "Appendectomy."

it's interesting how you can brag about a scar;
I'm fascinated with mine; it's diagonal and straight,
it suggests great skill, great speed,
it is no longer or shorter than it needs to be.

it is good how it follows my natural symmetry
parallel to the hip, perfect geometry;
it is not a wound; it is a diagram
drawn correctly, it has no connection with pain.

it's interesting how you can brag about a scar;
nothing in nature is a straight line
except this delightful blasphemy on my belly;
the surgeon was an Indian, and beautiful, and holy.

The next poems that I'll be reading are all from *The Shadowmaker*, a recent collection published by the MacMillan Company. The experience in this first poem is, I'm afraid, limited to people who are smokers, although I hope the implications will be within everyone's grasp.

You Held Out The Light

You held out the light to light my cigarette
But when I leaned down to the flame
It singed my eyebrows and my hair;
Now it is always the same — no matter where
We meet, you burn me.
I must always stop and rub my eyes
And beat the living fire from my hair.

Very many of the poems in *The Shadowmaker* deal with a sense of loss and of recovery or rediscovery. This is a century, I think, when there's a great sense of loss in the world, a great lack of belief in the spiritual and the divine. In many of these poems I try to reaffirm what for me is still holy.

Poem

It is not lost, it is moving forward always,
Shrewd, and huge as thunder, equally dark.
Soft paws kiss its continents, it walks
Between lava avenues, it does not tire.

It is not lost, tell me how can you lose it?
Can you lose the shadow which stalks the sun?
It feeds on mountains, it feeds on seas,
It loves you most when you are most alone.

Do not deny it, do not blaspheme it,
Do not light matches on the dark of its shores.
It will breathe you out, it will recede from you.
What is here, what is with you now, is yours.

Whenever I consider writing poems which are protests against the evils of the world and the social injustices and so forth, I become very much aware that these evils are embodied in each of us separately and in myself, so I don't feel we can really cure the world until we have cured ourselves first.

The Name of the Place

This is the world as we have made it,
As you and I together made it.
Do not speak to me of evil,
We know all the secret names of evil.
Do not speak to me of sorrow,
We invented all the shades of sorrow.
In my heart unspeakable deeds are sleeping
And why I have not yet performed them
Is only due to the shifts of season.
This is the world as we have made it
And we must enter it, endure.
There are unbearable things to bear,
There is a place I dare not speak of
And we have all been there.

But none of us have been there alone
Although it's a small place, fit only for one,
Like the thin black rib of a panther
Or the small receding eye of a dying whale,
Anyway, you know it well.

We each have a message to give to the other,
The size of the place, the colour of the place,
How to get in and out of it,
How long it is safe to remain,
But first of all its name.

I know the name of the place so well
That it's just now slipped my tongue,
But it doesn't matter as long as you
Tell me I have not been there alone.
All things are plotting to make us whole,
All things conspire to make us one.

This next poem was written recently, after I had a long, fascinating conversation with an elderly sailor on a train in the Maritimes. His view of the
world was rather strange, but I learned more from him than I could have
from a dozen books. This poem is actually a series of extrapolations from the
things he was telling me. It's called "The Compass."

"Now, Miss, the first thing you gotta understand
is that the earth moves round the sun.
I tell you this to help you get ahead in life.
And the next thing is that you gotta watch
your grammar, Miss, your grammar,
'cause that's important to get ahead in life.
And don't be afraid to face a big Congomeration
of people,
me, I'm not afraid even though I just got out
of the Hospitality,
because I know where I stand, Miss,
and everything's gotta go and come back home
like the tides."

"Now you give me a ship and I'll take her
to Germany or Africa, you name it
because I know how the Gulf Stream divides
the world in two,
and I'm not scared to cross the great Atitude;
yes Miss — Atitude —
they say the Atlantic but I know

it's the Atitude
'cause you go down the Longitude to reach
the Atitude, you follow me?"

"Stars? Sure, I can sail by the North Star
and the South Star
and the East Star
and the West Star.
Even on this train, Miss
you don't know it but we be sailing
by those stars
'cause they're the compass points
for all the world.
See this compass, you turn five degrees
and then you come back home.
You gotta always come back home, Miss,
like the tides."

"Look now, you'll be always at the centre,
even in a big Congomeration of people,
and all the words you talk here
go down to the sea, and the tide
brings 'em back tomorrow morning.
I tell you this so you won't fear
and you always know just where you stand
and how you're turning."

He turned the old German compass
over and over in his sure black hands.
"I had this fifteen years," he said,
"But I give it to you now so you
can get ahead in life,
and learn the Longitudes and Atitudes
and figure out just where you stand."

All I could think of
to give him in return
was my book of poems — a pointless gift.
But taking it he smiled and said,
"*I've* been doing some writing too
to get ahead in life!"
And pulled out from a suitcase old
as the crazy seas he sailed
something he handled with great respect —
a battered notebook where he'd written
in big scared lines
the first few letters of the alphabet.

For me, Canada is still a very mysterious country. We've no real history of our own, so we've had to plunge down into the lakes and into the forests and construct a sort of past. This poem is called "Dark Pines Under Water."

This land like a mirror turns you inward
And you become a forest in a furtive lake;
The dark pines of your mind reach downward,
You dream in the green of your time,
Your memory is a row of sinking pines.

Explorer, you tell yourself this is not what you came for
Although it is good here, and green;
You had meant to move with a kind of largeness,
You had planned a heavy grace, an anguished dream.

But the dark pines of your mind dip deeper
And you are sinking, sinking, sleeper
In an elementary world;
There is something down there and you want it told.

Dreams can be very important to some poets, and I wrote this poem after having a dream, which was tremendously simple yet at the same time terribly poignant and, I think, profound. It's called "The Child."[6]

He was turning and turning and turning and turning
outside my window on a big unicycle
suspended in air beside a black tree.

Hey, why are you turning and turning and turning
getting nowhere fast on that wheel
when you could be talking to me?

I've always been here, turning and turning
and I'll always be here, turning and turning
From the beginning and to the end, turning,
from alpha to omega turning and turning,
and I looked and saw it was me.

This book, as I mentioned before, is a book of loss and recovery. And for me, the process of growing up or aging has never involved having to lose the dreams and impossible hopes of childhood. This poem is a kind of restatement of that belief.

THE RETURN
I gave you many names and masks
And longed for you in a hundred forms
And I was warned the masks would fall
And the forms would lose their fame
And I would be left with an empty name

(For that was the way the world went,
For that was the way it had to be,
To grow, and in growing lose you utterly)

But grown, I inherit you, and you
Renew your first and final form in me,
And though some masks have fallen
And many names have vanished back into my pen
Your face bears the birth-marks I recognize in time,
You stand before me now, unchanged

(For this is the way it has to be;
To perceive you is an act of faith
Although it's you who have inherited me)

I'd like to read two recent poems, which are as yet uncollected in any book. The first is called "House of Mercury."

These days all those who come to me
should wear the blue of metal or the quick
silver of a sea which glints its mineral
histories — steel of blades from unknown wars,
scales like flint on the unknown fish, great
desolate wrecks of ships which set sail
for the depths, the thin grey clang of bells
calling someone somewhere, tin rivers of Aquarius.

Things that speak of forests I have long since lost
disturb me (eyes the colour of dry moss).
Leave me be, I want to be water,
I'm trying to flow though I'm dense and silver,
I'm trying to move a ton of metal
as easily as the sea.

This final poem was written very recently, after the enormous success of the moon shot.

Moon Landing, 1969[7]

Once his eye raised the cool towers of space
Over the roves of his youth, and he lay
Growing in the red shifting days beneath
Orbiting castles and giants and starbeasts.

Now he descends the steep mountain of the night
To the breathless valley of the moon; earthlight
Floods the lunar pools and craters accommodate
The visitation of his step, his alien weight.

Earthrise is an eye beyond the blinding brim;
Past sighing miles of silence the finite children
Watch him become the satellite of his own dream
And orbit the white world of his youth for them.

Computers map the territories of nether suns
Where galaxies are graphic castles giants own;
Now up the weightless slopes of time he climbs
Through vacuous doorways to the gasping dark beyond.

Transcribed by Griffin Kelly

AL PURDY
(1918–2000)

There are two likely reasons why Al Purdy is often described as the poet laureate of Canada. The first is that his distinctive, laid-back voice might be thought to embody the stereotypical attitude of the easygoing Canadian. The second is that his poems map out the Canadian landscape. Travelling was his way of life, and the stimuli for his poems were the experiences he accumulated throughout his travels across the country, from British Columbia to Newfoundland and Labrador. Taken as a whole, his body of work serves as a kind of poetic survey of the nation.

As a teenager during the Great Depression, he rode the rails across the country, gathering up the experiences that would be published in his first book, *The Enchanted Echo*. Though the work is generally considered an artistic failure, it showed the earliest suggestions of the immense gift for observation that would become the hallmark of Purdy's later genius.

In the late 1950s, Purdy and his wife built their famous A-frame house on Roblin Lake in Ameliasburg, Ontario. Here, Purdy focused on his writing while his wife supported the couple through a series of odd jobs. Their perseverance paid off, and the 1962 publication of *Poems for All the Annettes* announced the emersion of a refined, singular artistic voice that would propel Purdy to the highest ranks of the Canadian literary scene. Purdy's poems had gone from derivative to transcendent. From then on, he was able to support himself as a poet and an editor, with the occasional writer-in-residence position at various Canadian universities.

Purdy's conversation with Earle Toppings focused on the experiences behind his poems and showed his tendency, as myth-making traveller, to seek out scenes of plausible surrealism: what he describes in "At the Movies" as

the "really unreal" experience of seeing a group of Indigenous peoples of the Canadian North watch an American Western in a language they don't understand. His persona was that of the sentimental drunk, waxing vulgar and profound by turns. It is characteristic of Purdy to construct images of an idyllic beauty, decorated in flowery prose, only to puncture them with sly, acerbic wit. "Home-Made Beer" shows Purdy's tendency to express truth through rowdiness where marital discord takes the form of a facetious play-fight between husband and wife. His poems lie somewhere between comedy and tragedy, which Purdy expresses in his farcical war poem "About Being a Member of Our Armed Forces," in which he describes himself as a complacent and impotent soldier:

I took it and myself quite seriously
the way a squirrel in a treadmill does
too close to tears for tragedy
too far from the banana peel for laughter

Purdy won two Governor General's Awards, one for *The Cariboo Horses* in 1965 and another for *The Collected Poems of Al Purdy* in 1986. In 1982 he was appointed to the Order of Canada. He died in North Saanich, B.C., in 2000.

References

All poems except "Street Scene" and "Jubilate on Flight 17 (Eastbound)" come from *The Collected Poems of Al Purdy*. Edited by Russell Brown. Toronto: McClelland and Stewart, 1986.

"Street Scene" comes from *The Quest for Ouzo*, unpublished.

RECORDED ON SEPTEMBER 10, 1969

This is Al Purdy. Well, all my poems are autobiographical, at least to some extent, if my wife isn't listening. And in 1950, when I was in Vancouver, I worked for five years in this factory. At the end of that particular period, a friend and I put a union into that factory, and we were very unpopular henceforward. The factory manager's name was Watt, and eventually I wrote a poem about him, which is, however, *about* Percy Lawson.

PERCY LAWSON
(Contract Negotiator — Vancouver Upholsterers' Union)

Sitting with Lawson in 1954
        sitting with Percy Lawson
ill at ease in the boss's panelled office
after work hours talking of nothing
talking of practically almost nothing
a lousy nickel raise that is
        haggling over a lousy nickel
and maybe besides the long and hourly
bearable toil of an almost lifetime
(East Indians: 35 years
        Canadians: 70 — figures approximate)
Listen in again in the boss's panelled office
        listen to Lawson
listen to Percy Lawson
— thinking of girls in the cutting room
afraid of the union
        afraid for the jobs and
thinking of me — afraid of Watt or
not afraid
        only wanting to be liked
and knowing for sure I'm not
Thinking of Lawson

up from the coal mines
on the island and gotten fat
since talking and haggling and
being afraid of practically nothing
but death and his wife and damn near
        everything but not
not bosses
not Watt
And what's the contract news from Watt who
if I said what I thought he was would
sue me for damn near everything
would sue me right now in a poem and
get a judgement for one lying lyric
        I can't write
        (I'll be damned if I write)
in praise of Watt
in praise of
        practically nothing
But I listen to Percy Lawson
        haggling over a lousy nickel
listen to the sonuvabitch
        haggling over a lousy nickel
the twentieth part of a dollar that
        winks among the words
like a clean magician's coin
born from virginal nothing and not
mined or smelted and sweated and laboured for
for the twentieth part of a wasted hour back there
in the silvery guts of a labouring terribly useful lifetime
In a tactical pause between the chop
        of words Lawson turns
the little fat man probably dead now
        turns then and gives
me a gold-toothed grin

This poem, called "The Drunk Tank," is only autobiographical to a certain extent. After the war, I got in the taxi business, which was quite a turbulent thing. Anyway, I had a friend of mine who had stayed in the Air Force quite a bit after 1945 and eventually he got out … and we went on a party afterwards … and the beginning of this poem talks about that. And then the poem takes off. It's called "The Drunk Tank."

A man keeps hammering at the door
(he is so noisy it makes my ears ache),
yelling monotonously, "Let me outta here!"
A caged light bulb floats on the ceiling,
where a dung-fly circles round and round;
and there is a greasy brown mattress,
too small for the bolted-down steel bunk;
and a high barred window permitting
fungus darkness to creep in the room's corners.
The man keeps hammering at the door
until a guard comes:
"I just happen to know the mayor in this town,"
he tells the guard,
"and it's gonna be too bad for you
if you keep me locked up here."
The guard laughs and turns away.
"It's no use," I tell my cell mate.
"Just wait until morning.
Then we'll be up in the magistrate's court,
and being drunk isn't a very serious —"
"Who are you?" the man asks me.
"I don't know you —"
"I'm your friend," I say to him,
"and I've been your friend a long time,
don't you remember?"
"I don't know you at all," he screams.
"Stay away from me!"
"If that's the way you feel about it," I say,

and suddenly I'm not so sure as I was,
memory is a funny thing isn't it?
"Please sit down and wait until morning,"
I say to him reasonably —
don't you think that was the right thing to say?
But he turns his back and hammers on the door:
"Guard! Guard! I want a cell by myself!
You've put a crazy man in here with me!"
He is so noisy.
And I watch him pounding on the black steel door,
a patch of sweat spreading on his back,
and his bald spot glistening —
He looks at me over his shoulder,
terrified,
and I spread my hands flat to show him
I have the best of intentions.
"Stay away from me! Stay away!"
He backs off into a corner shaking,
while I sit down on the bunk
to wait for morning.
And I think:
this is my friend,
I know it is my friend,
and I say to him,
"Aren't you my friend?"
But there he is at the door again,
he is so noisy ...

This particular poem was also from Vancouver. There was a friend of mine present at the time, and maybe I acted a little bit differently than I would have otherwise, because my wife always denies that this particular incident happened the way I say it does in the poem. However, also, she's been very reluctant to stick her neck out again in any way because she's afraid a poem might get written about her. It's called "Home-Made Beer."

I was justly annoyed 10 years ago
in Vancouver: making beer in a crock
under the kitchen table when this
next door youngster playing with my own
kid managed to sit down in it and
emerged with one end malted —
With excessive moderation I yodelled
at him
          "Keep your ass out of my beer!"
          And the little monster fled —
Whereupon my wife appeared from the bathroom
where she had been brooding for days
over the injustice of being a woman and
attacked me with a broom —
With commendable savoir faire I broke
the broom across my knee (it hurt too) and
then she grabbed the breadknife and made
for me with fairly obvious intentions —
I tore open my shirt and told her calmly
with bared breast and a minimum of boredom
          "Go ahead! Strike! Go ahead!"
Icicles dropped from her fiery eyes as she
snarled
          "I wouldn't want to go to jail
          for killing a thing like you"
I could see at once that she loved me
tho it was cleverly concealed —
For the next few weeks I had to distribute
the meals she prepared among neighbouring
dogs because of the rat poison and
addressed her as Missus Borgia —
That was a long time ago and while
at the time I deplored her lack of
self-control I find myself sentimental about
it now for it can never happen again —

Sept. 22, 1964.   P.S. I was wrong —

I started to write poems at the age of thirteen, and when I got in the Air Force during the beginning of the war, I didn't think I'd be writing many more. I thought I'd be going overseas etcetera. However, eventually I wrote this poem about being in the Air Force. There are some terms in it that are a little difficult to understand, for instance, who ever heard of CWACs now? Canadian Women's Army Corps? And *zombies* were the conscripts who were not supposed to go overseas. And eventually I think they did get sent over. However, I was a very tame sort of soldier in many ways, a little awkward of course, as you'll see from this poem. It's called "About Being a Member of Our Armed Forces."

Remember the early days of the phony war
when men were zombies and women were CWACs
and they used wooden rifles on the firing range?
Well I was the sort of soldier you couldn't trust
with a wooden rifle
and when they gave me a wooden bayonet
life was fraught with peril for my brave comrades
including the sergeant-instructor
I wasn't exactly a soldier tho
                              only a humble airman
who kept getting demoted and demoted and demoted
to the point where I finally saluted civilians
And when they trustingly gave me a Sten gun[1]
Vancouver should have trembled in its sleep
for after I fired a whole clip of bullets
at some wild ducks under Burrard Bridge[2]
(on guard duty at midnight)
they didn't fly away for five minutes
trying to decide if there was any danger
Not that the war was funny
I took it and myself quite seriously
the way a squirrel in a treadmill does
too close to tears for tragedy
too far from the banana peel for laughter

and I didn't blame anyone for being there
that wars happened wasn't anybody's fault then
now I think it is

In 1965 I got some money from a public benefactor and went to Baffin Island. I rode a Nord airplane[3] to Frobisher Bay and then hitchhiked a ride on another plane. When I say hitchhiked, I mean I rode for nothing. But anyway, eventually I ended up at Pangnirtung. And after that I went with an Eskimo family in their canoe and stayed with them for two weeks on an island in Cumberland Sound. However, this is a poem about being at Pang. What struck me as really extraordinary about this was the Eskimos at the movies,[4] enjoying the movies a great deal, thinking they were so exciting and so adventurous whereas they themselves had just come from bringing caribou back over possibly a couple of hundred miles in their own Peterhead boats.[5] Anyway, "At the Movies."

The setting is really unreal
about 150 Eskimos and whites
jammed into a Nissen hut[6] to
watch Gary Cooper and Burt Lancaster
in a technicolour western shootemup
Eskimos don't understand the dialogue
at all but they like the action
and when noble Gary is in danger
or sinister Lancaster acts menacing
a tide of emotion sweeps the hot little hut
kids crawling on the floor are quiet
sensing what their parents feel
something tremendously important is happening
When the Anglican minister changes reels
(his blond head glinting as he administers
spiritual unction to his flock)
cigarettes are lit and everyone talks and
a kid crawls under my legs grinning bashfully

Jim Kilabuk says something I can't quite hear
a baby cries in the pouch on his mother's back
and is joggled gently
It's hot and stuffy as hell in the theatre
doors have to be opened
the odour of white and Eskimo
making a point for air conditioning
Lights go out and Gary Cooper rides again
the forces of evil are finally defeated
only the virtuous bullet kills
violence neutralizes violence
like a mustard plaster
(tho I kinda like the bad guy)
the way it always does in American movies
with an obvious moral a clear-cut denouement
Outside the fiord looks like poured blue milk
mountains like bookmarks under a cold sky
islands are moonscapes
where this story happens
It's 11 p.m.
some of the hunters visit their boats
where dead caribou drain into bilgewater
and the rest of the moviegoers go
home to tents on the beach or prefab houses
and dogs howl to make everything regional
But the point I'd hoped to separate
from all these factual things stubbornly
resists me and I walk home slowly feeling stupid
rejecting the obvious
threading my way between stones in the mud
with the beginnings of a headache.

Lately, when I've made a few more bucks, I've been doing a little bit of
flying. I don't suppose my wonderment at the idea of being high up in the
air and floating through the sky at tremendous speeds … I don't suppose

I'll ever get used to it. But this poem maybe is sort of a parody. Anyway, it's called "Jubilate on Flight 17 (Eastbound)":[7]

> I certainly am a jet age
> man technology's end
> product courtesy Air Canada
> and the U.S. board of directors
> The DC-8[8] paws the ground
> trembling hard then
> a thousand jet white horses
> break loose from the corral
> another thousand broncs
> pour in from open range
> escape down the black runway
> leap at the sky
> in an exaltation of worms
> (flying makes me chortle
> to be human I can almost
> forgive myself for being
> born naked without money)
> But I'm a flying chicken
> figure I'll get it sure
> this time and bound to die
> in five minutes enjoy
> every second to the last countdown
> that leads to a fowl death
> Then above the clouds by god
> my wonder evaporates for
> another big jet pops
> out of the east west
> bound we pass each
> other at a combined speed
> of 1,500 m.p.h. say
> And clear as your father's
> and appalled mother's

face at your own newborn
face I see the horse
and buggy we become pass by
on the mind's radar
screen
      clop
           clop
                clopping
thru the backwoods clouds
Something about the human mind
I can't understand suddenly
I am a stone age man
sitting glumly on a boulder
which is pure gold as like as not
having conceived half
a wheel can't complete
the rest of the circle
and it's raining in Toronto[9]

When I was in Europe, we rode a train down into Greece on West German railways. Eventually got to Turkey. Stayed at a hotel and near the hotel, when I was out walking, they had these horses pulling carts for tourists. I call them *droshkys*. And one of the horses fell down. And I wrote this particular poem shortly after.

STREET SCENE

The tired horse contentedly went to bed in the deep
white blaze of sun pouring down past the 14th
floor of a luxury hotel on the Izmir waterfront
It was unharnessed from the droshky carriage
used by tourists and lovers to pretend
the world is not what it is
and decided to stay on the pavement and sleep there
its mate standing above with blinders

like spectacles and a crowd gathering
The driver twisted the horse's tail forcing
its splayed legs into spastic search
for a sideways dimension to escape to
Another man yanked the brown tired head
and neck into an anguished eye-rolling corkscrew
caused its body to shudder across the blacktop
scraping friction burns onto raw hide
Perhaps the men weren't more cruel than necessary
after all the horse couldn't stay where it was
imagining green fields on the busy pavement
the sun dissolving connections with reality
it had to be gotten back on its feet
and this was accomplished
with minimum delay
traffic again moved briskly and unimpeded
I stood curiously on the pavement and watched
here consider me as spectator or involved
Or is there a moral issue anyway?
Now I fall into my own melodramatic trap
and lie on that street myself
bloody and dazed
and everyone acts as if I don't exist
I seem to be looking at the blind sun between
four legs of a tall brown table
which is really the other horse[10]
The sentimental mind makes such things an enjoyable
kind of game and these written down events
turn reality into poem-fiction
such moral questions the unimportant part
of a TV program staged in a vacuum
Perhaps some answer derives from the basic
error of being either a man or a horse
or even alive and not defenseless
the Turkish cop examining me
with casual eye to decide

whether I'm dangerous (?)
is both killer and victim himself
tho of course he doesn't entirely know that
Both the horse and I have made the mistake
of originally hailing from a foreign country
where victims romp by mountain streams with their killers
the forked man stands in his skin and smiles
wryly at himself
and we want to go home

Another poem about riding into Greece on this train, dealing, if you like, with the things you see looking out the window and the train itself. It's called "Hellas Express."

Bitter sleet pelting through Germany
makes the iron platform between cars icy
and iron steps down to the world
treacherous
In Austria snow is two feet deep
I wake up and throw off the wool blanket
Peering at Yugoslavia buried in snow
space folded up on itself by mountains
holds the wandering presence soon over
that may be walked around part way
then vanishes beyond now and keeps going[11]
Beyond the white villages
fields where cattle have traced 24 hours of their lives
a snowy diagram for whoever loves them[12]

Greeks who spent the summer in German fields
and factories are going home
Turkish workmen return to Antioch and Trebizond
past the Tigris and Euphrates
with new radios

Bending over my shoelaces
it occurs to me that when I was a child
I never learned to tie a simple bowknot
can't now; wonder how my shoes stay on[13]
and invent a landing net for breaking my neck
which seems typical of everything I do
but significance escapes me
in this iron pandemonium

Greece is summer
lovers join their bodies in one heartbeat
and every beat of the wheels reminds me
there is still enough time time time
for whatever I want to do with my life
if I can just remember the right telephone number
and forget to be clever[14]
Does the woman whose belly squeezes
past mine in the corridor know
I'm not responsible?
Someone asks me a question in Greek
or Sumerian but it has always been foolish
to expect intelligent answers from me[15]

Winter is reversed at the Macedonian border
the iron snake pants and lies there
orange trees have bronze age lights in them
rivers run south like old brown bones
in the land of Socrates Alexander and now me[16]
Greeks are lined up at every window staring
out at their homeland
at something not stamped on passports
the customs officials board the train
I fumble for it in my breast pocket

In 1965 when I went to Baffin Island, or at least before leaving for Baffin Island, my brother-in-law asked me to get him some Eskimo sculpture. This wasn't so easy as I thought it was because at Pangnirtung, which is right on the Arctic Circle, the sculptors were pretty lousy ... and it's farther south where they're more expert ... because all the sculpture at Pang had been sent back from Frobisher Bay because it wasn't very good. So I had to go through an awful bunch of it to find some good stuff for my brother-in-law, and I was pretty irritated about it. But eventually this poem came out of it: "The Sculptors."

> Going thru cases and cases
> of Eskimo sculpture
> returned from Frobisher
> because they said it wasn't
> good enough for sale to
> T. Eaton Co. Ltd.
> Getting itchy excelsior packing[17]
> inside my shirt and searching
> for one good carving
> one piece that says "I AM"
> to keep a southern promise
> One 6-inch walrus (tusk broken)
> cribbage board (ivory inlay gone)
> dog that has to be labelled dog
> polar bear (badly crippled)
> what might be a seal (minus flipper)
> I'm getting tired of this
> looking for something
> not knowing what it is
> But I guess they got tired too
> looking for rabbit or bear
> with blisters from carving tools
> dime-sized and inflating
> into quarters on their fingers
> waiting
> for walrus or white whale

under the ice floes to
flop alive on their lap
with twitching animal faces
unready to taste the
shoe blacking carvers use
for stone polish
I'm a little ashamed of myself
for being impatient with them
but there must be something[18]
one piece that glows
one slap-happy idiot seal
alien to the whole seal-nation
one anthropomorphic walrus
singing Hallelujah I'm a Bum
in a whiskey baritone
But they're all flawed
broken
      bent
         misshapen
failed animals
with vital parts missing
And I have a sudden vision
of the carvers themselves
in this broken sculpture
as if the time & the place & me
had clicked into brief alignment
and a switch pulled
so that I can see and feel
what it was like to be them
the tb out-patients
failed hunters
who make a noise at the wrong time
or think of something else
at the trigger moment
and shine their eyes
into a continual tomorrow

the losers and failures
who never do anything right
and never will
the unlucky ones
always on the verge
of a tremendous discovery
who finally fail to deceive
even themselves as time begins
to hover around them
the old the old the old
who carve in their own image
of maimed animals
And I'd like to buy every damn case

My wife and I left Vancouver in 1956 after I'd sold my first play to CBC. I decided I was going to make a fortune from my genius as a writer. We went to Montreal, my wife to work and myself to churn out works of genius. It didn't work out quite that way, though. I only sold two plays. Anyway, my wife quit her job, and we eventually used the proceeds of two sales, two CBC sales, and went and bought a pile of used lumber, the down payment on a lot and built a house on Roblin Lake in Prince Edward County. My wife had decided that if I could get away without working, so could she. So we built the house and looked at each other for two years waiting to see which one would weaken first and go back to work. And during that time at Roblin Lake, I wrote this little ... well not quite at that time, later ... "Winter at Roblin Lake."

Seeing the sky darken & the fields
turn brown & the lake lead-grey
as some enormous scrap of sheet metal
& wind grabs the world around the equator
I am most thankful then for knowing about
        the little gold hairs on your belly —

When I was a kid way back before the flood in Trenton, Ontario, I wanted to be a hockey player. But I couldn't skate. In fact, I didn't learn to skate until I was eighteen years old. But I learned to skate by going under the town bridge and falling flat on my face and getting up until finally I was able to stay on my feet. There was a hockey player with the Toronto Maple Leafs at that time called Red Horner[19] who was a great body checker, and I wanted to be a body checker. Oh well, I suppose that doesn't have much to do with the poem but it's probably the reason why I wrote the poem, so it has quite a bit.

HOCKEY PLAYERS
What they worry most about is injuries
                broken arms and legs and
fractured skulls opening so doctors
can see such bloody beautiful things
almost not quite happening in the bone rooms
                as they happen outside —

And the referee?
                He's right there on the ice
not out of sight among the roaring blue gods
of a game played for passionate businessmen
and a nation of television agnostics
who never agree with the referee and applaud
when he falls flat on his face —

                On a breakaway
the centre man carrying the puck
his wings trailing a little
                on both sides why
I've seen the aching glory of a resurrection
                in their eyes
                as they score
and crucifixion's agony to lose
— the game?

We sit up there in the blues
bored and sleepy and suddenly three men
break down the ice in roaring feverish speed and
we stand up in our seats with such a rapid pouring
of delight exploding out of self to join them why
theirs and our orgasm is the rocket stipend
for skating thru the smoky end boards out
of sight and climbing up the Appalachian highlands
and racing breast to breast across Laurentian barrens
over hudson's diamond bay and down the treeless
                              tundra where
auroras are tubercular and awesome and
stopping isn't feasible or possible or lawful
but we have to and we have to
                         laugh because we must and
stop to look at self and one another but
              our opponent's never geography
                         or distance why
              it's men
              — just men?

And how do the players feel about it
this combination of ballet and murder?
For years a Canadian specific
to salve the anguish of inferiority
by being good at something the Americans aren't —
And what's the essence of a game like this
which takes a ten year fragment of a man's life
replaced with love that lodges in his brain
              and takes the place of reason?
Besides the fear of injuries
is it the difficulty of ever really overtaking
a hard black rubber disc?
Is it the impatient coach who insists on winning?
Sportswriters friendly but sometimes treacherous?
— And the worrying wives wanting you to quit and

and your aching body stretched on the rubbing table
thinking of money in owners' pockets that might be yours
the butt-slapping camaraderie and the self indulgence
of allowing yourself to be a hero and knowing
everything ends in a pot-belly —

Out on the ice can all these things be forgotten
in swift and skilled delight of speed?
— roaring out the endboards out the city
streets and high up where laconic winds
whisper litanies for a fevered hockey player —
Or racing breast to breast and never stopping
over rooftops of the world and all together
sing the song of winning all together
sing the song of money all together ...

      (and out in the suburbs
there's the six year old kid
whose reflexes were all wrong
who always fell down and hurt himself and cried
and never learned to skate
         with his friends) —

Transcribed by Geoff Baillie

EARLE BIRNEY
(1904–1995)

P oet and novelist Earle Birney was born in Calgary, Alberta, and raised on a farm in Erickson, British Columbia. In 1922 he enrolled in the University of British Columbia intending to study chemical engin-eering, but after finding himself beholden to an undeniable passion for lit-erature, he walked out with a B.A. in English. He went on to earn an M.A. from the University of Toronto in 1926, at which time he became affili-ated with Marxist-Leninist student organizations; here he met his first wife, Sylvia Johnston, who introduced him to Trotskyism.

While working on his Ph.D. both in Toronto and at University of California, Berkeley, he was active as a Trotsky functionary. In the 1930s, he spent time in Europe, where he worked to reconcile different factions of the Trotskyist party in England, interviewed Trotsky himself in Norway, and was briefly imprisoned in Germany for refusing to salute a Nazi parade. He didn't begin writing poems until 1939, the same year Canada entered the Second World War. He joined the Canadian officer training corps after the invasion of Russia. His experience serving as a personnel officer was later used in his 1949 novel *Turvey*. He left Trotskyism over disagreements about the war, and though his entry into writing marked his exit from political life, the humanist spirit of Marxism continued to inform all of his poetry.

The poems Birney recited in this tape are reflective of his political beliefs. "David," the titular poem of his first collection (not read here, however), which has become a staple of high-school and university classrooms across Canada since its publication, is about mercy killing. "For George Lamming"

is an expression of the colonial guilt that Birney experienced while visiting Barbados. There is also the anti-capitalist expression of "Billboards Build Freedom of Choice" and the anti-war sentiment expressed in "Time Bomb."

His poetry became increasingly experimental during the 1960s, which led him, influenced by contemporary trends, to republish some of his earlier poems, modified to remove punctuation and sentence structure or fit into concrete poems. Many of these poems were published in *Selected Poems* (1966). The idea was that punctuation delayed communication between writer and reader. He replaced punctuation with spaces in the type, meant to emulate the gap between words and connect with the reader on a more immediate level.

While teaching at the University of British Columbia, Birney established the Department of Creative Writing in 1946, the first of its kind in Canada. He won the Governor General's Award twice, once for *David and other poems* in 1942, and again for *Now is Time* in 1945. In 1970 he was appointed to the Order of Canada. He died in 1995.

References

Birney, Earle. *The Collected Poems of Earle Birney.* 2 vols. Toronto: McClelland and Stewart, 1975.

———. *Fall by Fury.* Toronto: McClelland and Stewart, 1977.

———. *Ghost in the Wheels: Selected Poems.* Toronto: McClelland and Stewart, 1977.

———. "Meeting of Strangers." *Iconolâtre* 9 (March 1964).

———. *pnomes jukollages & other stunzas.* Toronto: Ganglia Press, 1969.

———. *Selected Poems 1940–1966.* Toronto: McClelland and Stewart, 1966.

———. *There are delicacies in you.* Cardiff: Mainly, 1966.

———. "Time Bomb." *Arizona Quarterly* 16, no. 1 (Spring 1960).

RECORDED ON OCTOBER 7 AND 14, 1969

This is Earle Birney, reading some of his poems, and talking a little about them. When I start writing a poem, I'm generally holding a specific thing at the centre of my consciousness. A scene perhaps, a visual memory, or maybe only a smell, even just the touch of a hand. But I can't get going with the writing unless I know something about the way the words should sound. What's the rhythm? Just ordinary speech? Or heightened? What's the tone? Tone, mood affect the choice of vowels, of consonants, too. Whose voice? Well, the voice is mine of course, unless I'm writing a dramatic poem, or dialogue, or verse play. But it isn't always easy to find one's deep-down, inner voice, the totally honest voice that one must have to write a convincing poem. One has to use so many voices to cope with the world, but a poem is written out of the naked self. For me, at least, it begins as a private compulsion, for which I must find words and try to fix them forever, for me, by writing them down. Even cast away on a coral island, I'd have to scratch poems in the sand and try to speak them, too, I guess, sing them even, especially if I were alone on the island, my singing voice being the poor thing it is. Sometimes when I'm writing, the rhythm comes easily just from the subject: what I see or saw.

This first poem of what I'm going to read you is an example. What I remembered seeing was a bear. A big, shaggy Himalayan bear, standing upright in a ditch, on a highway that goes from Delhi to Kashmir. Around the bear two little men were hopping, Kashmiri men. Teaching the bear to dance. Teaching him in the July heat of India, temperature at least 120. They were alone with their bear in a dust-storming desert, and I was a lucky tourist speeding by in an air-conditioned Chev. My Indian friend I was with told me the bear must have been trapped by some hunter high up in the Himalayas and bought by these two Kashmiri, probably with their life savings. Now they were walking with him all the way to Delhi, a thousand miles from where they'd got him. For the time they came to the city, they'd have to have turned him into a dancing bear, from whom they'd make their livelihood, if they were lucky. That's all I know about those men and that bear, and even some of that's guesswork, but it was enough to haunt me until I could find a spell of words to exorcise their ghosts. A year later it began to come to me, the mood of sadness and the grotesque hopping of men and bear, of all of us, of the human condition. And the rhythm, of course, was shambling bear rhythm, shambling bear, learning to dance.

THE BEAR ON THE DELHI ROAD

Unreal   tall as a myth
by the road the Himalayan bear
is beating the brilliant air
with his crooked arms
About him two men   bare
spindly as locusts   leap

One pulls on a ring
in the great soft nose   His mate
flicks   flicks with a stick
up at the rolling eyes

They have not led him here
down from the fabulous hills
to this bald alien plain
and the clamorous world   to kill
but simply to teach him to dance

They are peaceful both   these spare
men of Kashmir   and the bear
alive is their living   too
If   far on the Delhi way
around him galvanic they dance
it is merely to wear   wear
from his shaggy body the tranced
wish forever to stay
only an ambling bear
four-footed in berries

It is no more joyous for them
in this hot dust to prance

out of reach of the praying claws
sharpened to paw for ants
in the shadows of deodars[1]
It is not easy to free
myth from reality
or rear this fellow up
to lurch   lurch with them
in the tranced dancing of men

In some other poems I've written, the rhythm was supplied not so log-
ically perhaps, as with the bear poem, but subconsciously, out of musical
impulses I'll never fathom. This next poem, for example, was written to
a twentieth-century ballad tune. I won't tell you which until I've read it,
because the original ballad is so different from my poem the thought of it
would put you in the wrong mood from mine, which is more a lyrical elegy
than a ballad. If I were singing this poem to you, say with a guitar instead
of just saying it, then you'd know without my having to tell you what ballad
it was. I was thinking about a girl I once loved, and still love, of course, but
long ago lost touch with. Then I heard a rumour she might be dead.

The poem started with the memory of the first moment of seeing her, as
I walked down Hazelton Street in Toronto, on a hot and lazy day. And she
had hazel eyes. Hazel. Lazy. Hazelton. There were sounds echoing here, and a
rhythm growing, and I was off. In five minutes the whole poem was written,
except for the last stanza. The problem was how to stop it, actually, because I
was caught in my tune, and tunes go on forever. Images don't, though. They
expand, have a natural growth, and then stop. The next day, I saw how my
image must end and how it must tie in with the original mood, with the
beautiful sadness of just being born, out of the loving of others and coming
alive oneself by loving, and then having to die, someday, to give room for
others to come and grow and love. The poem, of course, may mean something quite different for you, for each one of you. That's fine, too. The art of
poetry is an open-ended art. It's not giving you a rigid moral nor clean-cut
story. Nor logic. Nor surface clarity, necessarily. It's trying to suggest in as few
words as possible, as much of the whole vast, terrible, exciting, wonderful
complex of being alive. Really alive. Of living under the hazel bough.

FROM THE HAZEL BOUGH

I met a lady
  on a lazy street
hazel eyes
  and little plush feet

her legs swam by
  like lovely trout
eyes were trees
  where boys leant out

hands in the dark and
  a river side
round breasts rising
  with the finger's tide

she was plump as a finch
  and live as a salmon
gay as silk and
  proud as a Brahmin

we winked when we met
  and laughed when we parted
never took time
  to be brokenhearted

but no man sees
  where the trout lie now
or what leans out
  from the hazel bough

It happens that four quite different pieces of music have now been composed for those words I just spoke. One in Toronto in trad jazz, one in Vancouver in folk rock, one in classical fugue in Montreal, and a New York one, which is part of a far out, atonal operetta. I like them all because they tell me that the poem is musically flexible, and whatever its own failures, it spurred others to do their own thing from it. So, the tune I started with is not really relevant. But for the book it was "Casey Jones" [Birney sings]: "I met a lady on a lazy street, hazel eyes, and little plush feet."

Now I'm going to read you more poems and yack less about them, for in the long run the poems should be able to speak for themselves. Here's a short one to start after I'd been sitting and having some coffee in Madrid on a plaza, or as they pronounce it, *platha*. Something happened that made me rename the square, privately, the Plaza of the Inquisition. So here is "Plaza de la Inquisición."

> A spider's body
> limp and hairy
> appeared at the bottom of my coffee
>
> The waiter being Castilian
> said passionately nothing
> And why indeed should apologies
> be made to me
>
> It was I who was looking in
> at the spider
> It might be years
> before I slipped and drowned
> in somebody else's cup

The voice there was of course just myself talking, since the waiter was so discreetly silent. Sometimes in a poem, I want to have more than one voice, but it's hard to know how to play voices off, especially if they're strange ones. So I just have to hope I got the accent, or I get it now as I read of that Trinidad character in this next piece. I was walking alone in the dockside quarter of Port au Spain, which was almost deserted as the dark was coming on. And only occasional glimpses of those tough, hungry fellows that lurk around the ports of big towns; I've seen them on Vancouver skid row sometimes and now here in Trinidad. And sometimes they rob silly tourists like me who go wandering there at such hours alone looking desperately for a taxi. So here's "Meeting of Strangers."

"Nice jacket you got dere, man"

He swerved his bicycle toward my curb
to call   then flashed round the corner
a blur in the dusk   of somebody big
redshirted   young   dark   unsmiling

As I stood hoping for a taxi to show
I thought him droll at least
A passing pleasantry?   It was frayed
a sixdollar coat   tropical weight
in this heat only something with pockets
to carry things in

Now all four streets were empty
Dockland   everything shut

It was a sound no bigger than a breath
that made me wheel

He was ten feet away   redshirt
The cycle leant by a post farther off
where an alley came in   What?!

My turning froze him
in the middle of some elaborate stealth
He looked almost comic   splayed
but there was a glitter
under the downheld hand
and something smoked from his eyes

By God if I was going to be stabbed
for my wallet (adrenalin suffused me)
it would have to be done in plain sight
I made a flying leap
to the middle of the crossing
White man   tourist   surrogate   yes
but not guilty enough
to be skewered in the guts for it
without raising all Trinidad first
with shouts   fists   feet   whatever
— I squared round to meet him

and there was a beautiful taxi
lumbering in from a sidestreet
empty!

As I rolled away   safe as Elijah
lucky as Ganymede
there on the curb I'd leaped from
stood that damned cyclist solemnly
shouting

"What did he say?" I asked the driver
He shrugged at the windshield
"Man dat a crazy boogoo
He soun like he say
'dat a nice jump you got too'"

Now another contrasting poem, also set in the West Indies. When you
go to an independent country whose citizens are black, and you are a whitey,
you can experience curious feelings of guilt. They occur especially when you
find how well you are treated, how hospitably, and how friendly and nice to
you most people are. Maybe there's no reason why they shouldn't be nice, no
reason why you should feel guilty when they are. Certainly I have no memory of ever having racist attitudes to anyone. But poems have much more

to do with non-reason, with the irrational within us, than with the rational. What I was feeling, I suppose, was collective guilt; shame for my own white race that had for hundreds of years enslaved or otherwise exploited and mistreated the ancestors of these very people. These warm, comradely Jamaicans I met in Kingston. I went away from there filled with curious gratitude, especially to George Lamming who made himself my chief host there. I hadn't met him before, knew him only as the author of a famous book about what it's like to be born black and poor in a British colony, which Barbados was at his birth. He called his book *In the Castle of My Skin*. The phrase gave me the concluding image for the kind of thank you letter poem I sent him when I sailed away from Kingston Town. But what really triggered the poem was an instant of time in the small hours of a long party, the night before I left. The instant when, linked in an impromptu sort of song and dance act, with George and some friends of his, I happened to glimpse myself in a wall mirror. Now here's the poem "For George Lamming."

To you
     I can risk words about this

Mastering them   you know
     they are dull
         servants
who say less
     and worse
         than we feel

That party above Kingston Town
     we stood   five (six?) couples
linked singing
     more than rum happy

I was giddy
     from sudden friendship
wanted   undeserved

     black tulip faces
self swaying forgotten
     laughter in dance

Suddenly on a wall mirror
     my face assaulted me
stunned to see itself
     like a white snail
          in the supple dark flowers

Always now I move grateful
     to all of you
who let me walk thoughtless
     and unchallenged
in the gardens
     in the castles
     of your skins.

I think it's time I read a poem set somewhere near home. Once I was driving with another fellow in Ontario, on the Trans-Canada, and came rather late in a midsummer evening to a part of the highway that follows the old fur trading route of discovery into western Canada. But also, I came to a town that is much more symbolic of the new nickel trading trail of pollution, uglification, and general rape of our country. I call the poem "Way to the West." The name of the town will emerge.

11 pm & sunset still going on?
but that could be the latitude
whats wrongs the color
everywhere horseshit ochre   & roiling
like paper that twists/browns
before firing up on hot ashes
theres somebodys hell ahead
     meantime our lips prick

& the trees are dead
but its another 20 miles before the sign
SUDBURY & christ there on the skull of a hill
3 manhattan-high stacks   a phallic calvary
ejaculating some essence of rotted semen
straight up like a mass sabotage at cape kennedy

the damned are all over   the young
shrieking (looking much like anyone)
drag-race with radios up
from one smoldering stoplight to another —
under neon the older faces (a map of europe)
are screwcheeked/pitted all the same way
& something restful about their devilship
stares me down   till they come human
    houcking brown on the cement

      WELCOME TO ... 73% OF THE FREE
      WORLD'S NICKEL IS CREATED HERE
and the free world invented a special cough
not even a hundred taverns dampen
nor all the jukes drown
in the doorways of Pandemonium   *Milton*
thou shouldst be living etc

DEAD END   wheres west?   sunsets folded
our headlights finger dumped cans
& wriggle through streets like crevasses
blasted in bedrock pink & folded
like glazed guts on a butchers counter
    out of the starless dark
    falls the roar of Golgotha
    how long before you stop
    noticing?   & the sting in the eyes

by a stripped truck an Indian kneels
    praying?   puking

YOU ARE LEAVING SUDBURY ... CENTER OF
(20 more miles of battlefield)
& if there is need of a bigger ...
FREE ENTERPRISE WILL BUILD IT!!!!

      at last a moon looms up
      we are into the dumb firs again
        HISTORIC SITE
        Turn out 300 yds
          FRENCH RIVER
what? canoe route the hurons found
& showed the whites —
the scrapped way to the west   silks
vietnam   buffalo   the moon
shines over the middle of nowhere —
dumb as the trees

      we stop for a leak   silence
      too late for other cars
      the trees listen back
      nothing   did they get all the owls?
      suddenly some kind of low growl
      coming up!   we head for the car —
      air canada's night jet
          but after it passes we begin to know
          we'd been hearing the river all along

That poem had certain elements that weren't so easy to read out loud because they were being suggested in the poem on the page by capitalizations and other printer's devices to represent road markers, big sign boards, and so on. I try when I'm writing a poem never to forget that the printed poem is not only a notation for the way a poem sounds, and that's why it has lines sometimes, so you know how to pause with your breath, but it's also a visual confirmation and even a heightening of the poem's mood and meaning. Our eyes are actually affected I think, emotionally, by how the poem looks on the page. And so our eyes can help to report, or what you put on the page can help to report, what the poet has seen, as well as what he's heard, tasted, touched, and felt and thought. I'll read you a poem that, in fact, got started simply from seeing a billboard. Or really a long succession of billboards, all saying the same thing. They stood between me and one of the world's most beautiful views, as I drove down the coastal highway of Oregon. It was in 1961. And what those billboards said was "Billboards Build Freedom of Choice, courtesy Oregon Chamber of Commerce." And I was alone, driving, and I brooded about the enormity and stupidity of these ugly signs and their phony message. What kind of human donkey could really be brainwashed into believing this, this message? Well, I must invent one and let him talk, expose his own stupidity. And so as I began to see it, by the irony of a dramatic monologue, by using his imaginary voice and keeping quiet myself, I could perhaps blow off my own growing head of steam. So, I invented a particularly cretinous, loyal American adman sort of hitchhiker, and I picked him up. And this is what he said to me in "Billboards Build Freedom of Choice."

Yegitit?
Look see
        AMERICA BUILDS BILLBOARDS
so billboards kin bill freedoma choice
between — yeah between billbores no
        WAIT
its yedoan hafta choose no more between
say like trees and billbores lessa course
wenna buncha trees is flattint out inta
        BILLB —
yeah yegotit
youkin pick between well
hey!   see!   like dat!
        ALL VINYL GET WELL DOLLS $6.98
or — watch wasdat comin up?
        PRE PAID CAT?

PREPAID CATASTROPHE COVERAGE
yeah hell youkin have damnear anythin
    FREE 48 INCH TV IN EVERY ROOM
see!   or   watchit!
     OUR PIES TASTE LIKE MOTHERS
yeah but look bud no chickenin out
because billbores build
    AM —
yeah an AMERICA BUILDS MORE
buildbores to bill more —
sure yugotta! yugotta have
    FREEDOM TO
hey! you doan wannem godam fieldglasses!
theys probly clouds on Mount Raneer
but not on
    MOUNT RAINIER THE BEER THAT CHEERS
and not on good old yella
    SHELL
keepin de windoff yuh from allose clammy beaches
Hey look, you want cows
Zoom dem was Borden's contented[2]
Landscapes is for the birds fella
yegotta choose between well like
between two a de same
hell like de man said Who's got time
for a third tit? *two* parties is *Okay*
that's   DEMOC   sure but yegit three
yegot COMMIES I'm tellinyeh
is like dose damfool niggers in
in Asia someweres all tryin to be nootrul
I tellyeh treesa crowd   a crowda
godamatheisticunamericananti
    BILLBORES
yeah an yewanna help Burma?   help
    BURMA SHAVE
yewanna keep the longhairs from starvin?

BUY HANDMADE TOY SOLDIERS
yegotta choose fella yegotta
choose between
     AMERICA and UN —
between KEE-RISPIES and KEE-RUMPIES
between KEE-RYEST and KEE-ROOST-SHOVE
and brother if you doan pick
     RIGHT
you better
git this heap
tahelloffn
our
     FREEWAY

Now some little poems. The first one's so small it was actually made into a mobile out of cardboard discs and wire coat hangers, and is, I hope, really swinging somewhere now. It's called "Like an Eddy."[3]

Like an eddy, my words turn about your bright rock

Two more love poems. The first called "there are delicacies in you," and the second, "i think you are a whole city."

there are delicacies in you
    like the hearts of watches
there are filigrees without patterns
    and tiny locks[4]

i need your help
    to contrive keys
there is so little time
    even for the finest
      watches

i think you are a whole city

& yesterday when i first
touched
you i started moving
thru one of your suburbs
where all the gardens are fresh
with faces of you
flowering up

some girls are only houses
maybe a strip
development
woman you are
miles of boulevards   with supple
trees unpruned & full of winding
honesties

so give me
time   i want   i want
to know all your squares &
cloverleafs   ime steering now
by a constellation winking over
this night's rim from some great
beachside of you with highrisers & a spotlit
beaux arts

i can hear your beating centre will i
will i make it   are there maps of
you i keep circling   imagining parks
fountains   your stores

back now in my single bed
i wander
your stranger   dreaming
i am your citizen

And after love poems why not a poem about love in general? This was made a few months before the Americans dropped the atom bomb on Japan. Before. But there were already rumours that scientists were trying to produce such a weapon so my piece isn't quite as eerily prophetic as it may sound, but it's certainly one of the first anti-atom-bomb poems. I wrote it in a military hospital in England.

TIME BOMB
In this friend's face I know
        the grizzly still   and in the mirror
lay my ear to the radio's conch
        and hear the atom's terror

Within the politician's ribs
        within my own   the time-bombs tick

O men be swift to be mankind
    or let the grizzly take

What I don't need to tell you, I guess, is that my politics is internation-
alist. but that doesn't mean that I don't feel roots somewhere. They go down
all over Canada, and a good number of them are in Ontario. But there are,
of course, the special roots one grows in childhood. Those in my case are
buried in the Albertan bush and the B.C. Rockies and the Pacific beaches.
So I'll end this half-hour with a poem in one of those settings. It's a piece
called "Bushed." Its title is western slang not for tired out but for nutsy, that
is, a state of being out of your skull from living too long alone in the bush.
Bushed. In this case, I'm trying to imagine the thought processes of an old
trapper, who really existed around Banff when I was a boy. Who gradually
became so paranoiac about the woods, so sure that the mountains were out
to get him, that he at last couldn't leave his cabin, and stayed inside and
starved to death before anyone could find him. So here's in conclusion then,
the poem "Bushed."

He invented a rainbow but lightning struck it
shattered it into the lake-lap of a mountain
so big his mind slowed when he looked at it

Yet he built a shack on the shore
learned to roast porcupine belly and
wore the quills on his hatband

At first he was out with the dawn
whether it yellowed bright as wood-columbine
or was only a fuzzed moth in a flannel of storm
But he found the mountain was clearly alive
sent messages whizzing down every hot morning
boomed proclamations at noon and spread out
a white guard of goat
before falling asleep on its feet at sundown

When he tried his eyes on the lake　　ospreys
would fall like valkyries
choosing the cut-throat
he took then to waiting
till the night smoke rose from the boil of the sunset

But the moon carved unknown totems
out of the lakeshore
owls in the bear-dusky woods derided him
moosehorned cedars circled his swamps and tossed
their antlers up to the stars
Then he knew　　though the mountain slept　　the winds
were shaping its peak to an arrowhead
poised

And now he could only
bar himself in and wait
for the great flint to come singing into his heart

Transcribed by Geoff Baillie

F.R. SCOTT
(1899–1985)

Poet Francis Reginald Scott was born in Quebec City. A member of the Montreal Group of poets writing in a modernist tradition, he also taught law at McGill University, served as a U.N. technical assistant to Burma in 1952 (he worked to design a socialist state there) and wrote extensively on national and international affairs. His books of poetry include *Overture* (1945), *Events and Signals* (1954), and *The Eye of the Needle* (1957). He was also the dean of the McGill Faculty of Law from 1961 to 1964 and was greatly involved with the CCF (Co-operative Commonwealth Federation), the political party that gave birth to the New Democratic Party.

Scott started this recording by talking about his childhood living on the outskirts of Quebec City and trekking through the mountains while he was young. He talked of how this time made him feel that Canada was expansive and boundless, as if its newness could undo the mistakes of an old Europe. Scholar Sandra Dwja calls Scott a writer for whom there was no separation between his political and literary interests (Kelly par. 5).

Scott's poetry is a vehicle to express his views of social justice, since he conceptualized Canada as encapsulating an acceptance of inclusivity. For example, in his poem "Dedication," he uses the poetic form to envisage people sharpening their tools to move beyond the excesses of capitalism toward inclusive participatory democracy. Furthermore, he believed the government should encourage artists to advocate for social change; artistic culture should be understood as a stepping stone to engagement in a polity (par. 24). His views and political involvement meant that Scott had a hard time dealing with the establishment at McGill University where he worked, especially when he was the national chairman of the CCF political party (Djwa par. 14).

From this recording, we see how Scott was oriented toward these ideas and morals from the beginning, as both his earlier and later work explore similar themes. Scott is a poet who did not pass through radical shifts in his writing. Even when Scott experiments with form and structure, his sense of poetry shines through: this, for example, is shown in "The Indians at the Expo 67," which talks about the injustice faced by the First Nations of Canada and literally draws on their own words. Overall, Scott was one of Canada's preeminent political poets of the twentieth century, a remarkable voice in Canadian poetry.

References

Djwa, Sandra. "F(rancis) R(eginald) Scott." In *Canadian Writers, 1920–1959: Second Series*, edited by William H. New. *Dictionary of Literary Biography*. Vol. 88. Detroit: Gale, 1989.

Kelly, Erica. "'The art of making artists': Canadian modernism, F.R. Scott, and the New Deal." *Canadian Literature* 209 (2011): 31.

Scott, F.R. *The Collected Poems of F.R. Scott*. Toronto: McClelland and Stewart, 1981.

———. "The Poet in Quebec Today." *English Poetry in Quebec: Proceedings of the Foster Poetry Conference October 12–14, 1963*. Ed. John Glassco. Montreal: McGill University Press, 1965. 43–50.

RECORDED ON OCTOBER 15, 1969

This is Frank Scott of Montreal, reading his poetry. I'm going to begin with a group of poems that might be called nature poems. They were all written by me, quite a long time ago, some of them about forty years ago, in fact. I grew up in Quebec City, which is very close to the Laurentian Mountains, and I spent many summer holidays and many wonderful picnics in the mountains and in that north country. My father used to say to me, "Frank, look north, there's nothing between you and the North Pole," and in those days, that was more or less true. I had this great sense of emptiness and newness, and I felt that this country, Canada, could be something new and different and free from a lot of the inherited troubles and histories of Europe. So one of the poems I wrote was this one, called "New Names":

Let us give new names
To the stars.
What does Venus mean
Or Mars?

The tall pines on the hill
Have seen no blood.
Beneath them no men or maids
Have woo'd.

Who would read old myths
By this lake
Where the wild duck paddle forth
At daybreak?

I am more moved by the lake sheen
When night is come
Then by all the tales of Babylon
Or Rome.

Look! The moon's path is broken
By rippling bars.
I think we should give new names
To the stars.

And then here's another in the same vein about this kind of country. As you know, the Laurentians are the oldest mountains in the world, and they've been under ice caps two or three times, and that's why they're sort of rounded, why you have these wonderful smooth petals on the shores of the rivers. And you have this sense of the ancient laws of geography and the movement of the Earth that are still operating. This one is called "Old Song."

> far voices
> and fretting leaves
> this music the
> hillside gives
>
> but in the deep
> Laurentian river
> An elemental song
> for ever
>
> a quiet calling
> of no mind
> out of long aeons
> when dust was blind
> and ice hid sound
>
> only a moving
> with no note
> granite lips
> a stone throat

Here's another of that kind. This one's called "Surfaces."

> This rock-borne river, ever flowing
> Obedient to the ineluctable laws,
> Brings a reminder from the barren north

Of the eternal lifeless processes.
There is an argument that will prevail
In this calm stretch of current, slowly drawn
Toward its final equilibrium.

Come, flaunt the brief prerogative of life
Dip your small civilized foot into this cold water
And ripple, for a moment, the smooth surface of time.

Now, I am going to move on to a poem that links together the idea of
this Northland with the inevitable development that will take place when
people come into it. And, of course, now we are developing many parts
of it and looking at the rest to see what it might support in the way of
civilized life, quite apart from what we are thinking of doing with respect to
the Eskimo and the Indian in that territory. This one's called: "Laurentian
Shield." That is the geological name for this particular formation of rock
that stretches all the way from Labrador, right across Canada out to the east
side of the Mackenzie River. It's a rock formation common to most of the
Canadian provinces.

LAURENTIAN SHIELD

Hidden in wonder and snow, or sudden with summer,
This land stares at the sun in a huge silence
Endlessly repeating something we cannot hear.
Inarticulate, arctic,
Not written on by history, empty as paper,
It leans away from the world with songs in its lakes
Older than love, and lost in the miles.

This waiting is wanting.
It will choose its language
When it has chosen its technic,
A tongue to shape the vowels of its productivity.

A language of flesh and of roses.

Now there are pre-words,
Cabin syllables,
Nouns of settlement
Slowly forming, with steel syntax,
The long sentence of its exploitation.

The first cry was the hunter, hungry for fur,
And the digger for gold, nomad, no-man, a particle;
Then the bold commands of monopoly, big with machines,
Carving its kingdoms out of the public wealth;
And now the drone of the plane, scouting the ice,
Fills all the emptiness with neighbourhood
And links our future over the vanished pole.

But a deeper note is sounding, heard in the mines,
The scattered camps and the mills, a language of life,
And what will be written in the full culture of occupation
Will come, presently, tomorrow,
From millions whose hands can turn this rock into children.

My next poem is called "Trans Canada." It was written after my first
trip on a Trans-Canada[1] plane, a long distance trip from Regina back to
Montreal. This was about 1943 before there were jets; I had been working
very hard at a CCF Party Convention in Regina.[2] I was very tired and I got
on the plane that evening around ten or eleven o'clock. I got to Montreal
next morning. I wasn't able to sleep at all that night, and yet I felt completely refreshed at the wonderful experience of being up in the air and
seeing the incredibly beautiful landscape made by clouds. So this is called
"Trans Canada." You can imagine me leaving Regina.

Pulled from our ruts by the made-to-order gale
We sprang into a wider prairie
And dropped Regina below like a pile of bones.

Sky, tumbled upon us, in waterfalls,
But we were smarter than a Skeena salmon
And shot our silver body over the lip of air
To rest in a pool of space
On the top storey of our adventure.

A solar peace
And a six-way choice.

Clouds, now, are the solid substance,
A floor of wool roughed by the wind,
Standing in waves that halt in their fall.
A still of troughs.

The plane, our planet,
Travels on roads that are not seen or laid
But sound in instruments on pilots' ears,
While underneath
The sure wings
Are the everlasting arms of science.

Man, the lofty worm, tunnels his latest clay,
And bores his new career.

This frontier, too, is ours.
This everywhere where life can only be led
At the pace of a rocket
Is common to man and man.
And every country below is an I land.

The sun sets on its top shelf,
and stars seem farther from our nearer grasp.
I have sat by night beside a cold lake

And touched things smoother than moonlight on still water,
But the moon on this cloud sea is not human,
And here is no shore, no intimacy,
Only the start of space, the road to suns.

Now I would like to go back a little over that poem and point out one or two things perhaps you may have missed on the first hearing. Why did I say that we dropped Regina below like a pile of bones? Well, the answer is that Pile of Bones was the original name of Regina in the old days before they touched it with royalty and called it Regina, because it was the place where they used to drag all the buffalo skeleton and bones for use and development at Regina. Now, it isn't necessary to know that if you're reading the poem, but there can often be in a poem allusions that are buried which will repay discovery. Similarly, you may have noticed I talked about a solar peace and a six-way choice. Six-way choice. Well, that, of course, is north, south, east, west, up, and down. And that came into my mind because I had once been down at the Grand Canyon of the Colorado, and the Hopi Indians in that area, I was told, have six directions: north, south, east, west, up, and down, because they go up and down the canyon. And it came into my mind as I was up in the air. And often, in the middle of a poem some distant memory, or phrase, or some fact will come into your mind and get incorporated into the poem.

Now, those poems were mostly made out of the facts of Canada's scenery and the geography. Canada, of course, is composed of people, people often in struggle and in conflict. And quite a good deal of my verse is concerned with those matters, either directly or sometimes, satirically. Let me read a poem called "Dedication," in which I'm thinking about our responsibility as citizens for all those who are oppressed or exploited in society.

DEDICATION
From those condemned to labour
For profit of another
We take our new endeavour.

For sect and class and pattern
Through whom the strata harden
We sharpen now the weapon.

Till power is brought to pooling
And outcasts share in ruling
There will not be an ending
Nor any peace for spending.

Some of these poems, of course, were written during the Great Depression of the 1930s, which so upset the entire establishment in North America, and indeed around the world, quite as much, if not more, than it is upset at the moment. There are some similarities, perhaps, in the two situations between the thirties and the sixties. You may feel these overtones, or hear these overtones, in some of these 1930s poems. Here's one, for instance, called "Overture" and I am listening to a woman play a piano, play Mozart, and yet I'm feeling the terrible calamity in the world outside the room. And this contrast is expressed in this poem called "Overture":

In the dark room, under a cone of light,
You precisely play the Mozart sonata. The bright
Clear notes fly like sparks through the air
And trace a flickering pattern of music there.

Your hands dart in the light, your fingers flow.
They are ten careful operators in a row
That pick their packets of sounds from steel bars
Constructing harmonies as sharp as stars.

How shall I hear old music? This is an hour
Of new beginnings, concepts warring for power,
Decay of systems — the tissue of art is torn
With overtures of an era being born.

And this perfection which is less yourself
Than Mozart, seems a trinket on a shelf,
A pretty octave played before a window
Beyond whose curtain grows a world crescendo.

I'll read a very short poem, nevertheless with social content. It's called "Charity."

A code of laws
Lies written
On this beggar's hand.

My small coin
Lengthens
His harsh sentence.

You don't see beggars on the street as much now as you did in the 1930s, but if you think of charity, which is sort of giving handouts to the poor, you realize that by doing that, often we preserve the system that creates poverty, whereas what we must do is get rid of poverty so that there won't be any need for this kind of charity.

Now I'm going to read a poem about a touch of educational idea in it. I've spent all my life inside of schools and universities, both as student and teacher, and I've had quite an experience of different kinds of educational method. I sent my son to a school where he spent seven years without any examinations, without any subjects or without any punishments, etc. ... quite a contrast to the ordinary school system, though that is undergoing great changes these days. This one is called "Examiner," and I wrote it when I was invigilating at an exam at McGill, and watching all the students writing away furiously.

The routine trickery of the examination
Baffles these hot and discouraged youths.
Driven by they know not what external pressure
They pour their hated self-analysis
Through the nib of confession, onto the accusatory page.

I, who have plotted their immediate downfall,
I am entrusted with the divine categories,
ABCD and the hell of E,
The parade of prize and the backdoor of pass.

In the tight silence
Standing by a green grass window
Watching the fertile earth graduate its sons
With more compassion — not commanding the shape
Of stem and stamen, bringing the trees to pass
By shift of sunlight and increase of rain,
For each seed the whole soil, for the inner life
The environment receptive and contributory —
I shudder at the narrow frames of our text-book schools
In which we plant our so various seedlings.

Each brick-walled barracks
Cut into numbered rooms, black-boarded,
Ties the venturing shoot to the master stick;
The screw-desk rows of lads and girls
Subdued in the shade of an adult —
Their acid subsoil —
Shape the new to the old in the ashen garden.

Shall we open the whole skylight of thought
To these tiptoe minds, bring them our frontier worlds
And the boundless uplands of art for their field of growth?
Or shall we pass them the chosen poems with the footnotes,
Ring the bell on their thoughts, period their play,
Make laws for averages and plans for means,

Print one history book for a whole province, and
Let ninety thousand reach page ten by Tuesday?

As I gather the inadequate paper evidence, I hear
Across the neat campus lawn
The professional mowers drone, clipping the inch-high green.

Now, in the prosperous 1950s, a sort of slickness came into life; people weren't concerned much about society and its problems. They were out to make money, and so on, and the young people of those days hung around in drug stores and so forth. This poem is called "Saturday Sundae." Sundae is spelled S-U-N-D-A-E … it's a sundae eaten on Saturday. This is where listening to a poem … you can't sometimes get exactly what is meant by it. You have to see it.

SATURDAY SUNDAE
The triple decker and the double-cone
I side-swipe swiftly, suck the Coke-straws dry.
Ride toadstool seat beside the slab of morgue —
Sweet corner drugstore, sweet pie in the sky.

Him of the front-flap apron, him I sing,
The counter-clockwise clerk in underalls.
Swing low, sweet chocolate, Oh swing, swing,
While cheek by juke the jitter chatter falls.

I swivel on my axle and survey
The latex tintex kotex cutex land
Soft kingdoms sell for dimes, Life Pic Look Click
Inflate the male with conquest girly grand.

My brothers, and my sisters, two by two,
Sit sipping succulence and sighing sex.
Each tiny adolescent universe
A world the vested interests annex.

Such bread and circus these times allow,
Opium most popular, life so small and slick,
Perhaps with candy is the new world born
And cellophane shall wrap the heretic.

And now, I am going to read you a different kind of poem. It's called a found poem: it's a poem made out of somebody else's writing, usually prose, which the poet has simply taken and arranged in verse form with lines, as you would in a poem. There must be something in the original that can be brought out and emphasized this way so as to give a new character to the writing. The poet doesn't really write it, but he sees that it can be arranged and made to mean something a little special. The one I am going to read is called "The Indians Speak at Expo 67." There was at Expo 67, a pavilion put up by the Canadian Indians, and they displayed many of their types of art and instruments. And they displayed certain attitudes toward the white man. And in each of the rooms of the pavilion, there were two or three lines up on the wall. And I just took those lines and put them in this form and they came out as follows:

When the White Man came
We welcomed him
With love

We sheltered him
Fed him
Led him through the forest

The great explorers of Canada
Travelled in Indian canoes
Wore Indian snoe-shoes
Ate Indian food
Lived in Indian houses

They could not have lived
Or moved
Without Indian friends

The early missionaries thought us Pagans
They imposed upon us their own stories
Of God
Of heaven and hell
Of sin and salvation

The White Men fought each other for our land
We were embroiled in the White Man's wars

The wars ended in treaties
And our lands
Passed into the White Man's hands

I thought I would read with that another poem I wrote after meeting a distinguished woman journalist from India, who … well, the poem speaks for itself. I call it "Two Indias" because, don't forget, our Indians are called Indians because they thought they were getting out into the East … the early explorers.

Two Indias
A distinguished woman journalist
from India
visiting Halifax
asked to meet a Canadian Indian
to see his way of life.

She was taken to a shack
on the outskirts of the city
with mud floor and leaking roof
in which the local Chief
was eating cold spaghetti

all by himself
out of a tin can.

Astonished, she asked him how he voted
in the last election.
He replied "Conservative"
And when asked why, said
"What have they ever done to hurt me?"[3]

I've been much concerned in my poetry with expressing some of the historical facts about Canada. Here's a poem called "On the Terrace, Quebec":

Northward, the ice-carved land,
les pays d'en haut.

South, the softer continent,
river-split.

At Valcartier, three Laurentian hills.
Many years ago, as children,
looking out the Rectory window
on the longest day of each year
we saw the sun set
in the second dip.

I walk these boards under the citadel,
see the narrow streets below,
the basin, l'Ile d'Orléans,
the gateway.

I think of the English troops
imprisoned in the broken city
in the spring of 1760
waiting the first ship.

Whose flag would it fly?

And the other army,
victorious at Ste. Foy,
still strong,
watching.

Suddenly, round the bend,
masts and sails
begin to finger the sky.

The first question is answered.

And two lines to end:

ECLIPSE
I looked the sun straight in the eye.
He put on dark glasses.

Transcribed by Vipasha Shaikh

IRVING LAYTON
(1912–2006)

The poet-messiah was born on March 12, 1912, in the Romanian village of Tirgul Neamt. He burst into a challah-scented world where stories were "charged with significant meanings": an already circumcised baby boy whom his mother believed to be a new age prophet (Layton, *Waiting for the Messiah* 7). As he grew, his mother kindled his imagination with prospects of messianic grandeur, fostering a "feeling of strangeness" and significance that grew ever stronger, making him feel his "life had been set on rails of a different gauge" (7). This was Irving Layton's origin myth, his personal Genesis, the story he told to explain the genius that made him one of Canada's foremost poetic figures.

In 1913 Layton's family immigrated to Montreal, settling in a working-class, multi-ethnic neighbourhood on St. Elizabeth Street. Here, young Layton first registered the difference between the warmth and intimacy of his Jewish family and the "feeling of apartness" he experienced in the outside world, where he encountered "that strange spiky flower ... of anti-Semitism" (21). In this hostile outside world, where "the children of the poor [got] the virtue of submissiveness knocked into them" (41), Layton spent his school days repudiating convention and expectations, setting a pattern that would persist for the rest of his life. He discovered poetry when his high-school English teacher read a Tennyson ballad aloud to the class, recalling, "I'd never heard the English language read so beautifully ... I remembered sitting quietly ... enraptured as the sounds filled the room" (83). Thus, Layton lost his heart to literature (83), and later used his poetry to spurn conventions and legitimate his difference, just as he had used his class-clown antics

to distinguish himself and showcase "everything unique and precious in my own makeup" (47). Indeed, he declared that every poet's real concern was the preservation of the self in a world of ever-heightening uniformity ("Interview with Glenn Sinclair" 16).

To this end, Layton spearheaded vital movements on the mid-century Canadian literary landscape, catalyzing a shift away from what he described as philistinism and puritanism (Znaimer), towards unprecedented richness and depth in modern poetry (Jacobs). As Barry Callaghan declared, Layton "has been … the frontrunner of English poetry in our country, he has been good alcohol in our blood" (Callaghan). In 1957 Layton won a Canada Council Grant for *The Improved Binoculars*, and in 1959, he won the Governor General's Award for *A Red Carpet for the Sun*. He co-founded Contact Press in 1952 alongside Louis Dudek and Raymond Souster, a press dedicated to author-owned, non-commercial Canadian publishing, that featured literary luminaries like Margaret Atwood, Gwendolyn MacEwen, and Eli Mandel. Hence, he embodied a new ethos of Canadian poetry, as writers sought to sculpt their own literary identities, exploring contemporary styles and social issues, rather than turning to English poetic traditions (Jacobs).

The poet-messiah died in January 2006 in Montreal. He left behind a larger-than-life personal and literary legacy of championing freedom and repudiating convention. Layton's sense of significance and strangeness, first sparked by his mother all those years ago, is epitomized by an anecdote his fifth wife, Anna, recounted. She described Layton's pity for their pet goldfish, with their circumscribed lives in their glass bowl. So, every night, he filled his bathtub and let the fish swim free (Pottier). This was quintessential Layton: the man who "carried the fever of the prophet with him all his life," who "punched a rectangular space of quiet" (Callaghan) into the "sweaty swindle of modern living" ("Interview with Glenn Sinclair" 14) and set Canadian poets free from their glass bowl.

References

"Biography." *IrvingLayton.ca.* 2012. http://irvinglayton.ca/Biography/index.html.

Callaghan, Barry. "The Irving Layton Centenary: Part 1." Filmed March 14, 2012. YouTube video, 13:38. Posted August 14, 2012. https://youtu.be/HYyhsp3t6zg.

Cameron, Elspeth. *Irving Layton: A Portrait.* Toronto: Stoddart, 1985.

CBC. "Fighting Words: Whither Montreal Intellectuals?" Filmed December 9, 1956. CBC Digital Archives, 28:24. www.cbc.ca/archives/entry/whither-montreal-intellectuals.

Cohen, Leonard. "Irving Layton Centenary: Part 6." Filmed March 14, 2012. YouTube video, 17:56. Posted August 14, 2012. https://youtu.be/Ty92sMZVWrE.

Jacobs, T. "Irving Layton: Biography." *Canadian Poetry Online.* University of Toronto. May 2001. Web. 21 September 2015.

Layton, Irving. *Collected Poems.* Toronto: McClelland and Stewart, 1965.

———. "Interview with Glenn Sinclair." Irving Layton Collection, RC0708, file 3, tape 1. Archives and Research Collections, McMaster University Library.

———. *Periods of the Moon.* Toronto: McClelland and Stewart, 1969.

———. *Waiting for the Messiah.* Toronto: McClelland and Stewart, 1985.

———. *The Whole Bloody Bird.* Toronto: McClelland and Stewart, 1969.

McKnight, David. "The Poetic Achievement of Contact Press (1952–1967)." *Historical Perspectives on Canadian Publishing.* http://digitalcollections.mcmaster.cahpcanpubcase-studypoetic-achievement-contact-press-1952-1967.

Pottier, Anna to Leonard Cohen. Leonard Cohen fonds, MS coll. 122, box 10, file 50. Thomas Fisher Rare Book Library, University of Toronto.

Toppings, Earle. "Notes on Irving Layton." 1969. Earle Toppings fonds, 2015.06, box 1, file 2. E.J. Pratt Library, Victoria University, University of Toronto.

Znaimer, Moses. "Irving Layton Centenary: Part 3." Filmed March 14, 2012. YouTube video, 16:17. Posted August 14, 2012. https://youtu.be/Il9kQF1Kkow.

RECORDED ON OCTOBER 16, 1969

Hi, I'm Irving Layton, and I want to begin this reading with a poem that means a great deal to me in summing up much of my experience and possibly some of the wisdom derived from that experience. I've called the poem "There Were No Signs." My feeling is that one has to make the signs along the road that one travels and not wait for someone else to put the signs up for you.

THERE WERE NO SIGNS
By walking I found out
Where I was going.

By intensely hating, how to love.
By loving, whom and what to love.

By grieving, how to laugh from the belly.

Out of infirmity, I have built strength.
Out of untruth, truth.
From hypocrisy, I weave directness.

Almost now I know who I am.
Almost I have the boldness to be that man.

Another step
And I shall be where I started from.

I believe that the poet lives in two realms — the realm of the imagination, and the realm of fact or reality — and that he is not happy, truly happy, completely happy, in either realm. And, to that degree, he is something of a misfit, particularly in a world such as ours is today, organized around the centrality of fact, the importance of fact. And, therefore, anyone who wants to live in the world of imagination finds it even more difficult today, in our century, than say, the imaginative poets of previous centuries.

I wrote a poem several years ago called "The Swimmer," and the swimmer is my symbol for the poet who cannot live either on dry land, which he finds skull-like and deathly; nor can he live all the time in the creative element of the imagination, here symbolized by water.

The Swimmer

The afternoon foreclosing, see
The swimmer plunges from his raft,
Opening the spray corollas by his act of war —
The snake heads strike
Quickly and are silent.

Emerging see how for a moment
A brown weed with marvellous bulbs,
He lies imminent upon the water
While light and sound come with a sharp passion
From the gonad sea around the Poles
And break in bright cockle-shells about his ears.

He dives, floats, goes under like a thief
Where his blood sings to the tiger shadows
In the scentless greenery that leads him home,
A male salmon down fretted stairways
Through underwater slums ...

Stunned by the memory of lost gills
He frames gestures of self-absorption
Upon the skull-like beach;
Observes with instigated eyes
The sun that empties itself upon the water,
And the last wave romping in
To throw its boyhood on the marble sand.

Several years ago, I taught English to newcomers, and one of my students was a Mrs. Fornheim. She had been driven out of Vienna when the Nazis occupied that city, fled to Paris with her husband, and then (when the Vichy government was formed that collaborated with the Nazis) she fled to Spain, then Portugal, and finally to Montreal, where I taught her and her husband English. If you've ever had the experience of teaching English to newcomers, you know that their common complaint is "Oh, if I only had someone to talk to," meaning of course "If I only had someone on whom I could practise this newfangled tongue of English on," and I've incorporated that plea or plaint in my poem. She died of cancer, and this is my poem for her.

MRS. FORNHEIM, REFUGEE

Very merciful was the cancer
Which first blinding you altogether
Afterwards stopped up your hearing;
At the end when Death was nearing,
Black-gloved, to gather you in
You did not demur, or fear
One you could not see or hear.

I taught you Shakespeare's tongue, not knowing
The time and manner of your going;
Certainly if with ghosts to dwell,
German would have served as well.
Voyaging lady, I wish for you
An Englishwoman to talk to,
An unruffled listener,
And green words to say to her.

I taught high school for many years. One year I was very fortunate in having several handsome young ladies in my class. And they were very attractive, and what is more, they knew exactly where their attractions lay. Very often, one of them more mischievous than the others, would make some rather provocative movements that would send my thoughts scurrying from the solemn history lesson that I was attempting to give to something more delightful. This is my poem for these fine, attractive, provocative young ladies who were in my class in those golden, golden days so many years ago.

To THE GIRLS OF MY GRADUATING CLASS
   Wanting for their young limbs praise,
Their thighs, hips, and saintly breasts,
   They grow from awkwardness to delight,
Their mouths made perfect with the air
     About them and the sweet rage in the blood,
     The delicate trouble in their veins.

   Intolerant as happiness, suddenly
They'll dart like bewildered birds;
   For there's no mercy in that bugler Time
That excites against their virginity
     The massed infantry of days, nor in the tendrils
     Greening on their enchanted battlements.

   Golda, Fruma, Dinnie, Elinor,
My saintly wantons, passionate nuns;
   O light-footed daughters, your unopened
Brittle beauty troubles an aging man
     Who hobbles after you a little way
     Fierce and ridiculous.

I've taken the title for this next poem from the early work of the great German philosopher Frederick Nietzsche. The title of the poem is "The Birth of Tragedy." Nietzsche believed that tragedy, or the writing of tragedy by the great Greek tragic poets Aeschylus and Sophocles, came about because of the fusion of the Apollonian, Dionysian elements: the elements of dream and intoxication, or reason and ecstasy. I have a reference to the gods in this poem, and they are of course the gods Apollo and Dionysius.

The Birth of Tragedy

And me happiest when I compose poems.
      Love, power, the huzza of battle
      Are something, are much;
yet a poem includes them like a pool
      water and reflection.
In me, nature's divided things —
      tree, mould on tree —
      have their fruition;
I am their core. Let them swap,
bandy, like a flame swerve
I am their mouth; as a mouth I serve.

And I observe how the sensual moths
      big with odour and sunshine
      dart into the perilous shrubbery;
or drop their visiting shadows
      upon the garden I one year made
of flowering stone to be a footstool
      for the perfect gods:
      who, friends to the ascending orders,
sustain all passionate meditations
and call down pardons
for the insurgent blood.

A quiet madman, never far from tears,
      I lie like a slain thing
      under the green air the trees
inhabit, or rest upon a chair
      towards which the inflammable air
tumbles on many robins' wings;
      noting how seasonably
      leaf and blossom uncurl
and living things arrange their death,
while someone from afar off
blows birthday candles for the world.

This poem of course is a tribute to the creative artist. I hold that the world is full of contradictions, full of the opposites — such as life and death, good and evil, light and dark — and that the poet, perhaps because he is more mixed up and more full of these opposites and contradictions than anyone else, is the spokesman for this strange, antinomial universe of ours. Therefore I say, in me, nature's divided things, tree, mould on tree, have their fruition. I am their core. Let them swap, bandy, like a flame swerve. I am their mouth; as a mouth, I serve.

I think it's a truism today, uttered from so many podiums and platforms, that unless man's moral intelligence catches up with his scientific and technological achievements, he is in danger of blowing himself off this planet in a very short time. It is indeed a race between destruction and education. Unless men can curb — of course, the same goes for women — unless they can curb their egotism and their greed and their selfishness, and their aggressiveness, they are going to blow one another into oblivion. And one day, in a rather unhappy and melancholy frame of mind, I wrote this poem, "The Improved Binoculars."

Below me the city was in flames:
the firemen were the first to save
themselves. I saw steeples fall on their knees.

I saw an agent kick the charred bodies
from an orphanage to one side, marking
the site carefully for a future speculation.

Lovers stopped short of the final spasm
and went off angrily in opposite directions,
their elbows held by giant escorts of fire.

Then the dignitaries rode across the bridges
under an auricle of light which delighted them,
noting for later punishment those that went before.

And the rest of the populace, their mouths
distorted by an unusual gladness, bawled thanks

to this comely and ravaging ally, asking
  Only for more light with which to see
their neighbour's destruction.

All this I saw through my improved binoculars.

Many years ago, I took my family to the Laurentians for our two-week summer holidays. And I noticed when my daughter was by the lake that I didn't really see her, because the weeds and the flowers and so on were somewhat taller than she was. I had a moment of anxiety: supposing she fell into the lake. Neither I, nor her mother, would perhaps see the thing happen. However nothing happened that summer, and just before we were to pack up and leave for town, I noticed that my daughter, Naomi, was by the lake, and this time, her head was peeping just above the weeds. I got very inspired and began to write the poem while my wife did all the packing to get us back into Montreal.

Song for Naomi

Who is that in the tall grasses singing
By herself, near the water?
I can not see her
But can it be her
Than whom the grasses so tall
Are taller,
My daughter,
My lovely daughter?

Who is that in the tall grasses running
Beside her, near the water?
She can not see there
Time that pursued her
In the deep grasses so fast
And faster
And caught her,
My foolish daughter.

What is the wind in the fair grass saying
Like a verse, near the water?
Saviours that over
All things have power
Make Time himself grow kind
And kinder
That sought her,
My little daughter.

Who is that at the close of the summer
Near the deep lake? Who wrought her
Comely and slender?
Time but attends and befriends her
Than whom the grasses though tall
Are not taller,
My daughter,
My gentle daughter.

Sometime just before the Second World War broke out, I was working on a farm. And there was a bull calf that the owner of the farm felt was not needed; he was superfluous and he had to be destroyed; it wasn't profitable to rear him. Bull calves, as you know, are very magnificent creatures, full of pride, and they have warm, soft brown eyes; altogether, a very handsome, proud creature full of the instinct of life and vitality. Fortunately, I wasn't given the order to destroy the bull calf — someone else had to do that. My job was to dig a grave for the dead bull calf and bury it. Many years later I remembered the episode and wrote this poem:

THE BULL CALF
The thing could barely stand. Yet taken
from his mother and the barn smells
he still impressed with his pride,
with the promise of sovereignty in the way

his head moved to take us in.
The fierce sunlight tugging the maize from the ground
licked at his shapely flanks.
He was too young for all that pride.
I thought of the deposed Richard II.

"No money in bull calves," Freeman had said.
The visiting clergyman rubbed the nostrils
now snuffing pathetically at the windless day.
"A pity," he sighed.
My gaze slipped off his hat toward the empty sky
that circled over the black knot of men,
over us and the calf waiting for the first blow.

Struck,
the bull calf drew in his thin forelegs
as if gathering strength for a mad rush ...
tottered ... raised his darkening eyes to us,
and I saw we were at the far end
of his frightened look, growing smaller and smaller
till we were only the ponderous mallet
that flicked his bleeding ear
and pushed him over on his side, stiffly,
like a block of wood.

Below the hill's crest
the river snuffled on the improvised beach.
We dug a deep pit and threw the dead calf into it.
It made a wet sound, a sepulchral gurgle,
as the warm sides bulged and flattened.
Settled, the bull calf lay as if asleep,
one foreleg over the other,
bereft of pride and so beautiful now,
without movement, perfectly still in the cool pit,
I turned away and wept.

Here's a rather satirical poem I wrote for my country. I don't think I would write this sort of poem today, because many things have happened to make this country more alive, more dynamic, more colourful than it was when I wrote this poem about twenty, or perhaps twenty-five, years ago. I took the title from a book that our foremost historian, Mr. Lower,[1] who I believe taught and perhaps is still teaching at Queen's University, wrote some time ago. It's called *From Colony to Nation* and the poem is called "From Colony to Nation."

A dull people,
but the rivers of this country
are wide and beautiful

A dull people
enamoured of childish games,
but food is easily come by
and plentiful

Some with a priest's voice
in their cage of ribs: but
on high mountain-tops and in thunderstorms
the chirping is not heard

Deferring to beadle and censor;
not ashamed for this,
but given over to horseplay,
the making of money

A dull people, without charm
or ideas,
settling into the clean empty look
of a Mountie or dairy farmer
as into a legacy

One can ignore them
(the silences, the vast distances help)

and suppose them at the bottom
of one of the meaner lakes,
their bones not even picked for souvenirs.

And here's another sharply satirical poem which I wrote after observing
a family eating watermelons.

FAMILY PORTRAIT
That owner of duplexes
has enough gold to sink himself
on a battleship. His children,
two sons and a daughter, are variations
on the original gleam: that is,
        slobs with a college education.

Right now the four of them
are seated in the hotel's dining room
munching watermelons.

With the assurance of money
in the bank
they spit out the black, cool, elliptical
melonseeds, and you can tell
the old man has rocks
but no culture: he spits,
        gives the noise away free.

The daughter however is embarrassed
(Second Year Arts, McGill) and sucks harder
to forget.

They're about as useless
as tits on a bull,

and I think:
"Thank heaven I'm not
Jesus Christ —
I don't have to love them."

CAT DYING IN AUTUMN
I put the cat outside to die,
Laying her down
Into a rut of leaves
Cold and bloodsoaked;
Her moan
Coming now more quiet
And brief in October's economy
Till the jaws
Opened and shut on no sound.

Behind the wide pane
I watched the dying cat
Whose fur like a veil of air
The autumn wind stirred
Indifferently with the leaves;
Her form (or was it the wind?)
Still breathing —
A surprise of white.

And I was thinking
Of melting snow in spring
Of a strip of gauze
When a sparrow
Dropped down beside it
Leaning his clean beak
Into the hollow;
Then whirred away, his wings,
You may suppose, shuddering.

Letting me see
From my house
The twisted petal
That fell
Between the ruined paws
To hold or play with,
And the tight smile
Cats have for meeting death.

This poem that I'm about to read I wrote after my mother's death. My mother was a very remarkable woman with a tremendous joie de vivre and also with a marvellous gift for cursing and for vituperation. I have said somewhere that I owe my gift, such as it is, for cadence and rhythm to the vituperative curses my mother would shower upon me when I was a young boy. This is my tribute to my mother, who was full of the most marvellous contradictions, a very colourful, dynamic woman who raised the family of eight or nine of us, with very little assistance from my father, who was a dreaming, ineffectual mystic, who found it much more pleasant to commune with God and his angels than to have much dealings with his wife or with his children.

KEINE LAZAROVITCH: 1870–1959
When I saw my mother's head on the cold pillow,
Her white waterfalling hair in the cheeks' hollows,
I thought, quietly circling my grief, of how
She loved God but cursed extravagantly his creatures.

For her final mouth was not water but a curse,
A small black hole, a black rent in the universe,
Which damned the green earth, stars and trees in its stillness
And the inescapable lousiness of growing old.

And I record she was comfortless, vituperative,
Ignorant, glad, and much else besides; I believe
She endlessly praised her black eyebrows, their thick weave,

Till plagiarizing Death leaned down and took them for his mould.
And spoiled a dignity I shall not again find,
And the fury of her stubborn limited mind;
Now none will shake her amber beads and call God blind,
Or wear them on a breast so radiantly.

O fierce she was, mean and unaccommodating;
But I think now of the toss of her gold earrings,
Their proud carnal assertion, and her youngest sings
While all the rivers of her red veins move into the sea.

And here's a somewhat gloomy poem that I wrote. Poets write sometimes out of gloom and melancholy, and sometimes out of great joy. Don't
expect them to be consistent; they're not magicians or mathematicians or
philosophers or bank accountants. They have their varying moods; they can
be up one day, down in the deepest depths of depression the next day. So, I
wrote this poem when I was in the dumps, about the possibility of human-
izing —through literature, through poetry, through what I'm doing at this
very moment — mankind.

For My Friend Who Teaches Literature
I tell you, William,
there isn't a ghost
of a chance
people will be changed by poems.

Book Club editors
wish to believe otherwise,
Commencement Day orators
and commissars;
but we poets know the facts of the case.
People will remain stupid and deceitful,
their hearts will pump
malice and villainy
into their bloodstream, forever.

All the noble lines of poets
did not make Hiroshima and Belsen
not to happen,
nor will they keep back the coming holocaust.

Why should you add
to the mischief,
the self-deception?
Leave that to the culture-peddlers.

Be truthful:
tell children who their forbears were,
the curse they bear.

Do not weaken
even a single one of them
with fine sentiments!

Three or four years ago I was in Germany, and I took the trip that everyone who goes to Germany is supposed to take, and that is a boat up — or
is it down? — the Rhine River. And there were all the other holidaymakers
with me; they were singing and drinking and laughing and talking. And of
course my mind went back to the very gloomy, terrible, catastrophic days
not too long ago when Hitler and his Nazi storm troopers ruled that unfor-
tunate land. I thought of all the terrible things that had been done, by them
and by their accomplices. And I wrote this poem:

RHINE BOAT TRIP
The castles on the Rhine
are all haunted
by the ghosts of Jewish mothers
looking for their ghostly children

And the clusters of grapes
in the sloping vineyards
are myriads of blinded eyes
staring at the blind sun

The tireless Lorelei
can never comb from their hair
the crimson beards
of murdered rabbis

However sweetly they sing
one hears only
the low wailing of cattle-cars
moving invisibly across the land

And to conclude this reading, there are two poems. The first one, "Silent Joy," which records a great moment of ecstasy I felt one day when I was in Molyvos in the island of Lesbos, Greece.

SILENT JOY

Remembering
St. James street, Sunday mornings
— a vast empty cathedral,
my footsteps echoing in the silent vaults

rooms on quiet afternoons, alone
or with one I loved deeply

shadows, cool and long, in hot lanes

insect-humming cemeteries
and light dripping from vines
in globules of rose, of pale-green

I am so utterly filled
with joyful peace and wonder,
my heart stops beating

Friends, I stare at everything
with wide, with sightless eyes
like one who has just died

LEAVETAKING

Good-bye
fields, waves, hills, trees
and fairweather birds whose blasts
woke me each morning at dawn

So that I might see
the early sun

Good-bye, Sun

I am growing older
I must instruct myself to love you all
with moderation

May you be as kind
to the next poet
who comes this way
as you have been to me

When you see him,
give him my felicitations
and love

Transcribed by Amy Kalbun

MIRIAM WADDINGTON
(1917–2004)

Miriam Waddington was a poet and author whose work is marked by the inclusion of social justice themes and pastoral imagery. Waddington was born in 1917 and grew up in an insulated Jewish community in Winnipeg. Her family life revolved around their Jewish heritage and Yiddish culture. Her parents, Isaac Dworkin and Masha Dobrusin, were Russian immigrants and imbued Waddington with socialist values, which were expressed in her studies and work. Her Jewish identity and historical knowledge influenced her writing, as seen in poems such as "Elijah" and "My Travels," which employ religious imagery and biblical allusions.

Waddington faced anti-Semitism for the first time when her family moved to Ottawa, where she was exposed to attitudes of Anglo-Saxon superiority in the public school system and later at the University of Toronto. She channelled these experiences into her poetry, which she began to write in earnest with guidance from Yiddish poet Ida Maze[1] and the Montreal artistic community to which her family was linked. Waddington published her first volume of poetry, *Green World*, in 1945 with the assistance of publisher and modern poetry pioneer John Sutherland.[2] Over the next six decades, Waddington published fourteen volumes. Many of Waddington's poems revolve around the concept of intersectionality, the experience of oppression based on multi-layered social identities. This is notably explored in poems like "The Bond," which were based on her experiences of anti-Semitism in Toronto as a young woman.

Waddington acknowledged that the combination of her gender and her religion created a massive social barrier for her and generated feelings of conflicting identities and isolation. As a result, Waddington became passionate

about social change: besides writing, she had a career as a social worker, advocating for the Jewish Family Service, a prisoner's rehabilitation society, mental illness facilities, and other communities. Her experiences and emotional engagement with social work influenced her poetry, which explores drug abuse, mental illness, and isolation. She also wrote landscape and romantic poetry. Waddington met her husband, Patrick Waddington, a journalist and an activist, at an anti-fascist meeting in Ottawa. They married in 1939, had two sons together, but divorced in 1965.

In 1962 Waddington became a lecturer at the University of Toronto and York University. The 1960s were a time of rising Canadian nationalism, which Waddington explored in collaboration with the National Film Board for a collection of poetry and photography entitled *Call Them Canadians*. She surveys themes of travelling and migration, while questioning the creation of national myths or social cohesion for such a vast landscape and its varied peoples.

Waddington's work engages the Canadian landscape; volumes containing pastoral poetry, such as *Driving Home* (1972) and *The Last Landscape* (1992), are based on a childhood lived in both urban and rural communities. Waddington died in 2004, but her poetic work left an extensive impact on Canadian-Jewish culture and contributed to social change.

References

Menkis, Richard. "Miriam Dworkin Waddington." *Jewish Women's Archive.* March 1, 2009. https://jwa.org/encyclopedia/article/waddington-miriam-dworkin.

Monk, Lorraine, and Miriam Waddington. *Call Them Canadians: A Photographic Point of View.* Ottawa: Queen's Printer, 1968.

Waddington, Miriam. *Apartment Seven: Essays New and Selected.* Toronto: Oxford University Press, 1989.

Waddington, Miriam, and Ruth Panofsky. *The Collected Poems of Miriam Waddington: A Critical Edition.* Ottawa: University of Ottawa Press, 2014.

Whalley, George and Miriam Waddington. *Writing in Canada; Proceedings of the Canadian Writers' Conference, Queen's University, 28–31 July 1955.* Toronto: Macmillan of Canada, 1956.

RECORDED ON NOVEMBER 3, 1969

This is Miriam Waddington.

> UNDERSTANDING SNOW
>   how hard it is
>   to understand
>   snow   how it is
>   a burning pile
>   and a white
>   sea   a halo of
>   greeting   hello
>   from a far star
>   and a sudden-
>   ness of seeing
>
>   miracles   bands
>   of light curving
>   around us moving

inside us   and
even in spring
when grass covers
the snow winter
is not asleep
but waiting
folded and dark

about to sprout
from the plump
lap of summer
about to fountain
from the green jet
of maytime   or
throw down from
its white tent
handfuls of
angry flowers

whole mouthfuls
of frost   paralyzed
stars   icefeathers
burning pillows
and white seas:
and on my empty
bed   lost summers
armfuls of soft
ownerless love

Now, I'd thought I'd like to read a poem that I wrote a very long time ago, even though I don't consider it to be one of my good poems now, but I have a special fondness for it because it tells a little bit of history from a point of view that isn't often explored in Canadian writing. Perhaps it's more often explored now than it used to be, but it's about being Jewish and feeling unaccepted because I was Jewish and about the war, which began in

1939, and which I felt very sad about, and about poor people about whom
I was beginning to learn in a very special way when I started to work and go
to work on streetcars. It was a different world from the university, and this
poem is called "The Bond."

On Jarvis Street the Jewish whore
Smiles and stirs upon the bed.
Sleep is the luxury of the poor
But sweeter sleep awaits the dead.

Sweeter sleep awaits the dead
Than all the living who must rise
To join the march of hunger fed
Under the dawn of city skies.

Under the dawn of city skies
Moves the sun in presaged course
Smoothing out the cunning lies
That hide the evil at the source.

I sense the evil at the source
Now at this golden point of noon,
The misdirected social force
Will grind me also, and too soon.

On Jarvis street the Jewish whore
The Jewish me on Adelaide[3] —
Both of the nameless million poor
Who wear no medals and no braid.

Oh woman you are kin to me,
Your heart beats something like my own
When idiot female ecstasy
Transforms in love the flesh and bone;

And woman, you are kin to me
Those tense moments first or last,
When men deride your ancestry
Whore, Jewess, you are twice outcast.

Whore, Jewess, I acknowledge you
Joint heirs to varied low estate,
No heroes will arise anew
Avenging us twice isolate.

    ....

I who start from noonday sleep
To cry of triumph, 'aeroplane!'
Hear nothing but the slippered creep
Of famine through the surplus grain.

Exultant females shriek, 'parade!'
And crowd a hundred windows high,
From offices on Adelaide
They wave the khaki boys goodbye.

    ....

The heavy night is closing in,
Signal omens everywhere,
You woman who have lived by sin,
And I who dwelt in office air,

Will share a common rendezvous
Arranged by madness, crime, and race.
Sister, my salute to you!
I will recognize your face.

I spent last year on leave — I'm a teacher now — on leave in England,
and I'm very fond of the drawings and paintings of William Blake; and I
used to go and look at them at the Tate Gallery and I suppose he was on my

mind. And so at Passover time, with the fact that Jews seem to be having a hard time in some of the communist countries, I wrote a poem about the prophet Elijah, who traditionally comes to Jewish homes on Passover and drinks out of the beaker of wine that's especially set out for him.

ELIJAH

Elijah's gone to Poland,
as naked as William Blake,
his beard is as black as a chimney,
his eyes are a Baltic lake.

He sifts the mounds of rubble
broken bottles and lead,
Elijah counts his children,
but his Warsaw children are dead.

The Jewish *seder* is over
Jerusalem's song is still,
Poland spills with echoes
but Elijah's beaker is full

Of night as black as chimneys
and the wailing of William Blake,
Elijah sits in Poland
and sips his own heartbreak.

I'd like to read a few more poems about being Jewish, growing up Jewish in Winnipeg, later in Ottawa, and perhaps, never feeling completely comfortable anywhere, and this is a much later poem called "My Travels."

I have looked at
beautiful things
in the museums of

foreign countries
all over the world
and I can report
they are still
mourning for Christ
on the tapestries
of Bucharest while
in Moscow the gold
icons are blazing
with the intense
motherhood of dark
medieval madonnas.

On the mountains
of new Jerusalem
in a house of
glass and stone
I read in a broken
alphabet the deed
of sale written
in the hand of
my forefather Bar
Kochba a brave
warrior[4] and later
on the cliffs of
Jaffa (spelled Joppa)
an old papyrus
dating from the
time of Ramses
the Second warned
me what may befall
the traveller in a
strange country:[5]
thou dost sleep
for thou art worn
out a coward steals

thy bow thy sheath-
knife and thy quiver
thy reins are cut
in the darkness
thy weapons are
become dry land.

And from Warsaw
where I went much
later I can report
that the war is not
over yet the stones
of the ghetto still
whisper at night
the old city cries
from the cellars
the Vistula moans,[6]
the music of summer
hides nothing in
Warsaw on Saturday
afternoons when the
Lazienki Park[7] is
empty and Chopin[8]
is dead and I study
the clever walls
of the Satirical
Café in the Square
of the Three Crosses.

And in Hamburg
I discover the
Germans are still
hating the Jews and
in Kiel the same
and in the quiet
gardens of Munich

still the same   it
was no pleasure
being a Jew in
Bucharest I did
not mention it to
anyone in Moscow
I softpedalled it
in Warsaw while
in Jerusalem where
everyone is some
kind of Jew or
other it was no
pleasure either:
thou dost sleep
for thou art worn
out a coward steals
thy bow thy sheath-
knife and thy quiver
thy reins are cut
in the darkness
thy weapons fall
to the ground
thy weapons are
become dry land.

I am homesick I
am packing up
I am going home
but now I don't
know anymore
where home is.

LOVERS[9]

Lovers tread the waters, lovers go
In all the seasons where the waters flow,
They neither swim nor fly
But magically they go
Where all the world envies where they go.

The world loves its lovers
And I love the waters
Where the lovers go.
In spring they conquer colour
And imprison all the cries
Of birds and fish within their rainbow eyes.

And deep at night
You hear them wander
In the city's woods,
The alleys and the streets,
You hear them cry beneath the eaves
They sigh and startle husband and his wife
From sleep, "the lovers," says the wife,
And the husband answers, "so were we."

The world listens and at night it hears
The silvering voice of love that pierces sleep,
All lovers weep, they neither swim nor fly
But magically they float in trees
And tread the water of the wavering will.
With all the cries of birds
Imprisoned in their rainbow eyes
They go where all the world envies
Where they go.

And here is still another one called "The Season's Lovers":

In the daisied lap of summer
The lovers lay, they dozed
And lay in sun unending,
They lay in light, they slept
And only stirred
Each one to find the other's lips.
At times they sighed
Or spoke a word
That wavered on uneven breath,
He had no name and she forgot
The ransomed kingdom of her death.

When at last the sun went down
And the chilly evening stained the fields,
The lovers rose and rubbed their eyes:
They saw the pale wash of grass
Heighten to metallic green
And spindly tongues of granite mauve
Lick up the milk of afternoon,
They gathered all the scattered light
Of daisies to one place of white,
And ghostly poets lent their speech
To the stillness of the air,
The lovers listened, each to each.

Into the solid wall of night,
The lovers looked, their clearer sight
Went through that dark intensity
To the other side of light.
The lovers stood, it seemed to them
They hung upon the world's rim —
He clung to self, and she to him;
He rocked her with his body's hymn

And murmured to her shuddering cry
You are all states, all princes I,
And sang against her trembling limbs,
Nothing else is, he sang, *but I.*

They lifted the transparent lid
From world false and world true
And in the space of both they flew.
He found a name, she lost her death,
And summer lulled them in its lap
With a leafy lullaby.
There they sleep unending sleep,
The lovers lie
He with a name, she free of death,
In a country hard to find
Unless you read love's double mind
Or invent its polar map.

And here is another one called "The Drug Addict." This was a young man that I met while working in a prisoner's rehabilitation society.

The Drug Addict

Kingly were his rags, his uniform
Was tatters, and fair his unshaven face;
His eyes were lighted as if some other world
Informed them of perfection closed to us.

What other world could turn his twenty years
From orphanage and factory, nurtured by machines,
To such a bright disorder, what genius could abash
His heaven inspired eyes ablaze with heroin?

His glory tumbled later, tumbled with the hair
Moist as cornsilk and flushed against his skin,
Age could not tutor him, nor gods confine
Him to those places — his will outshone

His chances, its brilliance bruised our eyes;
He went down like a hero defending his own kind,
And in some paradise which still eludes our lust
He climbs the beanstalk and with a shadowy knife
Stabs at the giant, cuts the glittering dust,
And cries at the blood of his own life.

Here's another one I wrote at the same time; I was also still then working in the prisoners' rehabilitation society. This one is called "The Women's Jail."

This garden is outlandish
with its white picket fence
and straggling orchard,
who would guess this painted house
with convent walks
is a women's jail?

Unless you have seen their faces,
old women grey as sponges
dropping in this habitat,
young ones sullen
with a worm gnawing them.
I often wonder why the drug takers
have such skyblue eyes.

And the cheque forgers:
how velvet they are
how apples and cream,
secretly I envy them
their blossoming bodies
and their talents with men.

Being especially human
I am no judge of evil
but hear how it has

a singing life in them,
how it speaks out
with an endowed voice.

Doubt my poor, my gentle one,
my overtrained, my fine,
my inner ear.
I have been insufficiently dowered,
my limbs are pale as winter,
sun-starved,
my blood is free from alcohol,
I am law abiding I am completely
resistible, is there anything
praiseworthy in that?

And here is a poem called "Saints and Others." It is about Toronto, to
which I returned after an absence of about fifteen years.

SAINTS AND OTHERS
I'll write no more poems,
I'll love no man.
I'll live in tall Toronto
where it rains against the sun,
here saints are very many
but I am not one.

I was once proud and
loved myself   I lived
five thousand feet
above sea level   loved
my prairie city and the wild
windscattered rose,
and no one read the sky
so clear so true as I.

In summer I travelled,
I mined the ocean
and shone like Lucifer,
talked with fish   stacked
sunsets like poker chips.
I loved myself and loved
the great seabirds
and the cool dark places
under their wingspread
I loved the eyeblue waters
which opened to my hand.

What now my human thirst?
seadeep; and my love hunger?
drowned; what of the saints?
they live in the wide world.
I live in tall Toronto
where it rains against the sun,
and saints there may be many
but I'm not one.

My love of birds has flown
no wing now stirs the sky
the fires I lit are dead.
Extinguished Lucifer
stagnates and lies alone
under the rotting pier;
he dreams of sunlit hell
and the sea is his blind eye,
my hand his fist of stone.

So we were noble; like the Titanic
we sank and slept alone;
who knows what voyages await
drowned travellers like us?
I dream I am the wild wind-

scattered rose   the parting
waters but wake to traffic noise.
Ruined and glorious
I make my soapbox speech
where no one hears me;
it is no use.
I'm my dishonoured brother,
my hand his fist of stone.

SEA BELLS

Five fathoms deep my father lies,
and of his bones are my bones made,
this is his blindness in my eyes,
his limping paced my grave.

Oh daughter toll the sea-green bell
and shake the coral from your hair,
the sea was once your bed of birth,
your given name your knell.

My body was your sepulcher,
the wide world was your cell,
my hand has written in your blood
what time and tide will tell.

The tide has since cast up its scroll,
and told what time could tell;
five fathoms deep my father lies
his daughter deeper fell

To see the seeing of his eyes
and take what pearls might have to give;
five fathoms deep in sleep he lies
whose death waked me to live.

And here is another poem about my father, who was a great gardener.

THE GARDENERS
Last spring I wished
for myself a fullgrown garden;
night and day in my mind's eyes
summer turned out its pockets
for me   spilled flowers and birds,
impaled the four winds in fossils.
I dreamed of rare specimens
and ordered forsythia lilac
and flowering almond bushes.

Strong with hope I began to dig
but the clay would not move
under my hand or foot or shovel;
I hacked away in my backlot
to the heart of North America
(virgin stone dammit) until my hands
trembled with failure; then I cried
as bitterly as a nine-year-old.

And later wondered is this
my father's daughter   this
rag-petalled wind-blown tear-
stained love-me love-me-not daisy?
This everything-ventured-nothing-gained
sorrykins   this no-more-young ineptitude?
This is not me or she my father's
daughter   it is some drag and hag
throwback to Abishag[10]   the devil took
and take hellish mistake!

And for my father?   For him
whole fields of cucumber

ripened by the riverside and
the small-leaved orchards grew.
Nowhere inherited   I am
his redhaired melancholy
ten generations deep and steep,
his course historical nourished
with skill   a proud harvest
heaped and reaped for ruin.

Yet he my father when aged sixty-eight
was bleached and humming as a field of wheat,
grew a grapevine in a city lot
with stems thick as your arm,
had flowers rioting   incited evergreens,
and against all nature harvested
in Toronto an Arizona melon.

And now, I'm going to read a poem about words and problems with words, which I suppose every poet comes to at some point in his writing life.

LOOKING FOR STRAWBERRIES IN JUNE
        I have to tell you
        about the words I
        used to know   such
        words   so sheer   thin
        transparent so light
        and quick   I had such
        words for wind for
        whatever grew
        I knew a certain
        leaf-language from
        somewhere   but now

it's all used up
I have come to the
end of some line or
other like walking
on railroad ties in
the country looking
for strawberries in
June and suddenly
the ties end in the
middle of no-place
and I stop to look
around to take my
direction but I

don't recognize the
landscape   it is all
grey   feathery   the
voices of birds are
foreign   yet I used
to know such words
japanned   brushed and
papery   whitefolded
Russian flowerwords
cabbage roses   huge
holes in the head of
the universe pouring
out rosy revolutions:

and I used to know
swarthy eastern words
heavy with Hebrew   then
I was kidnapped by
gypsies   I knew the
up and down of their
dark-blue anger   the
leathery touch of

the fortune-telling
begging wandering
words   but what's
become of them?
I don't know   I'm

just standing here
on the threshold of
a different country,
everything is made
of plastic and silence;
what month is it any-
way? I'm knocking at
the door but nobody
answers   I mutter *Lenin*
Karl Marx   Walt Whitman
Chaucer   Hopkins   even
Arichbald Lampman[11]   but
nobody comes   I don't

know the password
I only know it has
nothing to do with
being good or true
nothing to do with
being beautiful.

And here is one about an old landmark in Toronto, called "The Eight-Sided White Barn."[12]

I know now for whom
I was saving that eight-
sided white barn at the
corner of Dufferin and

Steeles Avenue   every time
I passed it the morning
would shiver and dance
and I want to frame
it all into a poem so

I have just given you
an eight-sided white barnboat and it has a ramp
(or gangplank) in front
of it for the animals
to come in on   and it
has a turret on top
of it for someone to
gaze out of   and see
the dove   the leaf   and
the lay of the land

and it has a field
around it   full of
ploughed-up earthen
waves crowned with the
foam of snow   and
the blown straw of
Toronto's skimpy winter
and it has an endlessly
unrolling slapdash table-
cloth sky   stained with
wind   blown by rain
covering everything.

Between the plangent sky
and the ploughing sea in
the sun-ice of Ontario on
the snowish shield of the
brittle world we are land-

ploughers   nightskaters
we are seafarers in the
flood who journey out
in a barnboat to touch
the broken leaf   to hear
the dove   to brush through
the boundaries of what-
ever keeps us from being
the wide new world.

And now I want to read a rather longish poem. It's about — I suppose it sums up pretty much what I believe in or what I am — and perhaps it sums up part of our whole Canadian society, because it is about driving home and looking at all the signs, the gasoline signs, Esso, and Shell and so on.

DRIVING HOME
Classic ESSO
          bloodlit SHELL
signs
      omens
              mysteries
on daylight roads
              look at them hang
conchy
      paunchy worlds
drunken planets
      insane balloons
electric lovecharms
              dangling
from sunlit skies
              (don't shout
my name   whisper it)
              I'm coming
driving to the Volga[13]

on the world throughway
past the grain elevators
     through Levitan's
painted nights[14]
     to his charcoal beaches
driving from Winnipeg
     to Chekhov's nineteenth-century
consumption
     in the swampy summers
outside of Moscow[15]   driving to
Stanislavsky[16]   his wild-eyed strike
for future   act of the new

And there's my grandfather's mill
     beside the marshy road
in the village Hitler burned
and there's my grandfather
     with his flourdusty beard
printer's-ink-smell of books
     and my mother running
barefoot
     in a forest of birches,
        she's a force
on fire with rage
     with joy
and here's my father
     building an arbour
in our backyard in the
     new world
coming in with
     his Sunday cucumbers
     and here's me
with my firstborn
     running after his
gesturing arms

and never catching him
and here's my second son
                placid smiling
                                (deceptive)
and here's my English husband
                stepping out of the picture
leaving us all
                classic

Classic ESSO
                geometric oracle
lined   and circled   and
                                alphabeted
monoyellow moonyellow
                        SHELL
(transformed lyre)
                poet's cymbal
culture flag
                against the billboard hangovers
programmed lovecharm
                        (don't tell me
it doesn't work
                it works   but
you have to ask the right questions)

Colours hang heavy
                heavy over my head
what shall this person do?
                this person
shall be captive
                a seal in the park zoo
asleep under the water
                a passenger in a
locked car or a camel
                in the city's compound
shedding its hair

in a northern country;
and this person
                    shall be a prophet
wake all of the dead rabbis
                    of Lithuania[17]
take dictation from them
                    plan strictness of study
how
          not to forget

And this person
                    shall be a singer
journey forth
                    when night falls
when the temple voices
                    rise thin
                              tenorous
above the rafters
                    when the gates are open

(Don't shout
                    my name   whisper it
to the world's rivers)
                    I'm coming
Father Volga
                    wait for me
                              Mother Assiniboine[18]
I'm coming
                    through the Northwest Passage
from east of the Labrador where
                              the arctic birds
are folding
                    their daylight feathers
between sky and earth
                    in cold lullabies,
where the blacksmith

                              of all possibilities
is thundering
                    stoking his furnace
for a new kind of people

The mosquitoes rise
                              in clouds
celestial
       ESSO
                    ambiguous
                              SHELL
the traffic roars
              in the mirror
tells me
       I am on my way home;
                    home?
Fool
       you *are* home
              you were home
in the first place
                    and
if you don't look out
              it's going to be
now this minute
              classic ESSO
                    bloodlit SHELL
forever

    A poem about a Canadian poet who died at about age thirty-six. I call it
"A Landscape of John Sutherland."

       We are
       in flight
       we are

a space of
dreamed-of
light
autumn canyons
crevices
we are the blue
between
the sliding doors
of sky.

We fall
among the shells
the molluscs
of our concerts
on the earth
our bones
are toys
and trumpets
for the wind,
our song
sand
on a shore.

Our eyes
are owls
who scold
the lit-up
winter night,
our skeletons
snow animals
prowling
through the
quiet moment
of landscape.

That is
what I like

best   to find
the quiet moment,
shadowless,
in the roar
of landscape;
to be the
landscape.

Now a poem that I wrote for a book of photographs for the National Film Board. It's called "Canadians," and in it, I suppose I try to say something about myself and everybody else who's a Canadian.[19]

Here are
our signatures:
geese fish eskimo
faces girl-guide
cookies ink-drawings
tree-plantings summer
storms and winter
emanations.

We look
like a geography
but just scratch us
and we bleed like
history are full
of modest mystery
sensitive
to double-talk, double-take
(and double-cross)
in a country
too wide
to be single in.

Are we real or
did someone invent
us was it Henry
Hudson Etienne Brulé[20]
or a carnival
of village girls?
Was it a flock of nuns
a pity of Indians
a gravyboat of
fur-traders professional
explorers or those
amateur map-makers
our Fathers
of Confederation?

Wherever you are
Charles Tupper Alexander
Galt D'Arcy McGee George
Cartier Ambrose Shea
Henry Crout Father
Ragueneau Lord Selkirk
and John A:[21] however
far into northness
you have walked
when we call you turn
around please and
don't look so
surprised.

Transcribed by Griffin Kelly

RAYMOND SOUSTER (1921–2012)

Despite being one of the most important contributors to the twentieth-century Canadian canon, on the surface nothing about Raymond Souster seemed out of the ordinary. As Oberon Press's Michael Macklem comments, "though he's recognized ... as one of Canada's most significant poets, he's hard to distinguish ... He wears suits, his hair is short, and he works every day at the Bank of Commerce at the corner of King and Bay ... He shows us things that are already familiar ... he himself is familiar" (2). This sense of familiarity is an essential ingredient of Souster's poetry, rendering his work, in the words of poet James Deahl, "at once pithy and humorous, silly and wise" (14–15). In short Souster was a seemingly ordinary man with an extraordinary talent for making the familiar memorable.

Souster was born in Toronto on January 15, 1921. Besides four years spent with the Royal Canadian Air Force during the Second World War, Toronto remained Souster's home until his death in October 2012. Toronto served as the preferred stage upon which he set many of his poems. In an interview with Tony Tremblay, Souster recalled first being inspired to write poetry as a child after reading Archibald Lampman's "Heat" in an old school anthology of poetry (Souster, "The Heart Still Singing" 4).[1] With his parents' encouragement, he submitted his poetry to Toronto newspapers such as the *Globe and Mail* and the *Toronto Star* (186), embarking on his professional poetic career in 1946 when John Sutherland's *First Statement* published his chapbook *When We Are Young* (Deahl 12). Through *First Statement*, Souster forged connections with other budding literary luminaries, including

Miriam Waddington, Patrick Anderson, Louis Dudek, and Irving Layton;[2] he collaborated with the latter two to form Contact Press in 1952 (12, 25). Contact was dedicated to author-owned, non-commercial Canadian publishing and featured work by Margaret Atwood, Leonard Cohen, Eli Mandel, and other prominent Canadian poets. In 1966 Souster also collaborated with Dudek, Ron Everson, and Michael Gnarowski[3] to form the League of Canadian Poets, which organized poetry readings and worked to promote Canada's next generation of literary talent (Souster, *Making the Damn Thing Work* 11, 13). Indeed, Souster was a tireless supporter of his fellow poets: as Deahl describes, he championed "cooperation, not competition among writers" (28), providing support and encouragement to many emerging authors (Souster, "Correspondence"; Fiorito; Deahl 27).

Souster wrote more than seventy books, including works of prose under the pseudonyms Raymond Holmes and John Holmes. His themes were as diverse as love and war, baseball and jazz (Deahl 16–17). Winner of the 1964 Governor General's Award and the 1979 City of Toronto Book Award, he was named an Officer of the Order of Canada in 1995 (Fiorito). One of the first Canadian poets to be inspired by American populist poetry, Souster drew on the brevity, imagism, and witticism of poets like Kenneth Patchen and Carl Sandburg[4] and adapted this style to a Canadian, and specifically a Torontonian, context (Deahl 12, 15). Thus, many of his most characteristic poems capture the quotidian sights, sounds, and smells of the city. As Souster explained, "I feel very close to what might be called 'the man on the street.' Ordinariness and human struggle have always interested me" (Souster, "The Heart Still Singing" 191). Hence, his poems were a celebration of the ordinary and the overlooked, providing readers with a condensed capsule of time and space, taking seemingly unremarkable events and injecting them with wit and import.

Despite his deteriorating health, Souster continued to engage with the literary world during his final years, hosting poetry afternoons under his backyard mulberry tree when he retired, and writing more than a hundred poems, even after losing his sight (Deahl 28, 30). For indeed, this was what he had been doing all his life: gathering people together under the boughs of his poetry and allowing them — in the words of Souster himself — to "explore ... feelings through words" (Souster, "The Heart Still Singing" 186).

References

Deahl, James. E-mail interview with Raymond Souster. February 25, 2016.

Deahl, James, ed. *Under the Mulberry Tree: Poems For and About Raymond Souster*. Toronto: Quattro Books, 2014.

Fiorito, Joe. "Happy Birthday, Raymond Souster." *Toronto Star*, January 13, 2012.

———. "Raymond Souster, 1921–2012." *Toronto Star*, October 24, 2012.

———. "Stairs First Step in Honoring Toronto Poet Raymond Souster." *Toronto Star*, October 23, 2013.

Macklem, Michael. Introduction to *Selected Poems of Raymond Souster*. Edited by Michael Maklem. Ottawa: Oberon Press, 1972.

McKnight, David. "The Poetic Achievement of Contact Press (1952–1967)." *Historical Perspectives on Canadian Publishing*. http://digitalcollections. mcmaster.ca/hpcanpub/case-study/poetic-achievement-contact-press-1952-1967.

Shanahan, Noreen. "He Gave His Life To Poetry." *Globe and Mail*, November 7, 2012.

Souster, Raymond. "The Heart Still Singing: Raymond Souster at 82." By Tony Tremblay. *Studies in Canadian Literature* 27, no. 2 (2002): 183–201.

———. *Making the Damn Thing Work*. Toronto: Junction Books. 2001.

———. Raymond Souster to Leonard Cohen. June 30, 1956. Leonard Cohen fonds, MS coll. 122, box 10, file 87. Thomas Fisher Rare Book Library, University of Toronto.

———. *The Years*. Ottawa: Oberon Press, 1971.

RECORDED ON NOVEMBER 11 AND 17, 1969

This is Raymond Souster. The collection is divided into three sections: the sixties, the fifties, and the forties, in that order. So I shall begin with poems written in the 1960s. The first poem is called "The Hippies of Nathan Phillips Square" and commemorates the hippie sit-in held in Toronto in 1967 in front of the new City Hall.

THE HIPPIES AT NATHAN PHILLIPS SQUARE
 Completely unaware
 and I'm sure not caring
 that the Superintendent
 of Sanitary Sewers
 together with his colleague
 the Assistant Director
 of Garbage Disposal
 watched them from the ninth tier
 of City Hall windows,

 the young bearded
 unkempt boy
 camped out below
 waved a greeting
 from his sleeping-bag
 to the long-haired blonde
 with bare toes showing
 in her sloppy joes,

 and helped her
 as she wiggled in beside him,
 and was then last seen
 as his hand reached out
 and zippered up the bag....

In the bright morning sunlight
that sleeping bag was seen
to shake, then to roll,
indeed was the most moving thing
in all of Nathan Phillips Square.

At that point the Superintendent
suddenly remembered he'd been
on the way to the washroom all the time,
and the Assistant Director
suddenly recalled
he was two minutes late
in his appointment with the mayor....

The next poem, "Yeah Tigers," is about one of the games of the 1968 World Series.

YEAH TIGERS

When our boy, Al Kaline, tagged that slider of
    Washburn's[5]
in the third today, tagged it good, sent it sailing
high and deep in the Tigers' upper deck —

Wilf, I heard that yelp of yours
clear across this crummy town,
over TV bedlam, traffic, everything —

even if it only came out
as the slightest half-whisper
from your cancer-bugged throat.

The incident which the next poem describes occurred during the first convention of the League of Canadian Poets, held in Toronto, October 1968.

The Petition

The petition we're told
is addressed to the judge
who is shortly to sentence
our fellow poet for trafficking in marijuana.

We are being asked
to certify as to his standing
among our community of poets,
the idea being
the judge may separate him
from the usual drifters
and give a lighter sentence,
six months for example,
instead of three years or four.

We are being asked
for very little, someone says,
it's no sweat to sign:
but I still can't feel
anything for this man
whom I've never met before
and know little of
beyond the talk
that he uses drugs heavily....

I look across the room
to where he sits
while we discuss his case
(a bad mistake)
and try to see
what the face tells
what the twitchy eyes reveal,
not what the beatnik sandals,
beads, long hair, beard,
do not say.

Then I ask him
(as a judge might ask?)
about the previous convictions,
and still can't feel anything,
can't believe what we do
in this room now may cut
his living hell in prison
to a bearable time,
repeat, can't feel the tie
of love for another,
can't move myself
off my rock of isolation.

Someone says it again nearby —
it's nothing, no trouble
to sign. Is that why
all this crowd of poets
moves so eagerly to scribble
on the required paper? I don't know,
but it seems this is all
we can do
for our fellow human,
and I can't move myself
to even this.

So the rest of the day
my mind keeps asking:
what's happened to you, what's changed you,
how long has this
been going on, how deep
has the cancer forked in,
how much of you
is still living flesh
beyond breathing
and excretion, eyes
still opening at daylight? —

what separates you now
from the brutes
from the unburied dead?

The Girls of the Morning

By bus and by train
I'm pushed into morning:
so I twist in my seat,
close my eyes, imagine sleep.
But the girls of the morning
wait at every bus and train stop,
and I know it, how I know it,
and I find my eyes opening
as the doors are swung back
and the cargoes are loaded
and unloaded:
                    O the girls
of the morning
are no girls dressed in mourning,
the skin of each shines
be it white, black or yellow
with the freshness of petals
newly-opened, their hair-dos
make them queens, flappers, innocents,
while their lips hint at passion,
eyes such tenderness.
                    O their perfumes
fill crowded aisles with dreams
of far islands, their dresses
shake the sleep from our eyes
as the mini-skirts ride, dresses hug,
saris flow like water!
One and all proclaim
breasts waiting to be pressed
legs waiting to be smoothed

thighs waiting to be parted,
while posteriors on stairways
sway with gentleness
badly needed in a world
of male rot and madness....
O the girls of my morning
crying love
crying love!

AND NOW WE TAKE YOU TO BIAFRA[6]
They are dying, the commentator says,
from simple protein deficiency,
these children all eyes looking up
two each from the hospital beds.

It's morning now in Biafra
a month from now all this won't be news any more.

No one will care that a million starved to death —
what's a million people more or less in this world?

Their leaders say they fight for independence,
So I suppose these children will continue to die
As long as there's a flag left to wave
And young men willing to murder other men.

Count the scarecrow bodies — thousands —
as the camera takes a shot of the camp.

A month from now it won't be even news.

During the commercial I select
a cool nectarine from the refrigerator.

The poem "His Great Grandfather" tries to show what the men who founded this country were made of and wonders just how well we shape up with them today.

HIS GREAT GRANDFATHER[7]
Arrived in Canada from England 1843
Settled first at Cobourg
Then moved to Rice Lake
Homesteading on a grant of
Two hundred acres of uncleared land.
At the age of twenty-two, mangled his right hand
Forced to saw it off himself before
The doctor got there two days later
Had a hook made to help hold a plough
And over the years, a dozen more like it for different operations
In between hooks and pushing the bush back,
He sired fifteen children.
When he died of a heart attack at age ninety-seven
After shoveling the snow from his front door walk
He'd completely lost track of all his grandchildren.
So tonight, as I talk to you, think together of ancestors,
Of your great grandfather, I look across this room
At the cocktail hour, and wonder how many of us,
Each with his little life,
His vanities, his small concerns,
He'd think of as men. Not too many,
I'm afraid. And the future no better.
How it sickens. How but backwards
We seem to have moved on.

Next we have a poem about box lacrosse as played at Maple Leaf Gardens in Toronto.

La Crosse

Box One A at Maple Leaf Gardens: the announcer
telling the crowd at intermission
"Tonight two full-blooded Indians
from the Five Nations Reserve are playing
for Detroit Olympics...."
                                   In the second period
one of them, Gaylord,[8] takes a cut
at a Maple Leaf player as though he knew
all about tomahawks as well —
                              swings his stick
much as those crafty Ottawas two centuries back,
staging their game on the English King's birthday
at Fort Michilimackinac —
                        all its gates wide open
for the holiday, the defenders drawn
to this game of a hundred savage men
knocking each others' brains out with gutted sticks —
then suddenly the ball innocently thrown
toward the fort, and the players swarming
through the gates —
                   but these players carried tomahawks
        as well,
and with a blood-stopping shout lacrosse was over
and a deadlier game, the massacre, began,
with British blood flowing on the ground to match
that already there from before....
                              Well, Gaylord's no
        Ottawa
of Pontiacs, he's from a friendlier tribe,
tonight shock-helmeted, shoulder-padded,
he's back at the wars, running end to end
in this giant arena with the roar following him
that of the white man who sits with his chips
his hot-dog, watching the sticks flip that rubber ball
so expertly, the savage sweep of the goal shot —

and now a player knocked down, lying motionless,
the crowd on their feet to a man, smelling blood....

The poem "Top Secret" should really be called "Mrs. Brown." It's about
an old cleaning lady I used to know in an office building where I worked for
many years, and which was torn down only this year.

TOP SECRET

Your building's coming down,
Mrs. Brown, sometime next spring;
first the roof, then the upper floors,
all the way down to your own,
the main one.
                    Why do I call it yours?
Who really but me besides yourself
has any real claim to it? And mine so slender
beside your own. I would guess you spent
a quarter of your life on your knees,
first scrubbing the surface dirt from that stubborn floor
with cleaner so ammonia-strong
I used to choke on one whiff of it,
then rubbing the paste-wax in till the sweat
ran down your glasses and you had to stop, fog-bound,
until you wiped them clear.
                              You gave your life
for that floor, Mrs. Brown, and it wasn't worth
one day of it; its smug face polished like glass
only laughed at you from the first
to that last time, when, head turning circles, stomach sick,
you left, never to return....

Your building's coming down
Mrs. Brown, and you should be buried under it
And your grave marked. But cleaning ladies are expendable,

A dime a dozen.
                    And sentiment, they all tell me,
as a major weakness, Mrs. Brown.

This next shortie describes my wife's childhood in several small towns in
Alberta during the hungry thirties.

SMALL HOUSE IN A SMALL TOWN
If the mud-swallows nested in your eaves
it was said you had bed-bugs for sure.

Mice made it hard to go to sleep
With their foot-faces up and down the walls.

Lizards scatter-scuttled like crazy
when a light shone down the earthen cellar stairs.

And one Christmas Eve the roof blew off
and we almost froze to death before morning.

PEACE DEMONSTRATION 1967
The six thin girls
of the Viet Cong who steal
into the Marine camp, calmly shoot
four men to death,
then escape in the dark,
know what they are doing
and why.
                    The young paratrooper
on the night patrol
looking for V.C.[9]
also knows: kill the enemy
impersonally, with the least use

of ammunition.
              His President
in the White House has no doubts,
or if he has hides them well
in his news conferences.
                  That aging
revolutionary of Hanoi
can't afford to waver; a lifetime's
sacrifices dearly bought
flash before his eyes.

So it's left for these,
our restless, unfulfilled
youths of the protests, sit-ins,
peace marches, to carry
the burden of guilt
for all of us, spelling it out
on their crude signs, hammering it home
as the police move in to drag them
night-stick them into
waiting paddy wagons:
these, the scarred,
the most bewildered,
the truly worse than dead.

FIRST SNOWFLAKE
The first snowflake
always has
the longest, loneliest journey.

A million comrades watch
on a night of shivers,
as it casts off from Mother Cloud
and flutters, slips and slides away
all very much down.

When, after several eternities,
the watchers see their brother
touch some part of earth,
it's as if a giant string were pulled
with dark turned inside out,
and all white now, all shine,
and falling falling falling.

And now some poems from the fifties.

CHRISTMAS LIGHTS OF YONGE STREET
You've seen the coloured lights
they hang up over Yonge Street
now at every Christmas time?

Paid for by local businessmen,
they say you can tell each night
how good the day's business has been:

if they seem to shine very green
the dollars were rolling in,
if the colour's more dark red
then it was slow, very slow.

So shine your greedy shine
Christmas lights of Yonge Street
under a cash or credit sky!

Caterpillar

Caterpillar inching
up the sunward wall

I wish you tonight
that same untroubled sleep

as my beloved
wrapped in dream's cocoon,

then the sun's first
thin stroke of dawn

laid on you soft
as the kiss I give
her sleepy lips now,

caterpillar
of enduring patience
on the sunward wall.

Centre Island, Late September

For Gael

From the ferry-boat see the high green of the park,
no-one at picnic benches, lying under trees.

Here and there a leaf blown free
by voyageur winds so lustily at work.

On the lake front where sun strikes the athletic cold,
all beach houses boarded up, all cottages deserted.

Even down on the breakwall of rocks whose KEEP OFF
can't stop the lovers,
they peck rather than kiss, lie apart rather than entwined.

Summer is indeed over.
                    Your poet's eyes say it,
that and much more. While your lips make this wish:
"I should like to study surgery in London
before they knock it off the world forever."

And mine add: "Or this place, any loved by man
in this winter of our time."

The next poem deals with Auschwitz, a notorious Nazi death camp in Poland, where thousands of Jews were burned to ashes in the three large ovens that worked around the clock, after they had first been gassed to death in large rooms, which the victims entered thinking they were going to take a shower. The incident in this poem was told to me by an Austrian girl who used to accompany her father on the train, which passed by quite close to the camp.

THE TRAIN PAST AUSCHWITZ
"Auschwitz?
Yes, I remember,
we used to pass it
on the train at night,
and once I noticed
a red glow in the sky
and asked some passengers
what it was.
They looked at me strangely
even for a child,
and said: the concentration camp,
which only left me puzzled,
the word meant nothing then."

Fraulein, I long to answer her,
too bad that train didn't stop
then and there. With the wind
blowing in the right direction
even you, the twelve-year-old child,
might have smelled what the word means.

And now some poems from the forties, beginning with "Our Sergeant-Major," a memory still very vivid to me from my service in the RCAF during World War Two. This incident took place in the Maritimes.

OUR SERGEANT-MAJOR
While it could have been worse
and I'd ended up one
of the ten-man party
firing blanks from their rifles
on the station platform
as his body's entrained —

Still, it's bad enough marching
through the streets of Moncton
in the funeral procession,
then switching to slow time
the last block to the church,

where I'm sitting behind
his widow from Ottawa
and her four bright-eyed children,
forced to listen to her crying
and sniffling in her handkerchief,
while the padré drones on
with one phrase coming through,
"Died on active service...."

It's said he locked himself
in his quarters, and drank
all alone for three days.

When they dragged him out
His speech was half gone,
the next day went blind
in the hospital:

and I wonder, when we make
our search under floor boards,
aircraft packing crates, how many
more hidden gallon cans
of typewriter cleaner
we'll discover that life
just didn't allow him
enough time to guzzle.

The next poem is a description of a troop ship returning to Canada from England in July 1945.

THESE WORDS, THIS MUSIC
Although we've been singing now for more than an hour
it's only as darkness builds, as stars pierce through,
that the music of the accordions, the words of our mouths,
raised in these thousand-throated songs, take on beauty

a pathos never intended, one never dreamed
would or could happen. So we sing on and on,
not wanting to end this warmth, this comradeship,
suddenly flowing like wine, a feeling electric

flashing invisible sparks
along the crowded deck length: while this good ship

carrying us home from war, pulses, shivers,
as its funnels lay plumes on the wake of seething water.

These words we sing, this music playing,
our thanks rising up to the heavenly angels.

I'd like to close this reading with a long poem called "Death Chant for Mr. Johnson's America," written in February and April 1968. The first part is in the nature of a warning to a great nation, which is approaching another crisis in its development, and uses a number of American poets to illustrate where the present dangers lie. Part Two was written on the day Martin Luther King was murdered,[10] and although a distinct poem of its own, seemed really to be a tragic footnote to the one already written two months earlier and so was made a part of the longer poem. If I seem to be running out of breath halfway through the seven minutes it takes to read the poem, let me assure you, I really am.

DEATH CHANT FOR MR. JOHNSON'S AMERICA[11]
America
you seem to be dying
America
moving across the forty-ninth parallel each day a stronger
        more death-laden stench; wafting inshore from off the
        Great Lakes the same unmistakable stink, so unlike the
        usual putrefaction of these waters
America
the cracks are beginning to show
America
I knew you were marching to doom the night a young
        American told me: "There at Buffalo I saw our flag
        flying, then fifty yards further on your Maple Leaf, and
        I thought: thank God I'll never have to cross that line
        going back again."
America

even your best friends of yesterday are now proud to be
    your enemies
America
that time is past when the sight of the Stars and Stripes
    flying at the masthead of your ships can calm the
    "natives," that time too is over when a detachment of
    Marines on landing can still restore law and order and
    a continuance of the prescribed vested interests
America
there will be no more San Juan Hills, no more Remember
    the Maines, no more sad empires of United Fruit[12]
America
your time is running out fast
America
you haven't changed at all since you sent your New York
    State farm boys across the Niagara[13] to conquer us
    once and for all, since you printed your handbills
    promising French Canadians sweet liberation from
    their oppressors, since you looked the other way as
    Fenians played toy soldier across our borders[14]
America
you're sitting on your own rumbling volcano
America
only you could create a New York where a new breed of white
    rats chase slum children through rotting rooms, biting
    infants' flesh with the same relish that some tailor's
    dummy at the same moment downtown taking his first
    mouthful of ten-dollar steak and beaming across at his
    equally overdressed partner as she too presses her teeth
    into the meat course, only you could create squads of
    drunks lying in doorways, addicts readying fixes in
    dirty washroom heavens, only you could build these
    terrifying buildings reaching up through dirt noise
    and smog-death for a breath of clean air somewhere at
    the thousand-foot level, only you could fashion East
    River mountains of used cars, graveyards of King Auto

more mysterious than elephant burial grounds, only
you could spawn the greed and corruption of a Wall
Street with its ticker-tape fortune-cookie dreams, and
short-sell nightmares, only you could conceive this
monster and only you will be the one to destroy it pier
by pier, block by block, citizen by citizen

America

you seem bent on self-destruction

America

today you are Ginsberg's nightmare[15] brought up-to-date,
today you would sicken Hart Crane,[16] make him puke
on his Brooklyn Bridge, today you are fast becoming
Jeffers' perishing republic[17] all set to vanish in one final
blast with the rest of a despairing world

America

you seem bent on taking that world along with you just
for the ride

America

phoney as a Hollywood cowboy mainstreet, laughable as
Rockefeller with his ten-cent pieces,[18] vulgar as a Las
Vegas nightclub, brave as your airmen machine-gunning
river-front refugees in broad daylight of Dresden's
holocaust[19]

America

you have learned from everyone's history but your own

America

all the Kennedys left cannot help you now

America

I've learned how you operate, I know how votes are
managed, who has his coat pockets stuffed with bribes,
who finds himself asked to be Assistant Secretary of
this or that, who is tossed out finally with nothing left
but bitterness eating at his heart

America

you kept Pound[20] locked up all those years — he had you
pegged, Usura, he had you dead to rights, betrayers

of Jefferson, he had you figured out so good so you
left him caged and cooking in the sun at Pisa hoping
to drive him mad — but he put the record straight
about Roosevelt;[21] you hoped to bury him but instead
he walks a free man now, his vision haunting you with
its signature of doom

America

was promises nobody has kept or ever intended keeping

America

how do you turn quiet home-loving men in five short
    years into hate-fired Black-Muslim avengers[22] who
    write, and scream out to their brothers: break doors,
    smash windows at night or anytime, bust in every
    store window, drag out all you can carry, set fire, kill
    or maim Whitey, pump holes in every dirty cop or get
    him good with a brick or your own two hands

America

give it all back to the Indians[23] if they can stand the smell
    and the flies around the corpse

America

how easily your myths tarnish, how expendable are your
    heroes, how quickly, how easily you swallow good
    people into your patented garbage disposal, then grind
    them down into nice little pieces to be carted away to
    the dump with the same care accorded to the ashes of
    dead Japanese soldiers (but none the less garbage, waste
    products of your restless unsatisfied ambition hanging
    like a cancer cloud, a plague of slowly spreading death
    over the world)

America

you have been tested and found wanting

America

the world has watched you in Vietnam[24] and even its
    hardened stomach has been turned, you have all but
    buried yourself in your own Coca-Cola beer can litter,
    your bar-to-bar Saigon filth so well aped by the small

men you came to save but instead have corrupted forever; after your crazy "weed killer" squadrons[25] have bared all the trees, after your Incinderjell[26] has roasted all available corpses, then perhaps we'll see at last every barbed-wire death camp, count every tin-can house left standing, see how much rice still grows — after the last plane has been shot down out of the sky we'll be able to see who owns all the graft concessions now, who hands out the government payoffs and opens unnumbered bank accounts in Switzerland daily — but until then we watch as your Marines advance, as the underground bunkers are cooked out one by one, as the aircraft let go their terror bombs hoping these latest villages have a few more V.C. than the ones raided yesterday — the whole world watches, wonders how it will end, while you twine yourself more and more with the dragon coils of your own pre-meditated meddling

America

there is really nothing left to do but die with a certain gracefulness

really nothing left to do

America

in the name of God you never trusted, e pluribus unum

February 1968

EPILOGUE

America

tonight fiery candles of the black man's mass burn crimson in the skies of Washington, Chicago, tributes from the ghettoes to your Gandhi[27] struck down by bullets of hate, the Gun used again to work out history, the Gun in the hands of the lawless once again making jungles of your streets, mockery of your laws, the Gun that gave you birth, that burned on its red-hot gun-barrel flesh of brother turned against brother, once again

supreme — so bring out machine guns, unsling the
shot-guns, line up the sights from the armored car,
shoot to kill, shoot to kill, shoot to kill, shoot to kill,
kill, kill, kill
America
April 5, 1968

Transcribed by Amy Kalbun

ELI MANDEL
(1922–1992)

Born in Estevan, Saskatchewan, Elias ("Eli") Wolf Mandel was an editor, a poet, and a teacher. After his return from military duty in the Second World War, he enrolled in a bachelor's program in English at the University of Saskatchewan. He continued his studies at the University of Toronto and was awarded a Ph.D. in 1957. His first publication, *Trio: First Poems by Gael Turnbull, Phyllis Webb, and Eli Mandel* (1954) was followed by *Fuseli Poems* (1960), a volume of violent imagery and dark themes, such as pessimism and guilt. Later, his books *In Stony Plains* and *Out of Place* examined Jewish identity through the lens of Nazi camps and Jewish diasporic settlements.

Mandel was fascinated with the fantastic and used mythological allusions throughout his works. These allusions challenge the reader to more deeply explore and understand his themes and metaphors.

What made Mandel unique was his own meta-commentary on poetry itself and how it engages with the world. One of his most absorbing poems is "City Park Merry-Go-Round" in which he uses the poetic style of a villanelle and adapts it to an image, in this case, the merry-go-round. A standard villanelle is nineteen lines with two rhymes, arranged in five tercets and a quatrain. Its poetic structure suggests circularity, making it particularly appropriate for Mandel's merry-go-round image. Mandel's obsession with poetic structure and meta-commentary can also be seen in poems such as "Poem Like a Stone," which focuses on the ingrained conflict between poem and poet.

Mandel used poetry to develop themes of identity and place. He wrote about his children, seeing in them a source of genuine joy. He reimagined

his hometown, Estevan, as a haunted house of horrors, a place of nightmares and terror, with scarecrows and corrupted royalty. Through his poetry, he explored his identity and the sense of displacement he feels, including that caused by his participation in the Second World War. Mandel's poetry suggests a sense of excitement in poetic forms and their capacity to reimagine everyday life. This attribute and his themes make him one of Canada's foremost poets of the twentieth century.

References

Kizuk, Alexander. "Desert Sands: Eli Mandel's Poetry." *Canadian Poetry Journal* 49 (2001).

Mandel, Eli. *Black and Secret Man*. Toronto: Ryerson Press, 1964.

———. *Fuseli Poems*. Toronto: Contact Press, 1966.

———. *An Idiot Joy*. Edmonton: M.G. Hurtig, 1967.

"Mandel, Eli(as Wolf)." In *Benét's Reader's Encyclopedia of American Literature*, edited by George B. Perkins, Barbara Perkins, and Phillip Leininger, 678. New York: HarperCollins, 1991.

Steele, Charles R. "Eli(as) (Wolf) Mandel." In *Canadian Writers Since 1960: First Series*, edited by William H. New. *Dictionary of Literary Biography*. Vol. 53. Detroit: Gale, 1986.

RECORDED ON DECEMBER 17, 1969

This is Eli Mandel and I want to begin reading from a selection of poems called "Minotaur Poems," which I published in a book called *Trio*, the first selection of poems I published. For me, I suppose, poetry begins ... has always begun ... with the fabulous, the legendary, the dreamlike ... and

I've been fascinated with the way in which legend and dream and myth interact with reality ... and fascinated for many years with the image of the maze or the labyrinth or the puzzle — the labyrinth being, of course, the mythic shape of reality itself — I suppose — in which a monster lurks. I wrote these poems —the Minotaur poems — not because I was reading Greek myth but because I saw in a newspaper, a cartoon drawing of a minotaur, a fabulous man-beast.

Minotaur Poems I

It has been hours in these rooms,
the opening to which, door or sash,
I have lost. I have gone from room to room
asking the janitors who were sweeping up
the brains that lay on the floors,
the bones shining in the wastebaskets,
and once I asked a suit of clothes
that collapsed at my breath and bundled
and crawled on the floor like a coward.
Finally, after several stories,
in the staired and eyed hall,
I came upon a man with a face of a bull.

Minotaur Poems II

My father was always out in the garage
building a shining wing, a wing
that curved and flew along the edge of blue air
in that streamed and sunlit room
that smelled of oil, and engines
and crankcase grease and especially
the lemon smell of polish and cedar.
Outside there were sharp rocks and trees,
cold air where birds fell like rocks
and screams, hawks, kites, and cranes.
The air was filled with a buzzing and flying

and the invisible hum of a bee's wing was honey
in my father's framed and engined mind.
Last Saturday, we saw him at the horizon
screaming like a hawk as he fell into the sun.

Another of the Minotaur poems is called "Orpheus," and it's about the
poet-singer Orpheus who, of course, was finally torn apart by the maenads.[1]

The Welshman by the pit whose Sabbath voice
Would set the week to peace, or end a day,
Picked over coal and said he knew within
The inside of our god, his transformation
Out of tree, the face in black, faced out of coal,
Stamped out of the walls he picked. His useful metaphor,
He said, the pit shaped underneath him into black
And pitied words that moved the leaves or sang
Together flocks, or shook the dull and herded animals.
His pity also took between the rocks
Some still alive who saw the black and second
Hand that clawed them, and he mocked in Welsh
Whatever shades fell back, and cursed and sang,
Back to their second death those grave ghosts.

Who found his body and who found his head
And who wiped god from off his eyes and face?

In the same early book, I wrote about my hometown, Estevan,
Saskatchewan, and tried to see this small town as a kind of place where
horrible and terrible and frightening, pitiful things could happen. In
other words, I tried to raise that small prairie town to the level of mythology, to the dimension of myth, and to see it as one sees the Oedipus
story or the Hamlet story or the story of Cain and Abel. This is "Estevan
Saskatchewan":

A small town bears the mark of Cain,
Or the oldest brother with the dead king's wife
In a foul relation as viewed by sons,
Lies on the land, squat, producing
Love's queer offspring only,
Which issue drives the young
To feign a summer madness, consort with skulls,
While the farmer's chorus, a Greek harbinger,
Forecasts by frost or rings about the moon
How ill and black the seeds will grow.

This goodly frame, the earth, each of its sons,
With nature as a text, and common theme
The death of fathers, anguished in betrayal
From the first family returns a sacrifice
Of blood's brother, a splintered eyeball
Groined in the fields, scarecrow to crows.
This warns Ophelia to her morning song,
Bawdy as a lyric, in a pretty brain gone bad,
While on those fields, the stupid harvest lies.

I suppose for some time I was obsessed with an image of the end of things, and in my second book, *Fuseli Poems*, I began to play around with the image of the end of things. It's sometimes called an apocalyptical image, an image of some revelation that's about to come. And I wrote a song on this theme:

When the echo of the last footstep dies
and on the empty street you turn empty eyes,
    what do you think that you will see?
    A hangman and a hanging tree.

When there are no more voices
and yet you hear voices singing
    in the hot street,

what you think will be their song?
Glory to the hangman who is never wrong?

When on the hot sands of your burning mind
    the iron footsteps clang no more
    and blind eyes no longer see
        and hot voices end,
    what do you think will be your plea?
    Hanging isn't good enough for me.

Well, not all my poetry is mythic or an attempt to blend myth and real-ity. Poets like to fool around with forms, and to work with forms, and figure out what form itself can do. In one of my poems — it's called "City Park Merry-Go-Round" — I try to do something with the form of the villanelle. The main point about the villanelle is that you have a set of lines, and you have to use these lines in a way which suggests that the poem is going round and round in a circle. It struck me, I remember one time, that the ideal con-tent for this form would be something that went around like a circle, like a merry-go-round. And I remember in Saskatoon, seeing a merry-go-round in the city park, and suddenly I knew I could write a villanelle on the image of the merry-go-round in the city park.

    Freedom is seldom what you now believe.
    Mostly you circle round and round the park:
    Night follows day, these horses never leave.

    Like children, love whatever you conceive,
    See then your world as lights whirled in the dark.
    Freedom is seldom what you now believe.

    Your world moves up and down or seems to weave
    And still you pass and pass that same old mark.
    Night follows day, these horses never leave.

You thought your past was here, you might retrieve
That wild illusion whirling in the dark.
Freedom is seldom what you now believe.

Sick on that circle you begin to grieve.
You wish the ride would end and you could park.
Night follows day, these horses never leave.

Mostly you circle round and round the park.
You'd give your life now to be free to leave.
Freedom is seldom what you now believe.
Night follows day, these horses never leave.

One of the themes that's interested me, though I haven't really pursued it as far as some people have said, is the theme of my Jewishness. I have written out of my Jewish background, and I want to read a couple of poems that use images from that background and from the Jewish tradition itself. These two poems are from a volume of mine called *Black and Secret Man*. The first one is called "Day of Atonement: Standing," and I think the poem is an interesting one because it plays with two aspects of the Jewish tradition. The day of atonement is the most solemn day of the Jewish year: it's the beginning of the new year, the year when your sins supposedly are remitted by God or when you finally pay for them and you're going to be punished for them in the coming year. At least, this is the story that's told. And so you stand before God. Now, when Jews pray, at the most solemn moments, instead of kneeling, they stand up. And of course, instead of uncovering their heads before God, they cover their heads, they must wear a cap ... a yarmulke I think it's called. And it struck me there was a marvellous kind of paradox here ... that to uncover yourself and confess your sins to God, you would cover your head ... and to bow down before his will, you would stand up. And so in this poem, I play with those paradoxes of standing to bow and covering to uncover. I suppose I had in mind, as well, a kind of play with religious paradoxes that you find in poets like John Donne and George Herbert[2] ... so the poem sounds a little bit like a seventeenth-century rather than a twentieth-century poem ... kind of a Jewish seventeenth-century, twentieth-century poem.

DAY OF ATONEMENT: STANDING
My Lord, how stands it with me now
Who, standing here before you
(who, fierce as you are, are also just),
Cannot bow down.   You order this.
Why, therefore, I must break
If I bend I will not, yet bend I must.

But I address myself to you thus,
Covered and alert, and will not bare
My self.   Then I must bear you,
Heavy as you are.
                              This is the time
The bare tree bends in the fierce wind
And stripped, my God, springs to the sky.

Another poem of this sort is a little song or lyric to my children. It's based on a curious Jewish tradition that you name a child after the nearest dead relative. As it so happened, my mother died and my daughter was born; my father died and my son was born. And so my children bear my parents' names. It seemed to me when one thinks about the magic that's in names and how one's own name is a magical thing that there was some kind of poem in this. So, I tried to write about the curious facts of the children being named after their parents, who are dead now, and the magic that's in the names. A little lyric, "To My Children":

A rose grew in my head
My father lay dead
My mother fell among stones
Two flowers grew in my loins

I sing to my blossoming wife
My father is dead
My mother abandoned her life
Why should I lay down my head

Stony and brittle my days
My children sing psalms
The rabbis are ancient and wise
Blessed be my flowering names

It isn't only one's Jewishness that possesses one; I've been equally pos-
sessed by marvellous images, like those that one sees in a circus ... and
occasionally these have blossomed into poems. I like the image of the tightrope walker, the girl on the high wire, or the image of the escape artist.
These seem to me to be really magical ones. One day I'd like to write about
a clown, I think. Clown images are great, as Picasso was aware, of course,
because he so often wanted to paint them. In my book *An Idiot Joy*, which
is the last book I published, I have a couple of poems on circus images. One
is called "Girl on a High Wire." It's about a tightrope walker and about, I
suppose, myself looking up at her as she's up on the high wire, and I think
about what it must be like for her to be there and what my relationship is to
that risk that she's taking.

GIRL ON A HIGH WIRE
Do you think I'd sit here staring
if I knew how to invent chair-lifts
or lacked this odd taste for vertigo?

What if I dare you to jump, saying, ah
my hurt bird, I will catch you —
And if I weren't there (someone calling,
my son pointing at camels or wanting
to pee) when your eyes became horizons?
Or if you fell
into the well of bankers, mid-wives,
my brother-in-law, the Prudential Life
Insurance Company?
                    I see them,
heroine, hefting you, their applause

ringing your head with the clatter of zircons,
mouths blowing little balloons of praise.

The great globe circles.
Soldiers fall into muddy rivers.
Boys walk the tightrope of their prison yard.

I can no longer look at telephone wires,
the vanishing point of your unfinished portrait.

I shall devote myself to entomology,
practice weight-lifting with dinky toys,
but who will keep me from my crooked prayers,
those mad doves that fling haloes around you?

Another of the circus poems is called "Houdini" after the great escape
artist himself.[3] And in this poem I'm really trying to work out what seems to
me to be a marvellous metaphor that's in the life of Houdini himself. As he's
trying to escape from all these chains that he's constantly binding himself in,
and all the trunks that he locks himself in, and all those pools that he throws
himself into inside trunks, he's really an image of the poet himself ... who's
a kind of magician or escape artist struggling with language and trying to
escape from the word even as he speaks the word, even as he binds himself
with the word. He's a magical figure for me and I wrote this poem, thinking
of him as a kind of poet:

HOUDINI
I suspect he knows that trunks are metaphors,
could distinguish between the finest rhythms
unrolled on rope or singing in a chain
and knew the metrics of the deepest pools

I think of him listening to the words
spoken by manacles, cells, handcuffs,

chests, hampers, roll-top desks, vaults,
especially the deep words spoken by coffins

escape, escape: quaint Harry in his suit
his chains, his desk, attached to all attachments
how he'd sweat in that precise struggle
with those binding words, wrapped around him
like that mannered style, his formal suit

and spoken when? by whom? What thing first said
"there's no way out?"; so that he'd free himself,
leap, squirm, no matter how, to chain himself again,
once more jump out of the deep alive
with all his chains singing around his feet
like the bound crowds who sigh, who sigh.

One isn't always quite so engrossed in the attempt to work out all the complications of poetic metaphor and language. Sometimes one tries to get it all concentrated in one or two little lines. In some ways I think I'm fondest of one poem that's only two lines long because it seems to me to say in two lines a very great deal. I don't know if it really does; it seems to me to say that in two short lines. Maybe I like it because it's one of my shortest poems. It's simply called "Poem."

You would have me deny my murderous thoughts
It is metaphor I distrust.

And another one that's called "Poem" works somewhat the same way, only it isn't as epigrammatic in a sense. Here, I'm trying in some way to get the feeling that one gets in Chinese paintings, and I refer to Chinese paintings that were on the wall of my office at the university. The poem sees the painting as somehow making a certain kind of comment on myself and on the world that I live in, in the Western world. This is called "Poem," too:

Lately, the polite Chinese paintings on my wall
utter profanities
        and yet no Western man
has set his foot upon those hills
or muddied with his hands that silent waterfall.

I suppose part of the feeling that one is after in a poem like that is the feeling you get in Keats' poem about the Grecian urn,[4] that paintings always remain the same and yet, in some way, they comment on the living world. It's the kind of thing you get in a good deal of Yeats,[5] too. A different tone and a different feeling in a poem which I call "Song." It's a lyric poem and here, part of the concern is to get as great a distance as possible between the subject and the tone so that while the poem sings, the subject is something that one feels perhaps one ought not to sing about. It is about injured, hurt children ... about the death of children ... and yet the poem sings. I suppose you'd call this an ironic lyric.

SONG

I will bless the girl with her tattered hands
whose fingers acclaim a rosy crime
that sings in her blood
in her vessels' lair
hums and hums again.
           This time
I will sing happily for the fresh blood
that runs from the nose of Jane
where she lies on the road.
Nobody cares to say where it ends.

For the rotten charms of Timothy,
I'll write a joyful song.
Come, let us admire his shining pain
and the shining blood of Jane.

In my gleeful song
will I sew and mend
Timothy, Jane, and the rosy hands
that hang from the arms of the tattered one?

When everything is done,
old men can rejoice, being old.
Let me be gay for the girls and boys
broken before me.

Who else will remember their joys?

A less sardonic lyric, a love lyric in fact, is one called "The Speaking Earth."

grandfathers fall into it
their mighty beards muffled in grass

and admirals, the sea-sounding men

lovers fall into the earth
like rain on wet dark bodies

listen, our lady earth flowers
into the sea-green language
of grass and drowned admirals

listen: in bearded branches
clasped like broken hands
admiring birds
lovers singing of their kiss
before and after all the words

I have several love lyrics in *An Idiot Joy*, and I want to read three of them. The three lyrics use traditional imagery that one associates with love lyrics: images of the sea and the moon, and the tidal attraction between the sea and the moon, and images of the daughter of the sea, Marina. Though the images are traditional, I think I like these poems because they're experimental and, in some ways, they're so very much different from the sort of thing I was doing earlier, when I was writing poems like the Minotaur poems. The mythic, or legendary, or magical is in some ways still present because the moon, after all, has its magical powers, as one of these poems suggests. Even with the astronauts on the moon, the magic is still there. I do mention the drive toward the moon in the poem, but the poems, though using the old images, do try different things, I think clearer things. I like them because they're clearer than the earlier poems, less complicated in their use of the myth and magical image and so on. So we'll start with "The Explanations of the Moon":

The explanations of the moon
are uncompromisingly lucid

so some say she is cold

but having known her fire
how she lives in deep water
lingers in hollows
                    and
like my friend who mad
with drugs or drink loves
luminous seas but not his
family
            induces what we
say are dreams
                    I'm
no longer sure
                    when
she assumes horizons
or

    beyond us

          crazes

whole nations

           so that

they drive engines

toward her

         no I can't

say for certain

           why

we, love, sometimes

smile and know each other

and why we change

and why

         our eyes clear

we are struck dumb

remote, I think,

isn't the word

You might notice that in that poem the rhythms are rather different from the rhythms that I use in earlier poems. The reason is that I'm experimenting now with a new kind of line, very much more related to the spoken voice than the tighter line with its heavy stresses and heavy beats that I used in the earlier poems. In a poem like the one I want to read now, "Listen, the sea," I carry the experiment as far as I've been able to because the poem depends almost entirely on its imitative harmony, on the sense that the waves of the sea are coming toward one and receding from one … and on the way in which the language imitates that. The title itself, "Listen, the sea," comes from a line, I believe, in *King Lear*, and it was a line that attracted the poet Keats, who wrote a sonnet about it[6] but this, of course, isn't a sonnet. It's a very different form and an experimental one.

LISTEN, THE SEA
yes what is
I'm learning

by your leave
leaving
      rising
to leave
      return
and turn
    we
deliberate
by the waves
rhythm casual
move
    tidal
as
    traffic
as
    the sea-women

neither are they
certain uncertain
but with us
      withal
within
      their song
here
    oh hear
it is

The poem mentions the sea women, and there's a legend about a daughter of the sea named Marina. Shakespeare wrote about her, and T.S. Eliot wrote about her, and P.K. Page — a Canadian poet — wrote about her[7] ... and I thought because I was writing about the sea and the moon, I would write about her, too. So I have a poem called "Marina" about the daughter of a sea, a strange, marvellous creature, a woman mysterious and attractive.

Marina

Because she spoke often of the sea we thought she had known
    another country, her people distant, not forgotten

We did not know then who was calling her or what songs she
    listened to or why the sea-birds came to rest
    upon her long fingers

Or why she would shudder like a seabird about to take flight,
    her eyes changing with the changing light

As the sea-changing opal changes, as a shell takes its
    colours from the sea as if it were the sea

As if the great sea itself were held in the palm of your hand

They say the daughters of the sea know the language of the birds,
    that in their restless eyes the most fortunate learn
    how the moon rises and sets

We do not know who is calling her or why her eyes change
    or what shore she will set her foot upon

Transcribed by Vipasha Shaikh

JAMES REANEY
(1926–2008)

J ames Reaney was born on a farm in South Easthope, outside of Stratford, Ontario, the locale that would be the focus of nearly all of his poems and plays. An avowed regionalist, Reaney believed that burrowing into the fields of rural southern Ontario and exhausting all of the land's metaphoric possibilities would allow him to express the universal within the contained.

Reaney published his first book *The Red Heart*, at the age of twenty-three, in 1949, the same year he earned his M.A. in English from University College, University of Toronto. The book is an imaginative recollection of Reaney's rural childhood, with poems concerning the trees and animals in his backyard and the comic strips he read as a child. It marks the first assertion of a claim that characterized his career: that the childhood perspective is as legitimate a narrative voice as any other. This assertion led to seeming contradictions when, in subsequent collections, Reaney engaged more sophisticated literary concepts. This bizarre mixture, along with the fact that Reaney lived outside the cultural capitals of Toronto and Montreal, explains his status as an outsider in the world of Canadian literature.

After a brief commitment teaching English at the University of Manitoba, Reaney returned to Toronto to boost his academic credentials, earning a doctorate at Victoria College under the supervision of Northrop Frye. Reaney's years studying under Frye were tremendously important to his work. He took Frye's course called Literary Symbolism (later published as *Anatomy of Criticism*), in which Frye presented ideas that would govern Reaney's poetic efforts henceforward, particularly with respect to symbolic structures and archetypal mythology. Frye's ideas encouraged Reaney to

write his next work, *A Suit of Nettles*, published in 1958. The poem is an adaptation of Edmund Spenser's pastoral poem *The Shepheardes Calender*, with shepherds replaced by talking geese; and the political concerns of Elizabethan England are turned into those of contemporary Ontario, including the debate between progressive and traditional models of education.

In keeping with his maverick spirit, Reaney asked that his inclusion in the *Canadian Poets on Tape* series be recorded at a piano. In lieu of offering explanations of the experiences and influences behind his work, Reaney performed songs and scales on the piano between reading excerpts: this encourages the listener to attend to the affinities of his poems to different types of music, particularly rags and hymns. Christian tradition is an essential part of the southern Ontario spiritual landscape that Reaney expressed in his poems. Like a ragtime composer, Reaney adapted traditional religious ideas to a modern, syncopated form.

James Reaney won the Governor General's Award for four of his works: *The Red Heart* (1948), *A Suit of Nettles* (1959), *Twelve Letters to a Small Town*, *The Killdeer and Other Plays* (1962), and *The Dance of Death at London, Ontario* (1963). He was awarded honorary doctorates from four different Canadian universities and was appointed to the Order of Canada in 1975. He died on June 11, 2008, in London, Ontario.

RECORDED ON DECEMBER 14, 1970

[Reaney performs "Beulah Land," a fragment of an old hymn, on the piano.]

That's the first poem I ever heard, at an early denominational Sunday school. I'm sitting at a piano on Bloor Street near a subway that you'll hear thundering by occasionally, and I've got ... sort of ... my collected works around me. I'm going to read from the *Red Heart* first of all, and I'm going to occasionally call forth from the piano pieces of music that really make a comment on the poems in a sort of way. This is "Antichrist as a Child."

When Antichrist was a child
He caught himself tracing
A capital letter A
On a window sill
And wondering why
Because his name contained no A.
And as he crookedly stood
In his mother's flower-garden
He wondered why she looked so sadly
Out of an upstairs window at him.
He wondered why his father stared so
Whenever he saw his little son
Walking in his soot-coloured suit.
He wondered why the flowers
And even the ugliest weeds
Avoided his fingers and his touch.
And when his shoes began to hurt
Because his feet were becoming hooves
He did not let on to anyone
For fear they would shoot him for a monster.
He wondered why he more and more
Dreamed of eclipses of the sun,
Of sunsets, ruined towns and zeppelins,
And especially inverted, upside down churches.

[Reaney plays a musical bridge, an ad-libbed flourish, with punctuation.]

THE SCHOOL GLOBE

Sometimes when I hold
Our faded old globe
That we used at school
To see where oceans were
And the five continents,
The lines of latitude and longitude,
The North Pole, the Equator and the South Pole —
Sometimes when I hold this
Wrecked blue cardboard pumpkin
I think: here in my hands
Rest the fair fields and lands
Of my childhood
Where still lie or still wander
Old games, tops and pets;
A house where I was little
And afraid to swear
Because God might hear and
Send a bear
To eat me up;
Rooms where I was as old
As I was high;
Where I loved the pink clenches,
The white, red and pink fists
Of roses; where I watched the rain
That Heaven's clouds threw down
In puddles and rutfuls
And irregular mirrors
Of soft brown glass upon the ground.
This school globe is a parcel of my past,
A basket of pluperfect things.
And here I stand with it
Sometime in the summertime
All alone in an empty schoolroom
Where about me hang
Old maps, an abacus, pictures,

Blackboards, empty desks.
If I raise my hand
No tall teacher will demand
What I want.
But if someone in authority
Were here, I'd say
Give me this old world back
Whose husk I clasp
And I'll give you in exchange
The great sad real one
That's filled
Not with a child's remembered and pleasant skies
But with blood, pus, horror, death, stepmothers, and lies.

[Plays segment of "Maple Leaf Rag" by Scott Joplin.]

THE KATZENJAMMER KIDS[1]
With porcupine locks
And faces which, when
More closely examined,
Are composed of measle-pink specks,
These two dwarf imps,
The Katzenjammer Kids,
Flitter through their Desert Island world.
Sometimes they get so out of hand
That a blue Captain
With stiff whiskers of black wicker
And an orange Inspector
With a black telescope
Pursue them to spank them
All through that land
Where cannibals cut out of brown paper
In cardboard jungles feast and caper,
Where the sea's sharp waves continually

Waver against the shore faithfully
And the yellow sun above is thin and flat
With a collar of black spikes and spines
To tell the innocent childish heart that
It shines
And warms (see where she stands and stammers)
The dear fat mother of the Katzenjammers.
Oh, for years and years she has stood
At the window and kept fairly good
Guard over the fat pies that she bakes
For her two children, those dancing heartaches.
Oh, the blue skies of that funny paper weather!
The distant birds like two eyebrows close together!
And the rustling paper roar
Of the waves
Against the paper sands of the paper shore!

[Plays segment of "God Save the Queen."]

The Royal Visit[2]

When the King and the Queen came to Stratford
Everyone felt at once
How heavy the Crown must be.
The Mayor shook hands with their Majesties
And everyone presentable was presented
And those who weren't have resented
It, and will
To their dying day.
Everyone had almost a religious experience
When the King and Queen came to visit us
(I wonder what they felt!)
And hydrants flowed water in the gutters
All day.
People put quarters on the railroad tracks

So as to get squashed by the Royal Train
And some people up the line at Shakespeare
Stayed in Shakespeare, just in case —
They did stop too.
While thousands in Stratford
Didn't even see them
Because the Engineer didn't slow down
Enough in time.
And although,
But although we didn't see them in any way
(I didn't even catch the glimpse
The teacher who was taller did
Of a gracious pink figure)
I'll remember it to my dying day.

Those are poems from *The Red Heart*, and I feel they're poems written more or less within reach of a piano in a farmhouse in South Easthope just outside of Stratford. The experience that starts off with the hymn is, believe it or not, behind them all, while underneath the experience of some of them is something like the page from the "Maple Leaf Rag" that I've played, which would be in a piano bench around home. I've tried to sum up the feeling of Sunday school and the kind of life *The Red Heart* seems to be about in something called "Childhood Sunday," which isn't a poem at all ... it isn't really a musical composition ... but I'll just play you a few bars of it, and it turns full circle in a way.

[Plays "Childhood Sunday."]

And after you walk through the fields at the beginning of the piece, you arrive at a Sunday school where they're playing "Beulah Land."

[Plays a few bars of "Beulah Land," with musical flourish ad-libbed.]

[Plays arpeggios and scales, as in piano practice.]

As you can gather, I grew up to take piano lessons. Perhaps from the experience of going to high school and taking piano lessons and taking lessons in counterpoint and harmony, the following poems I'm going to read from my next collection, the *Suit of Nettles*, sort of grow. This little dialogue I can't do justice to because in *Suit of Nettles*, a series of dialogues between geese … you just have to accept that … and these two geese are talking about educational theories in, I think it's the month of July. There's a series of dialogues for each month of the year, where there's a bunch of geese that exist or live supposedly near the pond in the farm where I grew up, and I used to have to watch them when I was a kid. It's more or less a battle between a progressive education goose and a traditional education goose.

The traditional education goose says:
> When I was a gosling he taught us to know the most wonderful list of things. You could play games with it; whenever you were bored or miserable, what he had taught you was like a marvellous deck of cards in your head that you could shuffle through and turn over into various combinations with endless delight. At the end of the year, we each made ourselves little huts of burdock leaves, lay down on our backs with large stones on our bellies and recited the whole thing over to ourselves forwards and backwards. Some of the poorer students were in those huts till November but even those to whom it was an agony, when they at length did know that they knew all that a young goose was supposed to know, the moment when they rolled the stone away and climbed out of their burdock hut — it was a joyous moment as if they had been reborn into another world.

And the progressive education goose asks rather scornfully:
> Well, well, well, may I ask just what this reviving curriculum was?

And the traditional education goose replies:
> Yes, it was,
> Who are the children of the glacier and the earth?
> Esker and hogsback, drumlin and kame.
> What are the four elements and the seven colours,
> The ten forms of fire, and the twelve tribes of Israel?

The eight winds, and the hundred kinds of clouds,
All of Jesse's stem and the various ranks of angels?
The Nine Worthies and the Labours of Hercules,
The sisters of Emily Brontë, the names of Milton's wives?
The Kings of England and Scotland with their Queens,
The names of all those hanged on the trees of law
Since this province first cut up trees into gallows.
What are the stones that support New Jerusalem's wall?
Jasper and sapphire, chalcedony, emerald,
Sard, sardius, chrysolite, beryl, topaz,
Chrysoprasus, hyacinthine and amethyst.

The other goose says:
My goodness, how useless so far as the actual living
of life is concerned. Why we have simplicity itself
compared to what that maze of obscurity was. I mean,
since our heads are going to be chopped off anyhow,
we only teach the young gosling what he likes.

To which the other goose replies:
We liked what our schoolmaster taught though it took
some effort.

The progressive education goose replies:
Pah! If they like nothing, then teach them that. The
self must be free.

I feel like the walls of OISE[3] are going to fall down on me for reading
that but, I have read it.
[Plays a single chord, for effect.]
Next, I'm going to read you two descriptions of animals from *Suit of
Nettles*. I'm also looking at an old harmony text of mine and an old coun-
terpoint text. First of all, I'm going to just read out a tiny phrase from the
harmony book before I read you "The Pig," the description of a pig from
Suit of Nettles: "The student should easily recognize the position of the third

of the chord. If it is low down, the effect is somewhat thick and grumpy."
[Plays several chords for effect and punctuation.]

THE PIG

Pink protrusion, pachyderm pork crystal,
Crackling with conch sounds casual acorn;
Mice muzzle and masticate to your back
Unbeknownst by unquick ununquiet mind;
Hear nothing ears except earhasp twitch,
Smell nothing snout except swine incense,
Touch nothing trotters save tapioca style wallow:
Eyes examine the excellent nose horizon,
Heedless of huntsmen horning your oak hall,
Dreaming of the devoured peacock safe down in your belly.

Before I read another poem about an animal called "The Cow," here are very simple illustrations of, from my counterpoint text, the five species or orders of different, five different ways, methods, or styles of writing a counterpoint, above or below, a *cantus firmus*.[4]
[Plays counterpoint.]
Second species:
[Plays.]
Third species:
[Plays.]
Fourth species, syncopation:
[Plays.]
Fifth species, florid:
[Plays.]

THE COW

Fanciful flighty fairy cow,
Black & white bulging beautiful thing.
Burdock bites she busily out of barn door,

Slavers till sicked over salt block at gate.
New grass assaulted at stone boat by her,
Cagily corn she corrals over barbed wire,
Tree leaves tassel out twitching mouth,
New clover now navigates she through gate,
Gorges down googols of juicy green fodder,
Bloats her four bellies up balloonwise-zeppelin,
Mooing for mercy meanders to keeper-help
Who sticks her with sharp pen, soon rush out
All vapours as velvety voluptuous tongue darts
Out again.

[Plays unknown fragment of music.]

Here's a poem from *Twelve Letters to a Small Town* called "The Cloak Room at the High School."

The high school is the palace of Merlin and Cheiron
    Where governors and governesses teach
The young Achilles and young Arthurs of the town.

The radiators teach the rule of monotony
    Cheep cheep cheeping in the winter classroom
Timid fingers learn to turn a fire on.

A stuffed hummingbird and a stuffed sandhill crane.
    In the dusty looking glass of grammar,
Number, the young see the shape of their brain.

But what and where did I learn most from?
High, dark, narrow as its single window
In the old high school there was a cloakroom —

A cloakroom! In winter stuffed with cloaks
 Soft with outside things inside
Burs, mud, dead leaves on some of the coats.

At four o'clock there are forty-nine bare hooks
    As a hundred hands reach up
And I, lingering rearranging my books
    See sweeping face peer in of janitor
        Alone in the winter twilight
The old janitor! An image to ponder over.

Of course I learnt snow dripping windows
    Corridors of words, cobwebs of character,
The ninety-two elements in a long row,
        But most I learnt

The insoluble mystery of the cloakroom
    And the curious question of the janitor
        In some way so centre and core
           January man and cloakroom
From which the moon each month unlocks upon the wave
    A white bird.

[Plays tune fragment or ad-libbed bridge.]

I'd like to read two poems that are really songs from my opera that I wrote with John Beckwith,[5] called *Night Blooming Cereus*. These are sung by Mrs. Brown who is quite an old lady, all alone in a cottage, her daughter ran away from her years ago. And this very night her night-blooming cereus is coming out … it only comes out every hundred years … this coincides with the return of her granddaughter … not to give the plot away, because it doesn't depend on that sort of thing. But just the feeling of, say, the interior of a house, a cottage, in, say, a village like Shakespeare, Ontario. The first little song is called "A Blessing," and the second song is called "Washing Dishes."

My Lord I thank you for bread and meat
You give more bread than I can cut,
More for to drink that I can cup
More to myself than I can eat.

These pitchers and these platters hold
The milk and honey of thy love
And I am grateful for thy grace
As starving prophet was of old.

But in between my praying hands
And in between my fast shut eyes
The table of thy manna stands
From whose delight may I not rise. Amen.

*[She gets up and begins to clear up the dishes, shaking out the
tablecloth, going to the stove for hot water and dishpan.]*

WASHING DISHES

Now I will gather up and wash the dishes,
Plate cup knife fork spoon and jug.
Now will my plate and cup be just like fishes.
There used to be so many more to gather up.

Even I an old woman have servants and children,
Plate cup fork knife jug and spoon.
Unlike children away they cannot run,
Safe on the shelves of the cupboard in this room.

I suppose we are his china and cutlery,
Plate cup jug spoon fork and knife.
He washes us when we Him see.
Easier to wash these than wash a life.

But when I the old woman am taken from the table,
Cup fork knife spoon jug and plate
If they are not broken, before I break, will
Faithful remain behind to demonstrate

To others who may own them after,
Plate cup knife spoon jug and fork,
Daily to baptize themselves in the water
Of thinking how they can for Heaven work.

[Plays a fragment of ragtime]
I'd like to read two speeches from a play of mine called *The Killdeer*. The
first is by a lady who goes around selling cosmetics. Her name's Madam Fay;
she comes in the door and says:

That's my little car. I painted it myself.
I drive it all over the country selling beauty.
You see what I got printed on that car?
'Here comes Madam Fay,' and on the other side
Y'know what I got? 'To make you beautiful.'
If you need more beauty, you need me.
Now let me see — h'm, sort of mushroom coloured.
Say — the things I can fix you up with.
I got things in this case'd transform you.
You say your religion forbids face-painting,
But look at Nature, ma'am. Doesn't the maple leaf
Turn red in the fall? God don't like that?
All those pretty fall colours? The things I got here
For a beautiful you! Curl your hair!
Shadow your eyes! Powder your face!
Youngs you! Slims your eyebrows!
I got hair-remover here would take
The beard off Santa Claus in a second
And make him a fat beardless youth of sixteen.
Make your bosom larger? Well, you're well
Provided there I see. Hands! Toes!
I forgot the mouth! Jezebel! Rage!
Terrific lipsticks. Midnight Black!
What are you looking at me like that for?

The next speech is by a boy who comes home from working in the bank to his mother's cottage after the cosmetics lady has left, and he looks around at the room and he says to his mother:

> Oh gosh! This room! This front parlour of yours!
> I think I'll go mad if I don't get one day
> Of my life when I don't come home to this.
> Why don't I run away? Because I'm afraid,
> Afraid of the look on a face I'd never see.
> Dear old Mother's face! This room! This room!
> These brown velvet curtains trimmed with
> One thousand balls of fur! Fifteen kewpie dolls!
> Five little glossy china dogs on a Welsh dresser!
> Six glossy Irish beleek cats and seven glass
> Green pigs and eight blue glass top hats and
> Five crystal balls filled with snow falling down
> On R.C.M.P. constables. Two little boys on chamber
> Pots: Billy Can and Tommy Can't. That stove —
> Cast iron writhing and tortured curlicues!

His mother replies:
> I think the whole room's real pretty!
> I started it from nothing twenty-five years ago
> And look at it now!

The son replies:
> Look at it now!
> This is your room, Mother. Your mind is like this.
> It's where I've spent most of my life And it's not
> Real pretty.

[Plays recorder, rattle, and tambourine; effects.]

In 1963 I worked on a book called *The Dance of Death at London, Ontario* with the artist Jack Chambers.[6] I'd like to read two dialogues from it, one between a rich young lady and Death, illustrated by Jack Chambers.

The rich young lady's leaning on her Cadillac; Death is dressed up in evening clothes, with a skeleton face peeping out above the tuxedo. Then another little poem called "The Grocery Boy."

THE RICH YOUNG LADY
My father breaks hundreds of bonds,
    My mother subscribes to *The Queen*,
I spent last winter in Antigua,
    Our swimming pool's drinkably clean.
Death says:
Then come ride with me & my hounds
    Or if you wish to this car keep,
And we'll drive with the speed of the wind
    To my park where the shadows are deep.

[Continues to play recorder, rattle, and tambourine; effects.]

THE GROCERY BOY
At the corner of Richmond & Talbot Street,
    Oranges, cornflakes cellophane & ham,
I fill up the bags & the boxes.
    Is that black car the one you mean, ma'am?
Death says:
Long enough have you drudged for the stomach!
    Drop that box at your feet in this parking lot!
It's just dust that I need for my supper,
    Put yourself in this box that *I*'ve got.

[Plays ad-libbed bridges.]

I'd like to read two pieces from *One Man Masque*. One of them is a vaudeville sketch called "A St. Hilda's Girl," and the other is a poem called "Rachel."

A St. Hilda's Girl[7]

*The speaker picks up a Kresge[8] artificial flower from the
table and holds it in front of him.*

After attending Harbord Collegiate — Lower School, Middle
School and Upper School, I went to St. Hilda's College where my
sister had been head girl some years before.

At St. Hilda's the social year began with three receptions
given for the men at Trinity College. Out of this might grow
an invitation to the Athletic Dance at Trinity in November. In
December you might invite a man to the St. Hilda's Formal.
And then *perhaps* he invited you to the Conversat at Trinity in
January. There were two more dances at St. Hilda's and then the
Valentine Dance at Trinity and then there was Lent and then
you got engaged to whatever came to the surface out of all this.
Well, I invited a young man to the St. Hilda's formal but he
didn't invite me to the Conversat. I had a friend who said, two
days before the Conversat: 'I haven't got an invitation to the
Conversat yet and it's two days to go, but I'm going to get one.'
And she did. I often wonder how she did it.

Rachel[9]

When I was a young young man
    In passing the city dump
Out of smoking rubbish I heard
    A small and rusty wail.

    Naked without any clothes
    Unwashed from the caul
    Thy navel string uncut
A crusted, besmattered and loathsome thing.

I ruined my clothes and stank for a week
    But I brought you to my house.
I found that your mother was a gypsy,
    Your father an Indian.

"Live!" I said, and you lived.
    You grew like a flax field,
Your hair gold as the sun,
    Your breasts were blossoms.

I passed your foster house,
    It was the time of love.
I rewarded your music teacher for
    Pearly runs in your Scarlatti.

It was the time of love
I was so afraid you might say no
My heart beat like giant steps
I felt agony in your garden.

    Then you came to my house,
I was ashamed to ask you so often,
    I gave you a golden ring
        I gave you a glass pen.

    You dressed in silk
    You bathed in milk
    But on your shoulder as we
Embraced I saw the red speck.

    It had never washed off.
    But I went unto you
        With all the more love
You prospered into a kingdom.

I must go away to abroad.
    When I returned uptown
I met you and you knew me not,
    Your hair like flax tow

Crimped like an eggbeater, your
Mouth like a cannibal's — bloody,
Your eyelids massive with blue mud,
        And a handmuff made of bats fur.

I found out about your carryings on,
        Your lovers and infidelities.
My child you had sold to a brothel,
        You had to pay for your men.

In pity, I bribed men to go to you,
        But to your two biggest lovers,
        Lord Dragon and Count Dino,
I whispered your triple crossings.

They gathered their devils and mobs.
In the name of virtue they attacked
        Your tall town house
You bore then your seven month bastard.

They brought you out on your balcony,
        Your house devoured with flame.
Out they threw you and the dogs
        Licked your blood up.

        Then from your hand I took
My ring, from the hag's claw
        I took my golden ring.
        Her breasts like pigsties.

        I found her child and I
        Washed you in my tears.
Still there is the spot
        Red on your shoulder — a speck.

I wash you with my tears
    And still the speck remains.
My darling, it is my fault
    I have not tears enough.

[Plays more.]

I'd like to read in conclusion, two pieces from a play of mine called *Colours in the Dark.* One of them has a title, the other really hasn't. The first one I'm going to read is called "Gifts." the whole play was kind of built up on it. It goes like this:

Pebble   dewdrop   piece of string   straw[10]

The pebble is a huge dark hill I must climb
The dewdrop is a great storm lake that we must cross
The string is a road that I cannot find
The straw is a sign whose meaning I forget
Hill   lake   road   sign

What was it that quite changed the scene
So desert faded into meadow green?
The answer is that he met a Tiger
The answer is that he met a Balloon,
A Prostitute of Snow, a Gorgeous Salesman
As well as a company of others such as
Sly Tod, Reverend Jones, Kitty Cradle and so on

Who was the Tiger?   Christ
Who was the Balloon?   Buddha
Emily Brontë and the Emperor Solomon
Who sang of his foot in the doorway.
All these met him. They were hopeful and faithful.

Pebble   dewdrop   piece of string   straw[11]

Now the mountain becomes a pebble in my hand
The lake calms down   to a dewdrop in a flower
The weary road   is a string round your wrist
The mysterious sign   is a straw that whistles home
Pebble   dewdrop   piece of string   straw

And the other little piece is at the very end, and it goes like this.

1024 great great great great great great great great grandparents
512 great great great great great great great grandparents
256 great great great great great great grandparents
128 great great great great great grandparents
64 great great great great grandparents
32 great great great grandparents
16 great great grandparents
8 great grandparents
4 grandparents
2 parents
One child.

By the way, Mr. Toppings has just reminded me that I forgot to identify myself at the beginning of this tape. My name is James Reaney.

Transcribed by Geoff Baillie

AFTERWORD: INTERVIEW WITH DR. EARLE TOPPINGS

How does Earle Toppings remember his encounters with the writers and poets on the tapes after almost five decades? The following interview took place in January 2016 at the Goldring Student Centre of Victoria College in the University of Toronto. In attendance were Earle Toppings, librarians Agatha Barc and Colin Deinhardt, and the four Northrop Frye Research Centre Undergraduate Fellows who transcribed the tapes for this volume: Geoff Baillie, Amy Kalbun, Griffin Kelly, and Vipasha Shaikh. In this conversation, they turned the tables on the original interviewer. It brings to the fore the thoughts, memories, and comments of the man who sat in the recording studio so many years ago, helping ensure the voices of these Canadian writers and poets would become a significant part of the history of Canadian Literature.

RECORDED ON JANUARY 13, 2016

Agatha: Good afternoon, everybody. This is very exciting. So, first, thank you, Earle, for meeting with us. You guys seem very prepared, and the questions you have prepared for today are very thought-provoking, and they seem really well crafted. Although I am the facilitator for this interview, I hope to stay in the background as much as possible, and we want you to interact with Earle as freely as possible. So, we'll get started.

ET: Please ask me anything … there are absolutely no barriers. Every question is useful … there is no such thing as a dumb question, so you must jump in with anything. And follow up if I'm not clear, or I'm incomplete, or I haven't given an example. Hound me about it because that's what the interviewer's job is partly about. Some stuff I'll read just to make sure I convey it because my memory's fading a bit, and some of the things I don't want to forget. So I might simply read just so I can share them with you. And I am a little bit hard of hearing, so if you don't mind speaking up, I'll hear you all the better.

Amy: Thank you so much. The question I think we all wanted to start with was why did you decide to initiate this project? Tell us a bit about the genesis of that.

ET: Okay, good. I can tell you a wee bit about my background so that it would seem perhaps to fit. I did a B.A. in English and History at UBC in the 1950s. I took a radio course with Lorne Greene[1] in Toronto at a school called the Academy of Radio Arts; that was in 1950–1951. I worked in radio as a newscaster, news writer, news editor, news announcer. I was an editor at the Ryerson Press. This all sounds like a terrible jumble, and in a way it is, but I'll just spew them all out so you'll know there's a bit of motivation for my being interested in literature. At the Ryerson Press I was an editor. It, of course, was steeped in Canadiana and had published most of the writers we're going to talk about today … a great publisher of poetry. It was founded in 1828 and was the oldest English-language publisher in Canada. It was actually founded by the Methodist Church, and it was still owned by the United Church when I worked there in the 1960s. It was, at the end of the sixties, sold to McGraw Hill.

So, obviously I have a keen interest in prose and poetry. In the 1960s, late 1960s, public readings were beginning; readings of Canadian poets reading their own work were becoming more common ... even sometimes people reading stories, but especially reading poetry. I became an editor at the Ontario Institute for Studies in Education, which is part of the University of Toronto; they were publishing research material, as you know, all about teaching and learning.

And the creation of the two series is a sort of follow-the-yellow-brick-road adventure with cash that seemed miraculously to surface. The sixteen resultant programs were subsidized, in addition to thirteen thousand six hundred dollars of found money, by the Ontario Institute for Studies in Education and also the United Church of Canada. I don't want to forget the United Church. I'm not a churchy person, but it contributed enormously to this series, completely gratis, donated services way beyond dollar value. So, if one were to portray the genesis of the two taped series in a work of fiction, I don't think anyone would believe it.

In the 1968 fiscal year, OISE realized a budget surplus, and the director sent an urgent message throughout the institute — which was hardly five years old at that time — for research, writing, and publishing proposals that legitimately could consume the margin of the budget. As associate editor in the editorial division, I outlined a series of Canadian authors' recordings for use in high schools and colleges. I thought this sort of enrichment could be terribly useful, and it was practically non-existent. Certainly in recordings it was non-existent. There was the occasional thing that was in print, by way of an interview. And at the institute, any monetary surplus from that boom year would be swallowed up immediately by the Ontario government, because they would say, "Well you didn't spend x-thousand dollars last year — we'll deduct that in the coming budget." So they were in a great race to get this money legitimately used up.

The series — poets and novelists — was quickly approved and work began. Tapes and cassettes were in production by 1970. We were way on the road by then, so that was a pretty rapid flow. Each novelist and poet was offered an eight hundred and fifty dollar buy-out. OISE was not registered to pay royalties on sales, so a buy-out means it was a lump sum: and that's it, for all time. But in 1970 dollars, eight hundred and fifty bucks was a pretty nice little stipend. The sum seemed acceptable even to Mordecai Richler, who was used to movie options and film script fees, and he wrote for international periodicals. And the initial letter to each writer emphasized the sale, at subsidized price — and it was a subsidized price. I think the tapes were five dollars each, to high schools and colleges, with probably some use in universities. But all the writers quite understood that it was a subsidized product designed entirely for school use.

So, that's how it all began, and there was marvellous cooperation from the institute OISE, as I call it, which carried the entire overhead. In other words, the thirteen thousand six hundred dollars to pay sixteen writers went entirely to the writers, absolutely; and all the overhead of every kind — including the production of the tapes, manufacture, designing jackets, publicity, promotion, all the internal office work — was completely absorbed by OISE. And the technical work was completely absorbed by the United Church, because we used the Berkeley Studio at Berkeley and Queen Street; it's an old Methodist Church that still stands from 1871. I think now you can rent it for weddings, but in those days it was the United Church radio studio. And they very kindly — I guess partly because I was doing some freelance work for the church — they very kindly let us use their studio, their engineers, their Ampex recording equipment — all up-to-date radio equipment at that time — recording machinery, duplicating, dubbing, studio time, overhead of every kind. All we had to do was to buy the tapes. Microphones and recording equipment all supplied by the church.

Amy: That's a wonderful overview. Do you want to tell us a bit about how you first contacted the authors and what their responses were to being contacted? How did you obtain their permission to conduct the interviews … that aspect of things?

ET: Yes, sure. It was in the great old days of the business letter. So, we drafted a letter, outlining exactly what the series would be about. We sent it to, at that time, it would've been fifteen writers … because, the very final poet, James Reaney, was signed on latterly, way at the tail end of all the others. There seemed to be eight hundred and fifty dollars that hadn't been found yet and did turn up … so we got Reaney, but we wrote to him later. But initially, all the others were written to: the project was explained, what they would be paid, that it was a buy-out, and, of course, there would be a form of some kind that would be by way of a letter of agreement with OISE, because OISE, of course, was publishing it. We very quickly heard from them. No confusion ... no serious questions that I remember. Everybody seemed to think that eight hundred and fifty dollars was adequate, even, as I said, Mordecai, because he was a higher earner than certainly people who were teaching in universities at that time. And, from there, we just proceeded to book interviews and to get them recorded. So it was quite quick. I could add that it was an age in which it was beautifully handy and convenient to contact these writers, that they were perfectly open to being phoned, or written to, and you didn't have to go through an agent ... you didn't have to go through a PR person ... you talked directly to the writer. They were wonderfully, wonderfully available. I'll always remember that. So, everything began, really, very quickly.

Amy: And how did you come to choose these particular writers?

ET: Most of them, at that time, anyone would choose, because they were pretty senior, and enormously well known: Morley Callaghan, Hugh MacLennan, Margaret Laurence, Hugh Garner. Moredcai Richler had risen very fast, but even in 1970, he had already been writing twenty years. I don't think people realize that his first novel was published when he was nineteen: *The Acrobats*, published in Britain. These people — I don't want to use that corny term *icons* — but they were all absolutely the solid people that you couldn't ignore them. You couldn't ignore them. Now, if you could afford more, you could've of course added numerous other people. Somebody would say perhaps, "Why not Alice Munro?" Well, absolutely Alice Munro, but she was writing short stories, and these were supposed to be novels. I think short stories are more fun to read ... but anyway, that's another question.

The poets? Again, you had towering figures who had been on the scene for a long time, like Earle Birney, Irving Layton, Dorothy Livesay, F.R. Scott, Raymond Souster, Miriam Waddington. Miriam Waddington, a very significant poet ... not a winner of awards ... not that awards, really, mean very much ultimately. But then there was one much younger person, Gwendolyn MacEwen, who was utterly remarkable, because she quit school at sixteen to write full time, and she had enormous talent, and enormous romantic talent, in the literary sense. It was wonderful to be able to include her. Eli Mandel, somewhat younger than the rest, but an important, if you will, mythopoeic writer. There was a certain movement for mythopoeic poetry in the 1960s, meaning poets who were interested in merging myth and daily grubby reality. We used to think of myth as something that involves unicorns or kings or god figures, et cetera, that kind of dream-like myth. But I always come back to Northrop Frye's definition, which I think is so handy, that myth is plot, myth is storyline. I like that.

Amy: I just want to return to something you said a little earlier: you said awards don't matter as much … they're not as important, you don't think. Why don't you think awards are as important in determining an author's capability, their skill, what they have to offer?

ET: I wouldn't shoot them down, in that I think it's great publicity for the book. I think it's great to help make the writer known. I don't think that it necessarily tells you which are the most profound works to read. I remember that Ernest Hemingway said, "I'm always praised for the wrong reasons in my books." The things that people really fall in love with are the things that he didn't think were important at all or that were really quite lesser. So, I think sometimes awards … well, it's a little bit like the Academy Awards in Hollywood. Some of them become kind of political. Bette Davis might not get it in a given year because Hollywood hates Bette Davis anyway, so there are all these other factors that weigh into it.[2] I think mostly, awards can perhaps help sell books, but I don't think they guarantee that a given writer is, say, going to be a Morley Callaghan. I think that has to be proven over a long period of time.

Amy: And in terms of the preparation for your interviews, how did you prepare to conduct the interviews? Did you read their biographies? Did you read their works? Did you do nothing? How did you prepare for the interviews?

ET: I read, with the novelists, every novel I could get my hands on, every book of stories I could get my hands on, and essays, and travel writing, if they wrote it. Hugh MacLennan, for example, wrote very interesting travel articles in many American journals. Books of his essays have been collected. I tried always to make it the writing of the author or poet involved. I didn't spend very much time reading reviews, which often can be trivial anyway: reviews, or notices of other kinds, or stories in newspapers by journalists, or, or that kind of thing. You get a great deal from the books themselves. You'll notice in the tapes I usually start with a quotation, and the quotation is always taken from something the author wrote.

Vipasha: The first question that I want to ask is, what made you decide to structure the interviews as you did, and which recordings did you enjoy creating more? Did you enjoy creating interviews with the writers more or with the poets?

ET: And how the interviews were built?

Vipasha: How did you decide to structure the interviews?

ET: It does help to have a bit of a skeleton. I know today, for example, you have a set list of questions. A set list of questions can be like a trunk of a tree, but there should also be branches that can spring out from that trunk that you didn't expect in advance. And those are the things you follow up. You can never be really welded to a set of questions, in that some of the best things you will get from the writer spring up spontaneously, and you should immediately follow up. If those are going to be juicy, you should say something that will keep that flowing, such as "Could you tell us more about that?" or "Why was 1953 such a good year for you?" That sort of thing.

Anyway, as well as some questions, either in your head or on paper, it does help to have a bit of a ladder. For example, I started with a quotation from the novelist, read the quotation, and then said, "This is by Hugh Garner. Hugh Garner is with us, and I'd like him to comment on that statement." And then he does ... so it gets you launched, and you hope there is something off the top that will grab attention, because doing an interview is like singing a song: the two strategic points are the beginning and the ending, absolutely, the beginning and the ending. Big moments, in either.

So that gets you going. From then on, you try to structure it, and the ladder of your questions will help you, because you're trying to lead into something and get it to develop a sort of natural build. Then, as we mentioned before, you're trying to follow up, which is enormously import-ant. The greatest skill you can have is to listen. If you listen intently, with a lot of eye contact, not burying your face in your notes, or not looking at a picture on the wall, but directly at the author, that kind of eye contact and electric listening, you'll be surprised what material you get, because nobody listens that way anymore. And that listening is really *the* skill.

Then, the whole thing develops, as does your follow-up, which really is fun to do, and really should be fun for the author, too, because the author wants to talk more about some of the things he or she has done. Then, I tried to have a set ending, which was, "What do you most want to be remembered for?" Which may be a little corny, but they could always turn that on its ear if they wanted to. You know, somebody might say, "Oh I don't give a damn because I'll be gone anyway, you know." But, anyway, it was a way to wind the thing up.

The poets tended to end on a poem, and very often, because they are good writers, there would be a final line in the poem that I would find quite memorable, and that's where the reading ended. That's in the poems. The poets just began announcing their name, and then went right into the collection of poems they wanted to read, and giving their own background on the making of the poem, on their life situation, their education, whatever it is they're going to add to it.

Vipasha: Which recordings did you enjoy creating more: the interviews with the authors or the interviews with the poets?

ET: I don't think I really had a preference. The novelists were fun to talk to. I must say that everyone, everyone was wonderfully warm and approachable. The only —I'll talk a bit more about this — the only sad kind of interview I think was with Sinclair Ross. That was by far, far, far the most difficult one. But we'll get back to that later; everybody else was enormously open and neighbourly. I had the greatest feeling that all of these people were just like neighbours. And there wasn't any reason they should be excited to talk to me, not at all. I was not a Peter Mansbridge[3] of the time. I was not any kind of media icon. I was just a zero. So it was their generosity that they agreed to do it, and that they were so warm and outgoing. They were marvellous to work with, all of them.

The novelists were fun because I could dig around and ask them questions — some of my pet questions — and see what their responses would be. That was great fun. But the poets were interesting because you have to get them to feel comfortable, you want them to be entirely themselves. I think that was a nice feature about most of the tapes, the person, the man or woman, the star of the moment, is entirely his- or herself — they really do feel that way to me. I think only Sinclair Ross was not. But, anyway, we'll get to that. So, for the poets, it was mostly a matter of "Let's get the warmest, most real reading from this particular poet." For example, Irving Layton: a lot of braggadocio, loved his sexual prowess, had a big ego, and I thought, "This could be a bit problematic." In the studio, he was lovely. The work was intimate, it was very gentle, and with enormous feeling. Listen to the poem about Naomi, his daughter. Makes you cry … it's so beautiful, and so visual, you know … you can see her walking along the edge of the lake yourself. So that was a marvellous surprise.

Earle Birney: it's probably the best reading Earle Birney ever gave. Very lively, electric, dynamic reading, with a great many varieties of emotion in it. Gwen MacEwen: a very musical performer, a naturally beautiful reader. It's just given to her. Al Purdy: always being more rough and ready than he actually was, more of a rough diamond than he actually was. He's enormously well read, and enormously knowing, but you have this guy — very self-deprecating, always putting himself down, telling you how he worked in a mattress factory and all that sort of thing — so, no, I don't think I had any preference, really.

Vipasha: So when you met the authors, did they conform to or did they subvert your expectations? Were they different from what you imagined them to be in the interview?

ET: Let me talk just a bit about some of the ones I didn't know. I knew Dorothy Livesey; I knew Miriam Waddington; I knew Earle Birney; I knew a bit about Al Purdy. I knew Eli Mandel a bit; I knew Gwendolyn MacEwan a bit; did not know James Reaney; did not know Sinclair Ross. Knew *of* Raymond Souster. Knew Callaghan. I didn't know Hugh Garner. Let's take Margaret Laurence. I had seen a photograph of Margaret Laurence. It's on one of her books, taken by a Vancouver photographer. And she looked to me almost stern, with a spine of steel, a powerful woman, really. There's nothing wrong with that. I had this impression that she was this very strong, steely person. I had this impression like, "Don't mess with Margaret."

In the studio her hand shook throughout the entire interview although you don't hear that in her voice. Her voice was actually stable, secure — and her hand is shaking throughout the half hour. When we left the studio, [at]

Queen and Berkeley, hardly any traffic. I started across the street, and she said, "Wait, I can't do this! Let me take your arm." And she had to take my arm across the street. This was my image of Margaret Laurence: made of steel and she was terrified of traffic in a big city. I think a part of it was that she was raised in a very small town. But it was just interesting. And I don't mean by any means that she was any kind of pushover. I think she was a very strong person. But like all of us, she had these moments of vulnerability.

Morley Callaghan was just a delight because he had been in the United States, in the *New Yorker*, in the twenties, when people in New York did not even know where Canada was. He was published internationally, in England. He had been in Paris, in the twenties, and knew so many writers there from Scott Fitzgerald to Ernest Hemingway to Sinclair Lewis, Gertrude Stein. And I knew in advance that he didn't suffer fools gladly, and he wouldn't put up with junk questions. Very, very, shrewd, smart man. He had a lot of Irish humour. And once he realized that you're going to let him have the floor and let him have fun, he was marvellous. He was just so warm and delightful ... I just loved it.

Hugh MacLennan, I didn't know anything about except that he had a big reputation, published widely. A classics scholar, he was a Rhodes Scholar at Oxford, studied at Princeton, and in the middle of the Depression, with all that upper-class education, he couldn't get a university position and he taught high school at Lower Canada College. But he, too, was wonderfully down to earth. He's a Cape Bretoner, a Celt, and he was marvellous. And I think, similar to the Morley Callaghan situation, once he realized that this was going to be authentic, that there was going to be integrity, that it was all about his work and not about his social life, or his sex life, or gambling or anything else that would paint any kind of picture. He was just wonderfully relaxed and it was really great.

Vipasha: Did you learn anything about the authors that surprised you?

ET: I'm just wondering if there's anything else that surprised me. When I mentioned Irving Layton was a sweetheart in the studio, I expected him to be more rambunctious. He also took direction very well. I wasn't sure that he would do that. But if you were on his side, and if you were for a good production, he was marvellous, He'd do retakes; he'd do anything. Birney was very much the same. Birney was like an old pro. He didn't like his first script; he went home and rewrote it. Writing is rewriting. He remade the thing and came back and re-recorded it on the second day.

Goofy things surprised me. Gwendolyn MacEwan was a heavy smoker, and she had a racking cough at the end of every poem. A racking, racking cough that would knock you over. So I had to edit all those out. Most of them flowed straight ahead, but there is editing that doesn't show. This is analog tape: this is before digital and you literally cut tape with a razor blade and patched it together with a particular kind of gluey-tape. So it was easy to edit, but I had to edit all the coughs out. James Reaney, I never knew that he would come as a one man band. He never asked for a piano, and we were talking in a talk studio, a little talk studio at the Berkeley Studio. It's like a good-size closet 'cause all you had to do was sit someone down at a desk, put a microphone and record them. So, there was no room for a piano. So, at the last moment, I had to phone OISE, and we found out that there was a piano in the basement and we could use that. We had to move Reaney and his stuff over to OISE, over to Bloor Street near St. George to record his show. I think he's a kind of busker, he's an old vaudevillian. He came with a tambourine, a little drum, a flute; he wanted to play the piano. He has all these musical interludes in the tape, and plays bits of Scott Joplin and old hymns. So, yes, those were surprising.

Vipasha: I guess this relates to what you were talking about with Sinclair Ross. My final question is how did you find the authors reacted to being interviewed? Did you see any of them nervous, or shy, and how did you work around those obstacles?

ET: Going back to what we said about eye contact. You have to do a lot of editing in your head. You were very close to the guest. So, if they seem to be bored by something, either you change the question or you go to a different question. If their interest is high, you can get a little more on it. And the reverse. Most of the novelists went straight ahead, partly because they had received the questions in advance. I think I forgot to mention that. They had all received the questions in advance, which guaranteed for them that it was not about their divorce, about messy personal stuff ... it was entirely about their work. That meant they were quite relaxed when they came in because they had a clear idea of where the interview was going to go. Somebody like Mordecai Richler, I was a little wary of … I had never met him … I had only heard that Mordecai was a tough interview.

I think like Morley, he didn't appreciate fools. He probably had had enough of nosy reporters who were badly researched. And he had to do other things with his time. He could be short if he thought it was going to be a stupid situation. He was terrific to work with because I think he sensed that it was going to be a serious job and that it would be useful to students. And he was — he went out of his way to give them material that was useful.

Sinclair Ross, and then I'll wrap this up, I can't quite figure out. I listened to all the tapes again, and that's almost half a century later. I think a number of things were at play. Sinclair Ross was a very private person, rather reclusive, very shy. He's a really nice guy, I liked him enormously, integrity up and down. He's from the west and I'm from Saskatchewan. And I knew that western people were not great talkers.

I think he was not satisfied with his writing at that time. I think he was in a really bad patch. One or two of his books, he thought were failures, and he was doing another one that had a crime element in it. Not satisfied, not well, as far as his health was concerned. But I just couldn't seem to feel that he was interested in talking about his writing. Which is extremely rare for a writer — they like talking about their writing. He didn't seem to enjoy talking about it. And if I had been grumpy at the time, which I wasn't, but I was grumpy listening to it after, and I thought, "Why the heck did he bother getting interviewed?"

Vipasha: Maybe for the stipend?

ET: I thought it was the money. But as you remember from the tape, I would ask him a question and he would say, "Well, I never thought about that" and I thought, *Oh hell, where do we go from here? I never thought about that.* And I didn't think the questions were arcane or anything. I thought they were straight-ahead questions. I think he didn't like talking about his work and he thought his work failed. Which was really sad. That was sad. Even *As For Me and My House*, as you know, it was out of print for something like sixteen years. Didn't get into the universities, until it went into the New Canadian Library. And it originally came out in 1941.

Griffin: What did you see as the primary purpose of these interviews and poetry readings? What did you want student listeners from high school and college to take away from these interviews?

ET: Partly, the evolution of writing in the country in that there was a sort of background of Victoriana, what was called the Maple Leaf school of poets: Bliss Carman, Charles G.D. Roberts, Archibald Lampman.[4] Leaping from there to poets such as Gwen MacEwan, Earl Birney, Al Purdy, was a kind of enormous leap. If I can just read you something to illustrate what I mean by what they call the Maple Leaf school of Canadian poets: this is end of the 1890s, beginning of the 1900s. This is Bliss Carman, this is the first stanza of his poem "Vestigia" — *vestigium*, of course, meaning "footprint" — he says,

> I took a day to search for God
> And found Him not. But as I trod
> By rocky ledge, through woods untamed,
> Just where one scarlet lily flamed,
> I saw His footprint in the sod.

Okay, that's Bliss Carman. Now to modernism if you want, and I think the modernism of the twentieth century. Modernism is kind of a worn-out word, but whatever you want to call the twentieth century, I think that was the country we were really interested in for this series. This is the first stanza of Earle Birney's "The Shapers: Vancouver" (and notice they were both writing about landscape):

> a hundred million years
> for mountains to heave
> suffer valleys
> the incubus of ice
> grow soil-skin
>
> twenty thousand for firs to mass
> send living shafts out of the rock

Different kind of hardness, isn't it? And it was really, I think, intended to be an overall enrichment in that students tend to ask questions such as, "Where do your ideas come from?" We never had any resources really, to tell us where the ideas came from. So, it was nice to get the poets to talk about how they came to be writing a given poem. I think that's why a poem such as Birney's "The Bear on the Delhi Road" is marvellous for students because it's so graphic, it's so visual. It's an actual event: he's with a driver in a Ford in India on a dusty road and sees these two men with an actual bear in the ditch. And he finds out from his driver that what they're trying to do was to teach the bear to dance. And that poem has affected me strongly, not only because it immediately lets a student see how the poem came to be, but that it has the marvellous rhythms of dance. He says, "to lurch lurch with them / in the tranced dancing of men."

With the novelists, there was so much background that fed into their writing. For example, who in the classroom would know that Hugh Garner had actually fought in the Spanish Civil War of the 1930s? In the International Brigades on the Republican side? Even Hugh Garner said he had not realized until he did the interview that what he really wanted to support was the Spanish people. Now, Hugh was a leftist of some kind, or he wouldn't have fought on the Republican side; if he was a fascist, he would have fought for Franco. But he said in the interview, "I've never said this before." He said, "I had a deep feeling for the Spanish people," and it was almost like a mission for him. He didn't say, "I went because I was a staunch left-winger, practically a socialist, maybe a communist." It wasn't anything like that. And I thought that was very touching, "for the Spanish people." That he had ridden boxcars in the Depression. That he had any variety of jobs. That he had worked on a floor in a factory, et cetera. We mentioned that Al Purdy had worked in a mattress factory, for example. One of Al Purdy's poems is about Percy Lawson who's haggling on behalf of the union with the company that operates the mattress factory. Haggling for a lousy nickel, as Purdy said. Mordecai Richler saying, for his first novel, which I don't think he cares for anymore, because it was a first novel — he said, "Any number of kind of disagreeable jobs would have taught me far more than that first novel." Margaret Laurence saying that although she had lived in Africa, lived in England, back in Canada, whenever she sat down to write, it was still the village of Neepawa, which she called Manawaka, and that rural prairie community in Manitoba that came back to her mind. She said, "I'm lumbered with it … I'm lumbered with it" and so she just had to take it and use it.

Other surprises? Well, Morley Callaghan, a lawyer, didn't practise law. A lawyer — and as a young man, with a wife and two little boys — he took a chance on being a freelance writer, writing stories for magazines, doing bits for CBC. His son Barry still lives in the old family home in Toronto. Barry loved going to the races, and he bet on horses and he used to make money once in a while. He loved betting on the races, and his dad said to him one time, "You don't know what gambling is!" Because his dad had taken this crazy, crazy leap out of law into freelance writing, supporting a family. That was real gambling.

Griffin: So making a human connection for students with these authors that are maybe seen like figureheads, that they don't feel any connection to. Do you think a tape or audio is the best way to make the connection for students?

ET: I like the way you're putting it. I think you put it well. Tape is certainly not the only way; a personal visitation is probably even better. But those weren't being done at that time. They were being done later, and there usually had to be an agency, a fund, that would pay the travel cost and be able to get the writer there, et cetera. It was just one method of doing it, but it's good for students to realize that this person actually exists.

Griffin: Could you tell us about the experience of recording and recording to tape and about any technological limitations that you experienced while recording? You mentioned earlier how you had to splice the tapes and cut them with a razor blade. Were there any limitations in post-production, editing, especially for the interviews, like maybe condensing?

ET: Tape, like radio, compared with other media, was wonderfully simple and vastly cheaper than film or video. And far less cumbersome. So that, for example, when funny old James Reaney needs a piano and we have to go all across town to get him a piano, all I have to take is a portable recording machine — which is an Ampex, I mean it's top quality — but the whole thing is only so big — you can get it in a cab. That, and a microphone. So we get him at this little grand piano, we set the mike on the piano, and away you go! He plays the piano and talks into the microphone and reads his poems, et cetera. It was wonderfully simple that way. I was the only staff person on duty in the studio. Let's say this is the studio in which the author sits, and over where Geoff is, that's the other little studio where I am through a glass window with the Ampex recorder ... and here is the author with the microphone, and there's a glass wall in between. So, the poets, I could sit them down here, check their level on the mike to make sure they were close enough but not too close and that they weren't popping and all that sort of thing, and then I could sit behind the glass safely on the other side and record them. If you can believe it, partly because we were saving money, with the novelists, I had to sit with them. Here's the microphone, here's Toppings, here's Morley Callaghan. And I just run in, set the machine going and come out. First, I have to make sure his level is okay; I know what my level is generically and we let the tape roll, and it was okay. It was all kind of wacky. Then you have funny little incidents. Gwen MacEwan, who was a dear and naturally was this musical, beautiful reader — she was kind of a Billie Holiday[5] among poetry readers — she looked at this mike and she didn't quite know whether she approved of the mike or not. Now she's not really saying that, but I could tell she wonders if this is a junk mike or something. And I thought, "I think she's thinking of those nice nickel plated microphones that singers with dance bands used to sing from, that were all shiny." And the mike we used was the top mike of the day. It was called a RCA Victor 44, which was a ribbon mike. It doesn't look like much but it is so delicate that what vibrates inside that picks up your voice is an actual thin metallic ribbon that vibrates with the sound waves of your voice. So it was the best mike we could have gotten. And of course, she sounds lovely on tape.

The cutting of tape, again you have little metal blocks to do it with and you have special tools and special tape to mend it and all that kind of thing. And that's fairly direct. And it's all in your hands. It's not one of those terrible production processes in which you have to have thirteen different specialists and seventeen different machines to work on and so on. So it was sort of seat of the pants. It reminded me a little bit of the great Canadian folklorist, Helen Creighton[6] who travelled around the Maritimes and probably other parts of Canada, recording folk singers, and folk poets and local historians and whatever. She, too, had a little portable recording machine and a microphone and she got this stuff recorded for all time.

There was not a lot of post-production. For example, with James Reaney and his musical bits, there would be cuts in between the musical bit and beginning a poem because he would have to pick up his papers, and there'd be a bit of rattling around. So that was just cut out. That was okay.

Griffin: Could you tell us about converting the tapes to 2016 technology?

ET: As you get older, you're haunted by all kinds of things you haven't done — you keep thinking you must get onto this or it will never get finished. So, I still had these things on reel tape. Analog reel tape, which, of course, nobody can play anymore, really. And I thought, "How am I ever going to preserve them?" So, I thought of CDs. Already CDs are out of date; my son doesn't have a CD player. What can you do? You can't keep up with technology anyway. I got in touch with a local studio, and I said, "Could you transcribe these reel tapes onto CDs?" They said, "Yes, yes of course." I said, "I don't have the masters, the masters are lost." The masters would originally have been kept at OISE. Then later Van Nostrand Reinhold — which was a branch plant, an American publisher working in Toronto at that time — took over the sale of the tapes, and they must have had the masters, so I don't know where they've gone. So what we had to do was make copies of copies. It's a wonder they're audible as they are; it's truly kind of miraculous that they are. So that's what they are. And this studio did a nice job on them. That's how we got them on CD.

Griffin: Did you ever take photographs of the sessions with the authors?

ET: No, I didn't. It's a good question because it would have been a bright, bright thing to do, but I was such a one-man band, I couldn't have done that as well.

Geoff: You mentioned retakes; so is it the sort of thing where, just sort of part way during the conversation the writer or you would say, "I'd like to try that again," and you'd repeat a line … or was it you'd hear it back and realize you needed to do something over?

ET: In that little studio, I don't remember that there was a talk back system. If there is a talk back system, I can just push a button in my little booth, there's his glass wall and he's on the other side, and I can just say, "Dorothy Livesay, would you do that one again? I think we just got a rumble at the beginning." But all I would do is just stop the tape, go into the studio, and say, "Let's take that one from the top, and we'll get a little clearer start on that."

Geoff: You've mentioned a few instances already, but is there any particular moment during all of the interviews that resonates with you above all others?

ET: Some of them are little, little things that wouldn't seem terribly important at the time. For example, when we were finished with the Richler tape, he said, "That was certainly painless," and I really loved that. I really sort of took that to my heart because I knew he didn't like doing interviews. In a public area in some building, I forget where it was, I once saw Mordecai, about to be interviewed in a kind of on-the-street thing, by Kildare Dobbs, a fellow writer.[7] They knew each other but Mordecai was going to be interviewed. There were a few people gathered to watch, and Mordecai was going around the back asking people, "Has anybody got brandy? Anybody got some brandy?" He was that nervous about doing an interview. I always remember. So I was so pleased when he said, "That certainly was painless."

At the end of his interview, Morley Callaghan said, "I enjoyed that," and I knew he enjoyed it because he had a good time, he let himself rip sort of thing, and his Irish humour came out. A nice thing about Callaghan, he said, "I do not withhold," which is true; he would be frank, and he would say what he felt, but even if he jabbed an idea, or a person a bit, it was always with a bit of humour, which was a touch I really liked. That's something to try to learn.

I think Birney's performance was a high, high point. They talk in music about the highs and lows, the dynamics. I thought that the dynamics in his reading were marvellous, the great changes; the way, for example, when he does that poem about a drifter in Trinidad who almost mugs him, almost mugs him, and suddenly a cab comes around the corner, and Birney leaps into the cab. Birney does the local lingo, he does the local patois of this fellow who almost jumped him, which was great. Dorothy Livesay said that I worked well with women writers, which was nice. I think sometimes women writers thought they were a bit underplayed, the way women painters are often underplayed; but women, as you know, were far and away the leading writers in the country. They certainly are now; they have been, not just in number, but also in quality.

I've mentioned Hugh Garner. That was a very strong point, his deep concern for the people of Spain, I mentioned that. Callaghan said something I always remember: he said, "I realized as a young man that politics was a substitute for culture in this country." He said, "Nobody would start a riot about an opera, but everybody could maybe have a fight about politics." Margaret Laurence quoting Arthur Miller when I asked her what she would like to be remembered for: she said, "I don't think we're in it for the immortality stakes. As Arthur Miller said, 'It's like trying to carve your name on a block of ice, in the middle of the street, on a hot July day.'" This also was something I liked about Richler's interview. I said, "What made you become a writer?" And he said, "I thought I could do it. I thought I could do it." Fewer than ten words, and I thought, yes, that says a lot. I'm sure that's a whole little booklet, about the beginning of his writing life: "I thought I could do it." Layton reading the poem to his mother, the poem to his little daughter, Naomi, is very moving, but the poem to his mother, Keine Lazarovitch, I find enormously moving. He reads it a little lighter than I would have thought, but then he plays with his mother's anger, her fury, asking God: "Are you blind?" But at the same time, his words really caress her in that poem. This was one by MacLennan; one of his manuscripts was turned down by twenty-one editors in New York, twenty-one publishing houses, and one of the editors said: "Who is this writer? He's not British, not American. We don't know who he is." That was MacLennan.

Geoff: Once the project was finished, were there reviews? Did the writers have any particular reaction that was interesting to you?

ET: OISE did quite a good job, because it wasn't really in that game; it was in the game of teaching and learning. But it was reviewed by the *Toronto Star*, maybe one other newspaper, but the *Star* I remember definitely. It was reviewed in educational journals, in periodicals that review books, there was the odd interview in other publications. So, yes, it did get reviewed, and we always made a point of sending these reviews to the author in question unless they were completely stupid. I mean, if it was just a nasty review we wouldn't bother, but if it made some sense, we sent it off.

Geoff: Did you follow up with the authors after the project was over? Did you maintain relationships with any of them afterwards?

ET: They were paid immediately. We sent a letter of appreciation, with a handwritten note on it, et cetera. Some of them I would be bumping into in different kinds of ventures to do with books anyway, but it's a good point because it is terribly important to have a follow-up, and if possible, to send a handwritten note. I know that's not done anymore — everybody does it on a ruddy computer — but you'd be surprised. I read a story by Norman Snider, who is a Canadian writer and has done some big film scripts for Hollywood as well.[8] He wrote a little crime story in a journal that's edited by Barry Callaghan, and the story was called "Wolves." The wolves in it were predators — you know predators, grifters, businessmen, et cetera — and I sent him a little note, a little handwritten note of gratitude, sort of a fan letter. He got in touch with me and he said: "Where did you find stamps? Where did you find envelopes? How do you do this stuff?" He was so courteous that, because I sent it by mail, he then sent me one by mail, whereas ordinarily he would just send an email, he wouldn't have bothered. But those little touches are really nice. I think there's something to remember: a little handwritten card means a lot.

Geoff: Having talked to so many of the most iconic Canadian writers, do you think that there's any way to generalize or make any sort of characterizations of Canadian literature as a whole? Is there something about it that's distinct compared to British literature or American literature, in your mind?

ET: I think the immensity of the country is always there, even if it's a sort of shadow or even if it sort of hangs over a piece of work. I think the immensity of the country: that we are this thin strip of land connected by railroads, from coast to coast. That we're a northern country, I think that shows up. One American poet has said that he finds in prairie writers — and he was thinking of writers from say, North Dakota or Nebraska — sometimes there is a sharp clarity, a sort of down-home practicality. I think that would certainly be true about Sinclair Ross and Margaret Laurence, very much prairie writers. I don't know that there's really any umbrella; there are so many regions, and as you dig, regional traces. You'll find them, for example, very much in Hugh MacLennan. Listen to his voice on tape: it's a very Cape Breton voice. The voice you have somehow seeps into the way you put words together: Cape Breton sort of washed by the sea. I think Callaghan talked about a kind of stingy narrow nationalism in the forties, for example, in which it was assumed that to be called Canadian, a work had to have a certain kind of quality so that it could it only be understood and appreciated in Canada. In other words, it must be a kind of ghetto piece of some kind, very much I think, the term *ghetto* would fit. Whereas someone like Richler didn't want to get shackled by that kind of narrow Canadian nationalism that was roaring at the time; he was thinking of the fifties and sixties. Although he said he liked to write journalistic pieces, articles about Canada, he said most other countries aren't interested. But I think he was the kind of writer who would say that writing is international; it doesn't matter where you're sitting, because he was in England for a long time. He was in France ... certainly he was in Paris for a while when he was nineteen. Callaghan rattled around, so did Laurence, so did so many of them ... MacLennan. I think all of them would like to think they're international, that their work could be read anywhere.

Geoff: One last question: what do you hope future listeners will take away from the series?

ET: I hope they'll delight in the fact that these writers have developed in a kind of Canadian modernism; again that terrible term *modernism*, but at least in our time, to use Hemingway's old line. They have come largely unnoticed going back to the thirties and forties. Even when I was an editor at the Ryerson Press for six and a half years in the sixties, you know, up to about '67, it was still a very small game in this country. That's why it was not at all hard to list who the top novelists were, because there was only about six of them anyway. Try to figure out how many important novelists there are now. I think it's the exhilaration of realizing that these people are all, in a way, sort of self-taught, or they have everything by their own bootstraps. They have made their way against really an enormous amount of indifference, which F.R. Scott said used to hang over the country like a fog. Indifference, that is, to the arts.

Amy: Would you say that's perhaps one thread that can unify all these works in terms of Canadianism, generalizing Canadian literature by that quality, is that idea of fighting against the indifference? Do you think that aspect could be applied to weave all these different authors together?

ET: I think that's part of the muscle of it, certainly, yes. I think it's a connecting thread. I don't mean that they were grumpy or bitchy about it; I don't mean that at all, but they were just not noticed. Even at the time that I recorded Morley Callaghan, he was not really what you would call a household word. He was probably better known in New York in some ways than he was in Toronto. He was sort of invisible in Toronto. People used to ask him: "Why don't you live in one of the great centers, like Paris, London, New York?" He said well, he said, "I'd be a stranger in London; Toronto is a good place to work." I think one reason it was a good place to work for Callaghan was that people left him alone, they didn't know he was doing this. So, a number of these people sort of came up through the shadows. We're hearing so much more about them now; there's much more attention given to books now. You get stories in daily newspapers, which we never used to get.

There was a wonderful editor/producer at CBC, called Bob Weaver, who was very instrumental;[9] he was the first editor of Alice Munro. He put her stories on the air, he put young Mordecai Richler's stories on radio, on a program called *Anthology* on CBC Wednesday Night. He was a great, quiet influence in the Canadian way, and a term he often used was "staying power"; have they got staying power? I think that's what I mean when I said, rather clumsily off the top: this business of fighting through, not giving up, but having this kind of staying power, believing in what you were doing. Irving Layton taught high school for many, many years; Gwendolyn MacEwen died poor. She died actually when she was only forty-six, which was very tragic. Al Purdy never had any money, made his own beer, rolled his own cigarettes. Raymond Souster worked in a bank; Sinclair Ross worked in a bank. I think that more than anything, it's the itch to do it, that you can't resist, even Sinclair Ross, although it was so hard to get him to say anything. He said, "I've always scribbled."

A lot of them began writing when they were very young: Purdy, when he was about thirteen, Margaret Laurence when she was about ten, and some of them, before they were even writing it down, were telling stories, telling themselves stories. Mordecai Richler said, "A writer is a loner," and I think there is something true about that. You need a fair amount of solitude just to do it, perhaps by nature. As Laurence said about herself, "I always was a rather solitary child." I guess, one could say that a lot of these writers got published and continued to write, with very, very little encouragement. We could certainly say that. It was only in very recent times that any of them would become huge celebrities, such as Margaret Atwood. Nobody ever dreamed in the 1960s that any Canadian would win the Nobel Prize, which Alice Munro did.

Amy: I was just wondering, you spoke earlier in the interview about how you came from Saskatchewan; you said that people from the West are famously not very loquacious. So it's interesting that you've found yourself in this career of being in radio, and creating these tapes, and working with Ryerson Press. Do you have a first memory of the first audio recording, whether that was on radio or in any other medium; do you have your first memory of that? And what about that struck you? What about that resonated?

ET: Okay, well, even before the first recording made an impression, I remember hearing Lorne Greene doing the radio news during the war years; it was a national newscast all across Canada on radio; it was before television. And, it was Lorne Greene! I remember being enormously impressed by that. A bit farther along, when I was a teenager, hearing jazz recordings with the people next door, with Fats Waller, Nellie Lutcher, whom I had never heard before, great black jazz performers.[10] That made an impression. I think one thing that sort of hooked me, I had a crazy kind of dream of show business, the way most little boys want to be firemen or policemen. I wanted to do something in show business. When I was a kid, there was no show business, there was no live theatre, there was no television, there was no Canadian film, there was only radio. That was the only sort of professional show business that might pay you a scratch living, and so I headed in 1950 to the Academy of Radio Arts to Lorne Greene's school, and studied radio. That was my beginning to love recordings and sound.

Amy: At the end of your interviews with the authors, you asked them: "What do you want to be remembered for?" I'm going to ask that question of you: what do you want to be remembered for?

ET: What would I like to be remembered for? Well, in a little way, I would like to be remembered for this set of tapes. That's perhaps not the only thing, but I'm just so glad it got done. It was really kind of a crazy miracle, because the money dropped out of heaven. It was all completely accidental, and the fact that it all worked … that OISE was so efficient and so helpful … that the United Church was marvellous and never charged a dime. Only recently did I write them a serious letter and thanked them because for a long time, the United Church was so important but I hadn't really written them a formal thank you. I finally got that done, which I am glad of. The second thing was going to university. That was a major, major blessing in my life, which you all will find. Treasure it, work your butts off. I got in partly by mistake. It will sound really weird but at one time I was a candidate for the United Church Ministry. I went straight from senior matric to Lorne Greene's radio school, graduated from it in 1951, got a job as a newscaster, news editor, news announcer at CKNW, a little radio station in New Westminster in B.C., worked there for two years, had a very forceful minister in our church who was trying to push me into the ministry, and I was kind of drifting into it … I think because I didn't have enough power within myself to tell him: "Forget it!" And eventually I dropped out. I did not become a candidate for the ministry, but it got me into this wonderful ragtag little B.A. course at UBC, which I really loved because I took a bit of everything … if you can believe I did one course in listening to music, I did one theatre course; I had this nice smattering of English, I had some history, some psychology. It went all over the map, and it was glorious. It was as far from an Honours B.A. as you could ever get but I loved it. And the funny thing is, I got in by accident. If this pushy minister hadn't try to make me a clergyman, I would have never gone back to university, because I was good in radio and I had a job, and I probably would have just stayed in radio, with a senior matric education. That would have been it. So, yes, the university education would be the other big one.

Agatha: You mentioned a few themes. You mentioned Hugh MacLennan and how his novel was first rejected by twenty-one publishers, for instance. Would you like to follow up on that? Or anything else?

Amy: How do you account for someone like Hugh MacLennan being rejected by twenty-one publishers? What barriers would there be, even for someone who clearly had talent? What barriers exist within the industry that maybe prevent authors, writers, from getting their work out there, and do you see that as something that can be overcome, discussing either at that time in the past or now?

ET: It's a good question. I think part of it was echoed by that one New York editor who said, "Who is he, we don't know who this man is, he's not British, he's not American, where is he from?" I think they found somehow that the material didn't resonate with the American industry. But also you will find if you read through the histories of all kinds of writers, many of them have been turned down all kinds of time … maybe not as many as twenty-one … maybe more. And there's no guaranteed genius in editors. They're just human, too, so they pass somebody by, somebody else publishes him down the line, and maybe sells eighty thousand copies, you never know. You never know.

I've had the experience of sending stuff out, and it's very disappointing because mostly it comes back. I think that's why writers have to have an enormously tough skin, because if you asked any of these, I'm sure they would all have said, "Oh I've got bushels of stuff back: 'Rejected.'" A writer friend told me that Earle Birney had the wall of his office papered with rejection slips. He was one of our greatest poets. He was turned down by all kinds of places. Also, when MacLennan was submitting material, nobody gave a damn about Canada. They didn't know where it was, and they didn't care about it even if they did find out where it was. So, they probably thought, "Oh, no, no, this isn't American or British, or it's not international, or whatever."

Agatha: You mentioned Ryerson Press, where you worked. In contrast to American publishers, could you tell us more about some supportive Canadian publishers? I know Lorne Pierce[11] was active but it was earlier. Who was very supportive of Canadian poets and authors in the sixties and fifties? Publishing houses, in particular.

ET: You mean other editors who were very receptive?

Agatha: Yes.

ET: I'm glad you mentioned that, Agatha, because Lorne Pierce was a great pal of Canadian writers, and Canadian painters as well. He published so many; almost everybody in this list has been published at Ryerson in one way or another, with a story in an anthology, or a complete book, or a series of books, on and on. So, Lorne Pierce was the first editor-in-chief that the Ryerson Press had, and certainly the first with an attention to contemporary writing. He was there for forty years. His reign began in 1920, ended in 1960. He brought in so many writers. He was way back in the Maple Leaf school that we mentioned, of Bliss Carman and so on. He knew all of those writers, and published them as well. Very great encouragement, I think that's an enormous point. He was a clergymen also, so it was an ethical and a moral task for him to do something for the people of the country.

Jack McClelland. Jack McClelland[12] in much more recent times was another pillar of Canadian publishing. He published Irving Layton, Leonard Cohen. He published Earle Birney, too. All kinds of them, and actually lost money doing it. I don't think he died at all a rich man. So, McClelland of McClelland and Stewart was another great impetus. And there were little presses that began to pop up, like New Press, like House of Anansi, and some of the others that are alive right now. Coach House Books, who made an enormous difference, and were able to sort of completely bypass the big, cumbersome publishing houses and just present things because they really believed in them. Margaret Atwood worked at House of Anansi, for example, at one point.

Geoff: I remember in the Sinclair Ross interview, he talks about how he thought that part of his lack of financial success and popularity was owed to the fact that he was from the prairies and that there was just a lack of general interest in that part of the world. Do you think that was true? That it was because of a regional bias? Or if it was true then, do you think it still persists now?

ET: I think it's a good point. I'm glad you mentioned it, Geoff, because I did not. I think it's very true that at the time Ross was writing, nobody in this part of the world really knew where Saskatchewan was, and couldn't care. I was born there; I was born in Regina. It's only in recent years that people say, "Oh, Saskatchewan, they've got jobs. It's doing well isn't it?" Otherwise they never knew it existed. So, I think that's true, it was a regional thing.

Even James Reaney was as close as London, Ontario, but he was really on the outer fringes. The big concentration was Toronto and Montreal. It had been very strong in Montreal once. Montreal poets included F.R. Scott, Miriam Waddington, P.K. Page,[13] et cetera. That was a strong poetic movement. There was also a strong movement of painters. But apart from those two massive cities, in a lot of other areas — if you were in Regina, forget it. Or if you were in northern Ontario, forget it, I think, pretty much. It does make a great difference. I'm very interested in Canadian art, and I know that even in Toronto, we're not at all well acquainted with Quebec artists, and there are brilliant painters in Quebec. I mean, just go to the Montreal museums and you'll be astonished. But it's the business. The country's so damned big that it's too expensive to ship this stuff and insure it from one end of the country to the other. It makes an enormous difference in, for example, painting. Writing, the action of publishing, and the biggest newspapers, and the biggest industry to do with letters of any kind, and the biggest universities, tended to be in centres like Toronto, and not in Saskatoon, not even in Vancouver. So you're right, regional differences are very great. Not quite as much now. Not as much now. But in the forties, enormous.

Griffin: I know that some of the writers received Canada Council grants to write. Was regional bias also expressed in the distribution of those grants? Were those grants concentrated in areas like Toronto and Montreal?

ET: That's a good question. That's a very good question, and I don't really know enough about the inner workings of such as the Canada Council to reply to it. I did have work, just for one short stint, in judging material that was potential for a Canada Council grant, in Ottawa. I just happened to be recommended by Earle Birney. I was freelancing at the time. But the three of us were Joyce Marshall from Toronto,[14] Toppings from Toronto, and Al Purdy from Ontario. So that didn't look like a very wide distribution across the country. The only one who was a little *outré* was Purdy, in Ameliasburgh, I guess. I honestly can't say about the Canada Council. I'm sorry, I can't, no. Let me ask you a question: Are there writers you have found which really surprised you in this list?

Geoff: I was surprised by Sinclair Ross, just because I was familiar with his stories from syllabuses of English courses I'd studied. So it was kind of an iconic name to me already. Then to hear his sort of self-degrading … it seems like he had really low self-esteem about his writing … was kind of shocking to me. Because I guess his legacy came later than that interview. He really seemed to have it in his head that he was a failed artist. That surprised me. It was sad to listen to, I think.

ET: There are terrible contradictions, because — when I talked to Morley Callaghan he said, "In the Canadian university there are two Canadian novels they recommend: *As For Me and My House* and *The Double Hook*."[15] He said, "I tried to get through that *As For Me and My House*, and I couldn't do it." But what it did reveal was … I don't know what your experience is, but apparently, with dear old Sinclair Ross in the dumps, apparently they've elevated, in academe, they've elevated *As For Me and My House* way, way up! Is that right?

Agatha: I read *As For Me and My House* in my third year Canadian literature course.

ET: There you are. It was on the course, right?

Agatha: Yes, it was. I think it's considered now one of the great Canadian novels. I love Canadian literature, and I took three courses in Canadian literature when I was an undergraduate; we never read Hugh Garner or F.R. Scott, or even Livesay. We read Sinclair Ross, Richler, not even MacLennan, and I was surprised, because he was the first distinctive Canadian writer. We read Margaret Laurence; as you know she's iconic right now as well. She's considered to be in the Canadian canon. But yes, I was surprised how many of them are not read.

ET: Yeah. Do you find there's a kind of star system? There are fashions, aren't there? Like poor Dorothy Livesay had a period when she was enormously popular, and then they started to kind of downgrade her. Push her into the shadows a bit.

Amy: Well, even with someone like Layton. I mean obviously he had a reputation of flaunting his sexual prowess and of being quite the character. So, you have someone like that who is much more known than someone who is like a Garner or a Souster. I was reading some articles by Joe Fiorito of the *Toronto Star*,[16] who knew Souster, and was advocating for a park to be named after Souster. He was saying that if you want to be called a Torontonian in any sense, you should know Souster because of his writings about Toronto. And yet so many don't. So it's interesting. That two-tiered, maybe even more than a two-tiered system that ranks the different authors according to what's considered popular, what's considered iconic to use that word.

Agatha: I was surprised. This topic really reminds me of E.J. Pratt,[17] in particular. When I took a Canadian poetry course we didn't read him at all, and at one point in the sixties, especially in the fifties, he was considered Canada's national poet. At our book sale, last year, we had signed copies of Pratt's poetry, and I bought some of them, so I'm very lucky. I read them already. Like *The Witches' Brew* and *Towards the Last Spike*. I think he's an amazing poet. I think partly, however, this has to do with the changes that have happened in the country. For instance *Towards the Last Spike*, which is almost the national poem, doesn't talk about the Chinese labourers who were working under Canada's national railway, and I think maybe that's why what was then considered national or a point of pride, we look at it now and to us it seems dated and perhaps unjust or even historically inaccurate. Not that poetry pretends to be historically accurate, necessarily. But I think it's also changes in attitude; what is considered to be national or patriotic has changed as well. I think for Pratt in particular — I know I'm going off-topic — he was really a great poet. He was also a very interesting person. We also have his papers at our library. He was originally from St. John's, Newfoundland, but he spent his entire adult life in Toronto. And he's also very central to Toronto. I actually live in the building where he first lived in the 1920s with his wife. Because I'm not Canadian maybe ... I wasn't born here ... maybe I have a different appreciation as an outsider for Pratt. I think he's a really amazing poet. I think it's too bad that he and Souster and Garner have fallen out of the canon perhaps.

ET: I'm still interested in the way writers are elevated at the university level when they sort of establish a canon. I had a good friend who was in Halifax and decided to do an M.A. This was a number of years ago. Would've been forties or fifties. She wanted to do her thesis on Hugh McLennan and her thesis adviser said, "No, no, no," ... he says, "No, you have to do it on Philip Grove."[18] Is anyone studying Philip Grove now? Not much. *Over Prairie Trails*, et cetera. It was just that in academe at that time, he was *the* Canadian writer. And he was an import, he was Scandinavian or something, wasn't he? I think so.

Vipasha: I think the definition of what is a quintessential Canadian writer changes a lot over the years. I think it's hard to pinpoint writers, and on syllabi there's differences, sometimes even year to year. Like, this is what we learned in the eighties; this is what we learned in the nineties. It's definitely interesting.

ET: I think Agatha has a good point, too, that there are some huge events in the country and after a while we sort of just say, "Oh, ho-hum." Like the building of the railways. Or the St. Lawrence Seaway. Or whatever it happens to be that might get into poetry. And then it just sort of dates, and you think, well we're sort of past that now. Or the Great War, or something like that.

Griffin: Margaret Laurence said something in her interview which struck me as very modern. You asked her about writing when she was living in Africa. And she talked about cultural appropriation and about taking someone else's voice and how you have to pay respect to the place that you're in, and not subvert a country's voice by using your own to try and mimic or duplicate. I think that's something that Canada especially is really grappling with, because we have so many different immigrant writers. Where does your voice come from? And it may be taking advantage of cultural minorities in a country to try to echo or reflect their experience. I was really blown away because it's from the sixties, and she's speaking about something that we're dealing with now. I thought that was really cool.

ET: It's a very good point. She sort of put a stopper on herself, didn't she? Like she said, "I won't write about Africa anymore."

Griffin: She said, "I've gone as far as I can go, and to go any further, I would take other people." So she said, "Okay, I'll go back to where I am from, and my story that I can share."

ET: Yes.

Amy: To bring that back to the tapes that you've created … in their own way, that's what many of them do, bringing in these other voices. You spoke about Morley Callaghan: you could tell sort of the Irish sense of humour you spoke of. Or when Layton discusses his childhood in the Montreal slum, the Jewish ghetto. You see these influences that they're bringing in, each of these authors. And you almost need to take all the tapes together, to get a sense of the Canadian voice. Because it's all these different strands of culture coming together.

ET: Yes. Another very strong point. Asking about religion or politics would've been a bit like asking somebody about their third divorce. I think with Richler, I just asked him, "Were there events in your life that got into your writing, or changed your writing, or influenced you or whatever?" And he said, immediately, "Well, I think the fact that I'm Jewish is enormously important. And Canadian." And it's the interface of those two, the interlocking of those two, or the tensions of those two, that are in his writing. So that was kind of interesting, the way it slipped in. The way, as you say, Margaret Laurence admitted to knowing that somebody like Chinua Achebe,[19] born in that part of Africa and writing out of it, would have a different kind of authenticity than she could have, than she possibly could have. Although I love her African stories. Has anybody read them? Yes, they're lovely.

Agatha: Who would you interview today? If you were to do the interviews today, who would you interview?

ET: I have interviewed her before, and while she's still with us, God love her, I would interview Alice Munro. I have one interview with her, which is, I think, a half-hour interview. She was lovely.

Amy: In what context did you interview Alice Munro? Tell us more about that.

ET: Oh, just about her work. How she grew up. I was at some literary function. I was sitting beside a woman who actually was from the same town as

Alice and knew about her background. Alice was from Wingham, Ontario. And she said, "Well," she said, "Alice was from the wrong side of the tracks." And she was, and she was proud of it. And she wrote about it. She made the wrong side of the tracks scintillating, if you will. Because, as you know, she lived just outside of Wingham, where there were bootleggers and people who had mink farms and that kind of thing. That's where Alice grew up. But she read an enormous amount and she said, "I always felt that reading was a way of escaping from my life." And I thought that's interesting. I'm from a rural community. I grew up on a farm. You can't get any farther into the country than that. And Alice's background was on the edge of a small town. So, I identify a lot with her people. I can recognize some of the people in her stories, the types of people, immediately. And I've always appreciated the fact that she is so honestly true to the people in that community. James Reaney was sort of the poet of southwestern Ontario. He really gave voice to that area in poetry. And he had this wonderful, ironic, satiric sense of humour. He wrote poems with speaking ducks, and speaking geese, and the country people, et cetera. And small-town folk. He said that Alice gave voice to southwestern Ontario. And I think she really did. If you went there now, and went to Wingham, I'm sure you'd recognize all sorts of things because Alice told you about them.

Geoff: Do you have any feelings about George Elliott Clarke's[20] poetry? I'm just thinking because he was just named the Parliamentary Poet Laureate. I don't know if you've met him or if you know his poetry at all.

ET: I've read him a bit. I haven't read him enough to really talk about it. But I like some of the things he's interested in. He's really interested in expanding the poetic art and people's approach to it and the availability of it. I think he will be a very good person in that job. It could be a gormless kind of job but I'm sure he will really make something electric out of it.

Agatha: So, thank you, Earle, so much. We've learned so much, all of us.

ACKNOWLEDGEMENTS

T his book could not have become a reality without the work, advice, efforts and patience of many collaborators, and I am deeply indebted to all of them. Among these, I would like to thank the following in particular: Dr. Earle Toppings, for his wise counsel and unwavering support of our work; Geoff Baillie, Amy Kalbun, Griffin Kelly, Vipasha Shaikh, the wonderfully talented undergraduates who made this project a reality and brought their enthusiasm, energy, and engagement to every page; Agatha Barc and Colin Deinhardt, Reader Services and Instruction Librarians, at the E.J. Pratt Library, Victoria University in the University of Toronto, who were always ready to guide the archival work; Andrew O'Handley who patiently and expertly read and reread the manuscript, and the editorial staff at Dundurn, who believed in the project from its initial stages.

I would also like to acknowledge and thank everyone listed below who gave generously of their time and expertise as this project developed: Lisa Sherlock, Chief Librarian, and Roma Kail, Head of Reader Services at E.J. Pratt Library, Victoria University in the University of Toronto; Douglas J. Fox, Systems Librarian, E.J. Pratt Library, Victoria University in the University of Toronto; the Northrop Frye Research Centre, Victoria College in the University of Toronto, and in particular its Director Prof. Robert Davidson and Alexandra Varela, its Coordinator; Prof. Angela Esterhammer, Principal of Victoria College in the University of Toronto; Ontario Institute for Studies in Education of the University of Toronto, and in particular Glen Jones (Dean) and Monique Flaccavento (Librarian); James McAdams, Technical support, Victoria College; Laurie O'Handley, Technical Support;

Prof. Jeffrey Heath, Prof. Sam Solecki, Prof. John O'Connor, James Deahl; Graeme Slaght, Copyright Outreach Librarian, Scholarly Communications and Copyright Office at the University of Toronto Libraries; Dean Allen, Transit Audio Services, the United Church of Canada; Thomas Fisher Rare Book Library (University of Toronto); William Ready Division of Archives and Research Collections, Mills Memorial Library, McMaster University, Hamilton, Ontario; Queen's University Archives, Queen's University, Kingston, Ontario, Archives and Research Collections Centre; Western Libraries, Western University, London, Ontario.

PERMISSIONS

Photograph of Raymond Souster is reproduced with the kind permission of Donna Dunlop.

Photograph of Miriam Waddington is reproduced with the kind permission of Jonathan and Marcus Waddington.

Photograph of Earle Toppings by Mark Tearle is reproduced with the kind permission of Victoria University Library Special Collections, Earle Toppings Collection, box 2, file 9.

POEM PERMISSIONS

Materials from the *Canadian Poets on Tape* and *Canadian Writers on Tape* series are used with the kind permission of the Ontario Institute for Studies in Education (OISE) of the University of Toronto.

Poetry read by Earle Birney is excerpted from *Selected Poems 1940–1966* by Earle Birney. Copyright © 1966 Earle Birney. Reprinted by permission of McClelland and Stewart, a division of Penguin Random House Canada Limited and also excerpted from *Rag & Bone Shop* by Earle Birney. Copyright © 1971 Earle Birney. Reprinted by permission of McClelland and Stewart, a division of Penguin Random House Canada Limited.

Poetry read by Irving Layton is excerpted from *The Collected Poems of Irving Layton* by Irving Layton. Copyright © 1971 Irving Layton. Reprinted by permission of McClelland and Stewart, a division of Penguin Random House Canada Limited.

Poetry read by Dorothy Livesay is included with the kind permission of the Estate of Dorothy Livesay.

Poetry read by Gwendolyn MacEwen is included with the kind permission of the Estate of Gwendolyn MacEwen.

Poetry read by Eli Mandel is included with the kind permission of the Estate of Eli Mandel.

Poetry read by Al Purdy is included as follows: "Percy Lawson" by Al Purdy, *Beyond Remembering: The Collected Poems of Al Purdy*, edited by Sam Solecki, 2000, Harbour Publishing, "Winter at Roblin Lake" by Al Purdy, *Beyond Remembering: The Collected Poems of Al Purdy*, edited by Sam Solecki, 2000, Harbour Publishing, "Hockey Players" by Al Purdy, *Beyond Remembering: The Collected Poems of Al Purdy*, edited by Sam Solecki, 2000, Harbour Publishing, "Home-Made Beer" by Al Purdy, *Beyond*

Remembering: The Collected Poems of Al Purdy, edited by Sam Solecki, 2000, Harbour Publishing, "The Drunk Tank" by Al Purdy, *Beyond Remembering: The Collected Poems of Al Purdy*, edited by Sam Solecki, 2000, Harbour Publishing, "About Being a Member of Our Armed Forces" by Al Purdy, *Beyond Remembering: The Collected Poems of Al Purdy*, edited by Sam Solecki, 2000, Harbour Publishing, "At the Movies" by Al Purdy, *Beyond Remembering: The Collected Poems of Al Purdy*, edited by Sam Solecki, 2000, Harbour Publishing, "The Sculptors" by Al Purdy, *Beyond Remembering: The Collected Poems of Al Purdy*, edited by Sam Solecki, 2000, Harbour Publishing, "On the Hellas Express" by Al Purdy, *Beyond Remembering: The Collected Poems of Al Purdy*, edited by Sam Solecki, 2000, Harbour Publishing, www.harbourpublishing.com.

Poetry read by James Reaney is included with the kind permission of the Estate of James Crerar Reaney.

Poetry read by F.R. Scott is included with the kind permission of the Estate of F.R. Scott.

Poetry read by Raymond Souster is excerpted from *The Years* (Ottawa: Oberon, 1971) and is included with the kind permission of Oberon Press.

Poetry read by Miriam Waddington is included with the kind permission of the Estate of Miriam Waddington.

All efforts possible were made to find copyright holders for the poetry and photographs in this volume, either previous publishers or the estates of the poets. The author and the publisher welcome any information enabling them to rectify any references or credits in subsequent editions. In some cases, the spoken poems differ from the printed versions. We have indicated where there are major changes and respected the spoken word in the case of minor changes.

NOTES

MARGARET LAURENCE (1926–1987)

1. Laurence was living in Penn, Buckinghamshire (near London), at the time of the interview.
2. Chinua Achebe (1930–2013), renowned Nigerian academic, poet, and writer.
3. Mordecai Richler (1931–2001), author also featured in *Canadian Writers on Tape*.
4. Morley Callaghan (1903–1990), author also featured in *Canadian Writers on Tape*.

MORLEY CALLAGHAN (1903–1990)

1. Sinclair Lewis (1885–1951), American playwright and novelist.
2. Award-winning film starring Dustin Hoffman and Jon Voigt (1969).
3. A novella by American author John Steinbeck (1937).
4. Joseph Conrad (1857–1924), a Polish-born British author best known for his novella *Heart of Darkness* (1899).
5. Arthur Waley (1889–1966), known for his translations of Chinese and Japanese poetry.
6. Ezra Pound (1885–1972), expatriate American poet.
7. Canadian Pacific Railway.
8. Helena Rubenstein (1870–1965), philanthropist and founder of a beauty empire.
9. Callaghan received the Royal Bank Award in June 1970.

10. Claude Bissell (1916–2000), cultural commentator, president of Carleton University (1956–1958), president of the University of Toronto (1958–1971).

11. Edmund Wilson (1885–1972), American critic who notably reviewed Callaghan in *O Canada: An American's Notes on Canadian Culture* (1965).

12. F. Scott Fitzgerald (1896–1940), American novelist and short-story writer.

HUGH GARNER (1913–1979)

1. A novel by Thomas Hughes, published in 1857.
2. F. Scott Fitzgerald (1896–1940), American novelist and short-story writer.
3. Department of Veterans Affairs.
4. Margaret ("Peggy") Blackstock, an editor at MacMillan.
5. A model residential Toronto neighbourhood built between 1952 and 1965, now no longer considered suburban.

HUGH MACLENNAN (1907–1990)

1. Published in 1942, the book won the Governor General's Award in the same year.
2. A highly controversial novel published by Smith in 1944, the story dealt with interracial romance.
3. Waldo Frank (1889–1967), well known for his contributions to various magazines, was a novelist and literary critic.
4. Edmund Wilson (1895–1972), American literary critic and author.
5. Theodore Spencer (1902–1949), American poet and academic.
6. Lewis Mumford (1895–1990), American urbanist, historian, and sociologist.
7. Refers to the conversion to Christianity of Paul the Apostle who, according to the New Testament of the Bible, was blinded on the road to Damascus by a vision of Christ.
8. Benjamin Spock (1903–1999), American pediatrician whose 1946 book *Baby and Childcare* changed North American attitudes to child rearing.
9. Clifton ("Kip") Fadiman (1904–1999), American writer, editor, and radio and television announcer.
10. Robertson Davies (1913–1995), eminent Canadian academic, playwright, and novelist.

11. Herbert Jonathan Cape (1879–1960), renowned independent British publisher.

12. *David Copperfield* (1850) by British author Charles Dickens (1812–1870). The focus of his novels was on contemporary social problems.

13. John Galsworthy (1867–1933), British author and playwright, winner of the Nobel Prize in Literature in 1932.

14. Eugene O'Neill (1888–1953), American playwright. He won the Pulitzer Prize for Drama four times and was awarded the Nobel Prize in Literature in 1936.

15. Empedocles (495–430 BCE), Greek philosopher living in Sicily.

16. Rebecca West (1892–1983), British author and journalist.

17. Senator Télesphore-Damien Bouchard (1881–1962), active in Quebec and Canadian politics and known for his attempts to reform the education system in Quebec.

18. Rodrigue Cardinal Villeneuve (1883–1947), dean of the Canon Law Faculty at the University of Ottawa; he became a cardinal in 1932.

19. One of the protagonists of *Two Solitudes*.

MORDECAI RICHLER (1931–2001)

1. Saul Bellow (1915–2005), author of the bestselling novel *Herzog* (1964), was a Canadian-American writer. He received the Nobel Prize for Literature in 1976.

2. George Plimpton (1927–2003) was an American journalist and author, also known for his sports writing.

3. Norman Podhoretz (b. 1930) is an American writer.

4. Norman Mailer (1923–2007), American author and playwright also renowned for his counter-cultural essays.

5. Brian Moore (1921–1999), a writer born in Northern Ireland who moved to Canada and then to the United States, he is known for his novels *Judith Hearne* (1955),which was then retitled *The Lonely Passion of Judith Hearne* (1956), and *The Luck of Ginger Coffey* (1960).

6. In 1974 the university was renamed Concordia when it merged with Loyola College.

7. George Orwell (1903–1950), British writer best known for his dystopic works *Animal Farm* (1945) and *Nineteen Eighty-Four* (1949).

8. An allusion to French writer Voltaire and his sarcastic dismissal of Canada, expressed in *Candide* (1758).

9. Published in 1971.

10. Greene (1904–1991) was an award-winning British novelist. *The Power and the Glory* was published in 1941, *Journey Without Maps* in 1936, *A Burnt-Out Case* in 1960. The travel book about Mexico is likely *The Lawless Roads* (1939) in which Greene describes his trip to Mexico.

11. This 1953 film by the Italian director Federico Fellini (1920–1993) narrates the story of five young Italian men in postwar Italy.

12. British dramatic romance released in 1945. Directed by David Lean, it tells the story of a woman whose life changes after her chance encounter with a stranger at a train station.

13. Richler's review of *Paper Lion,* titled "A Hero of Our Time," appeared in the *New York Review of Books*, February 23, 1967, issue.

14. A popular American radio comedy broadcast between 1935 and 1959.

15. Arthur Koestler (1905–1983), British journalist and writer born in Budapest, best known for his novel *Darkness at Noon.*

16. Allan Ginsberg (1926–1997), American Beat poet.

17. Sinclair Lewis (1885–1951), American playwright and novelist.

18. Dorothy Parker (1893–1967), American writer known for her work in numerous civil rights issues and much appreciated for her witticisms.

19. John Updike (1932–2009), American critic, poet, and novelist.

20. Anthony Burgess (1917–1993), British writer who excelled in numerous genres. He was also a composer. He is best known for his novel *A Clockwork Orange* (1962).

21. Perhaps he is referring to *Victorian Underworld* by Kellow Chesney, published in 1970.

SINCLAIR ROSS (1908–1996)

1. Edward McCourt (1907–1972), Canadian academic and novelist.

2. Pearl Buck (1892–1973), American writer, winner of the Nobel Prize in Literature in 1938.

3. Published in 1958.

4. Published in 1970.

5. Roy Daniells (1902–1979), teacher, poet, writer, and professor at the University of British Columbia.

6. The protagonist and his wife.

7. Walter Scott (1771–1832), Scottish historian and novelist. Highly influential among his European contemporaries, he devised and promoted the historical novel as a genre.

8. Charles Dickens (1812–1870), English novelist highly critical of Victorian society, which he described in novels such as *Oliver Twist* (1837) and *Great Expectations* (1860). Also known for his character Scrooge in *A Christmas Carol* (1843).

9. Joseph Conrad (1857–1924), Polish-born British author best known for his novella *Heart of Darkness* (1899).

10. Thomas Hardy (1840–1928), English novelist and poet. *Return of the Native*, his controversial sixth novel, was published in 1878.

11. Margaret Laurence, *Long Drums and Cannons* (Toronto: Macmillan of Canada, 1968), 10.

12. Likely *Sawbones Memorial*, which appeared in 1974.

13. F. Scott Fitzgerald (1896–1940), American novelist author of *The Great Gatsby*. The line is actually attributable to Budd Schulberg in his novel *The Disenchanted* (1950), whose protagonist is a fictional representation of Scott Fitzgerald. See *The Cambridge Companion to F. Scott Fitzgerald*, ed. Ruth Prigozy (Cambridge: Cambridge University Press, 2002), 16.

DOROTHY LIVESAY (1909–1996)

1. Ezra Pound (1885–1962), expatriate American poet.

2. Amy Lowell (1874–1925), American poet, Pulitzer Prize winner (awarded posthumously) who wrote in free verse and who based her work on the imagist movement. Vachel Lindsay (1879–1931), American imagist poet who advocated for poems to be sung. Carl Sandburg (1878–1967), beloved American poet and biographer who won three Pulitzer Prizes for his work.

3. Henry Havelock Ellis (1859–1939), British medical doctor, researcher, and writer whose studies on human sexuality made him a pioneer in the field. *Dance of Life* was published in 1923.

4. Edwin John Pratt (1882–1964) noted Canadian poet and professor at Victoria College in the University of Toronto.

5. Federico García Lorca (1898–1936), prominent Spanish poet and playwright.

6. Francisco Franco (1892–1975), rebel leader who became dictator of Spain after the Spanish government was overthrown during the Spanish Civil War (1936–1939).

7. Malcolm Lowry (1909–1957), English poet and novelist.

8. The final stanza differs from the published version.

9. The final two lines differ from the published version.

10. Kenneth Kaunda (b. 1924) was the first president of Zambia, serving from 1964–1991.

11. Pacifist Russian Spiritualist Christian group residing in communes in the western provinces of Canada. They gave rise to controversy when some members began protests through acts of arson and nude marches.

12. Alice Lenshina (1920–1978), self-proclaimed spiritual founder and leader of the Zambian Lumpa Church, a sect that combined Christian and Indigenous rituals. Her name, which Livesay writes as *Lenchina*, means "queen." Livesay refers to her as such, using the Latin equivalent, Regina.

13. Government office for the district.

14. In this recording the following lines have been omitted: "But again I was drawn / pulled by the hair / up into grey / half-morning."

GWENDOLYN MACEWEN (1941–1987)

1. Yuri Gagarin (1934–1968), Russian cosmonaut, became the first man to enter space on April 12, 1961.

2. Valentina Tereshkova (b.1937), Russian cosmonaut, became the first woman in space on June 16, 1963.

3. Canadian National Exhibition held in Toronto each August.

4. Mario Manzini, performing escape artist, magician.

5. Harry Houdini (1874–1926), renowned American illusionist and escape artist.

6. Published as "Dream Three: The Child."

7. Published as "Apollo Twelve."

AL PURDY (1918–2000)

1. A Canadian-built submachine gun first used in the Second World War at the Dieppe Raid (1942).
2. The bridge that connects the neighbourhood of Kitsilano in Vancouver to the city's downtown area.
3. Originally a French military plane built by Nord Aviation.
4. The term is no longer in use. The Indigenous peoples of Canada's North call themselves Inuit.
5. Fishing and hunting boats used in Canada's northern regions; the design originated in Peterhead (Aberdeenshire), Scotland.
6. A corrugated steel hut used in the Second World War, shaped in a half cylinder. Similar to a Quonset hut.
7. Published as "Eastbound from Vancouver."
8. A passenger plane of the 1960s.
9. In the printed version, the final line is replaced by: "and a block I can't tackle / pulls down the stars."
10. The printed version has: "which is really the other horse / the one that behaved itself all along." Al Purdy, *Sex & Death* (Toronto: McClelland and Stewart, 1973), 73.
11. The three preceding lines are not found in the printed version of the poem and are replaced by the following lines: "where old kings with purple carbuncles / doze fitfully thru a dream of trains."
12. In the printed version, the lines read: "Beyond the white village unfindable again / fields where cattle have traced a diagram / in snow of 24 hours of their lives."
13. This line is found in the spoken version only.
14. The printed text reads: "if I can just handle the difficult problem / of not being clever."
15. The printed text reads: "or Sumerian but it has always been foolish / to ask me questions in Greek."
16. In the printed text, the following line is inserted here: "the latest anonymous arrival."
17. Packaging material made from wood chips.
18. The following line is omitted from the spoken version: "there must be something."

19. Red Horner was an ice hockey defenceman for the Toronto Maple Leafs of the National Hockey League from 1928 to 1940.

EARLE BIRNEY (1904–1995)

1. A species of cedar tree found in eastern Afghanistan.
2. The Borden Company's iconic Elsie the Cow was presented as the "contented" cow in ads for their condensed milk products. These two lines do not appear in the printed version.
3. Earle Birney, "Like an Eddy," *grOnk* 4, no. 3 (November 1969), https://www.flickr.com/photos/48593922@N04/6877957791.
4. In the published version, these two lines are replaced by: "there are wheels that turn / on the tips of rubies / & tiny intricate locks."

F.R. SCOTT (1899–1985)

1. Now Air Canada.
2. CCF (Co-operative Commonwealth Federation), from which developed today's New Democratic Party.
3. In the published version, the final stanza reads: "Astonished, she asked him how he voted / in the last election / thinking she would discover his social awareness. / Without stopping to eat, he replied / "Conservative" / and by way of explanation added / "What have they ever done to hurt me?"

IRVING LAYTON (1912–2006)

1. Arthur Lower (1889–1988), Canadian historian and author of *Colony to Nation: A History of Canada* (1946).

MIRIAM WADDINGTON (1917–2004)

1. Ida Maze (1893–1962) was known for her support of Montreal's Yiddish cultural community. She was also a poet and writer.
2. John Sutherland (1919–1956), editor and poet, was a member of the Canadian modernist movement. He was Waddington's publisher and mentor. She later collected his work into *John Sutherland: Essays, Controversies and Poems* (1972).

3. A street in downtown Toronto.
4. Simon bar Kokhba led the revolts of the Jews against the Roman empire (132–135 CE)
5. Refers to the satirical text of the Papyrus Anastasi I (now in the British Museum) which warns travellers of dangers awaiting them. Waddington quotes from the text in the two italicized sections of this poem.
6. The Vistula is the longest river in Poland.
7. A large seventeenth-century park in Warsaw.
8. Frédéric François Chopin (1810–1849), Polish-born pianist and composer of the Romantic era.
9. This poem was published as "Lovers II."
10. Biblical reference to Abishag, the beautiful young woman given to King David as a servant.
11. Vladimir Lenin (1870–1934), Russian revolutionary; Karl Marx (1818–1883), philosopher and revolutionary, author of the *Communist Manifesto* (1848); Walt Whitman (1819–1892), influential poet and writer best known for his collection of free verse *Leaves of Grass* (1855); Geoffrey Chaucer (1343–1400), the father of English poetry, known for his *Canterbury Tales*; Gerard Manley Hopkins (1844–1889), British poet known for his invention and use of sprung rhythm; Archibald Lampman (1861–1899), Canadian poet known for his nature poetry.
12. A reference to the building on the campus of York University, Downsview, where Waddington taught. See Miriam Waddington, *The Collected Poems of Miriam Waddington: A Critical Edition*, vol. 2, ed. Ruth Panofsky (Ottawa: University of Ottawa Press, 2014).
13. The Volga, which flows through central Russia, is Europe's longest river.
14. Isaac Levitan (1860–1900), Russian landscape painter.
15. Anton Chekhov (1860–1904), Russian writer and playwright. He suffered from chronic tuberculosis (consumption).
16. Konstantin Stanislavski (1863–1938), theatre director and actor whose system influenced many American teachers of film acting.
17. Refers to the torture and murder of Lithuanian rabbis during the Holocaust of the Second World War.
18. A reference to the Assiniboine River, which runs through Manitoba and Saskatchewan.

19. *Call Them Canadians: A Photographic Point of View.* Produced by the National Film Board of Canada; Editor, Lorraine Monk; Poems, Miriam Waddington; Designer, Leslie Smart. Queen's Printer, 1968.

20. Henry Hudson (1565–1611), English explorer of Canada who searched for the Northwest Passage. Etienne Brulé (1592–1633), French navigator who explored Lake Huron, Georgian Bay, and the area around the Humber River watershed of Lake Ontario.

21. Charles Tupper Alexander (1821–1915), Alexander Tilloch Galt (1817–1893), Thomas Darcy McGee (1825–1868), George-Étienne Cartier (1814–1873), Ambrose Shea (1815–1905) are included among the Fathers of Canadian Confederation (1867), along with John A. Macdonald (1815–1891) who became the first prime minister. Henry Crout was a seventeenth-century British explorer who established a settlement in Newfoundland; Paul Ragueneau (1608–1680) was a Jesuit priest who became the Catholic religious leader of Quebec; Thomas Douglas Lord Selkirk (1771–1820) promoted the settlement of the Red River Valley by Scottish farmers.

RAYMOND SOUSTER (1921–2012)

1. Archibald Lampman (1861–1899), one of Canada's Confederation poets.

2. See readings by Waddington and Layton in this volume. Patrick Anderson (1915–1979) was a poet and professor. He also co-founded the collective of poets known as the Montreal Group. Louis Dudek (1918–2001) was a Canadian Modernist poet.

3. Ron Everson (1903–1992), Canadian poet who was also a lawyer and co-founder of Delta Books (Montreal). Michael Gnarowski (b. 1934), Canadian academic, literary critic, and poet.

4. Kenneth Patchen (1911–1972) was an American poet known for his experimental incorporation of other artistic genres into his poetry. Carl Sandburg (1878–1967), beloved American poet and biographer, winner of three Pulitzer Prizes for his work.

5. In 1968 Ray Washburn was the pitcher for the St. Louis Cardinals. Al Kaline played for the Detroit Tigers.

6. The poem recalls the humanitarian crisis reported by Western media during the Biafran War (also known as the Nigerian Civil War), 1967–1970.

7. This poem is available in spoken form only.

8. Likely Gaylord Powless (1946–2001) an outstanding player elected to the Canadian Lacrosse Hall of Fame.

9. Viet Cong.

10. Martin Luther King (1929–1968) was an activist and a leader of the American Civil Rights Movement. He was assassinated, as Souster writes, on April 4, 1968.

11. Mr. Johnson is Lyndon B. Johnson, U.S. president from 1963 to 1969.

12. San Juan Hills refers to the decisive battle that took place in July 1898 during the Spanish-American War. The USS *Maine* was an armoured cruiser that sank in battle during the explosion in Havana Harbor in 1898. United Fruit refers to the social unrest that surrounded the U.S.-supported overthrow of the government of Guatemala in 1954, which involved the United Fruit Company.

13. Refers to the War of 1812.

14. In the late 1860s, the American Irish Fenian Brotherhood, a secret Irish nationalist society working for Irish independence, raided Canadian territories.

15. Poet Allen Ginsberg criticized the United States in a poem of 1956 entitled "America." Souster here clearly shows Ginsberg's influence on his own thought and poetry.

16. Hart Crane (1899–1932), American modernist poet known for his book-length poem *The Bridge* (1930), inspired by the Brooklyn Bridge.

17. Robinson Jeffers (1887–1962), American poet known for his social criticism of the United States, particularly in his poem "Shine, Perishing Republic" (1925).

18. Refers to the stories of millionaire John D. Rockefeller, who gave only a dime as a tip for services.

19. Refers to the bombing of Dresden in February 1945 by American and British forces, an event often considered egregious and unjustified.

20. Expatriate American poet Ezra Pound (1885–1962) was held as prisoner first in Pisa and then in Boston's St. Elizabeth's Hospital largely because of his anti-American, pro-Hitlerian, and pro-Mussolinian views. *Usura* is the Latin form of usury, the practice of lending money at high interest rates. "With Usura" is the title of Canto XLV of Pound's *Cantos*.

354	LITERARY TITANS REVISITED

21. Souster refers here to Ezra Pound's booklet *America, Roosevelt and the Causes of the Present War* (1944), published first in Italian, which also deals with usury.

22. A reference to the Black Panthers of the 1960s, an American nationalist and socialist group of the far Left, fighting racial segregation.

23. Souster alludes to the many unjust treaties signed with various Indigenous American tribes.

24. Refers to the Vietnam War, which had begun in 1955 but escalated in the 1960s.

25. Souster alludes to the use of Agent Orange by American troops to defoliate the jungles of Vietnam. The herbicide was highly toxic and has had long-term detrimental effects on plants, animals, and humans.

26. Incinderjell (or incindergel), also known as napalm, is a highly flammable chemical preparation that causes severe burns. It was used in the Vietnam War by American troops.

27. Mohandas Gandhi (1869–1948) was the leader of the independence movement in India. In his work, he promoted peaceful civil disobedience. He was assassinated in 1948.

ELI MANDEL (1922–1992)

1. In Greek mythology, the maenads ("the raving ones") were the female followers of the god Dionysus.

2. John Donne (1572–1631), a clergyman and British metaphysical poet, known for his elegiac and satirical works. George Herbert (1593–1633), Welsh poet and Anglican cleric, known for his religious poems, some of which have become hymns.

3. Harry Houdini (1874–1926), renowned American illusionist and escape artist.

4. Mandel refers to "Ode on a Grecian Urn" (1819) by British Romantic poet John Keats (1795–1821).

5. William Butler Yeats (1865–1939), renowned Irish poet. He was awarded the Nobel Prize in Literature in 1923.

6. From *King Lear* (Act 4, Sc. 6): "Hark, do you hear the sea?" Mandel here also refers to "Sonnet. On the Sea" by English poet John Keats (1795–1821).

7. Marina, daughter of Pericles, appears in Shakespeare's *Pericles, Prince of Tyre*. Marina is also the title of one the Ariel poems by renowned American poet T.S. Eliot (1888–1965). It was published in 1930 with drawings by E. McKnight Kauffer. P.K. ("Pekay") Page (1916–2010) was a Canadian writer and poet, and an artist under the name P.K. Irwin.

JAMES REANEY (1926–2008)

1. An American comic strip that first appeared in 1897 and remains in syndication.
2. Reaney refers to the visit of the British monarchs to Stratford, Ontario, in May 1939. Shakespeare is a small village nearby.
3. The recording of this reading is taking place at the Ontario Institute for Studies in Education (OISE) in Toronto.
4. *Cantus firmus*: a pre-existing melody that provides the basis for a more complicated polyphonic arrangement.
5. John Beckwith (b. 1927), Canadian composer and pianist.
6. Canadian artist Jack Chambers (1931–1978) initiated the style often referred to as *perceptual realism*.
7. St. Hilda's is one of the residences for students of Trinity College, University of Toronto.
8. Kresge's was a department store chain.
9. This recited poem differs significantly from the published version.
10. This line is the final line of the first stanza for the published poem.
11. In the published version, the first line of this stanza reads: "But love and patience do quite change the scene."

AFTERWORD

1. Lorne Greene (1915–1987), Canadian actor and newscaster (his deep voice earned him the nickname "The Voice of Doom"); among his best-known roles were those in the television series *Battlestar Galactica* and *Bonanza*. He founded the Academy of Radio Arts.
2. American actor Bette Davis (1908–1989) was overlooked for an Academy Award for her role in *Of Human Bondage* (1934). The ensuing controversy resulted in major changes to how votes were cast and tabulated.

3. Peter Mansbridge anchored the CBC evening news from 1988 to 2017.

4. The Maple Leaf Poets, who were more commonly known as the Confederation Poets, were the four most prominent poets who wrote in the years immediately following Canada's Confederation in 1867: Bliss Carman (1861–1929), Charles G.D. Roberts (1860–1943), Archibald Lampman (1861–1899), and Duncan Campbell Scott (1862–1947). Some critics also include other contemporary poets in the group.

5. Billie Holiday (pseudonym of Eleanora Fagan, 1915–1959) was an American jazz singer and song writer.

6. Helen Creighton (1899–1989) collected folklore, particularly from Nova Scotia, including stories, songs, and ghost stories.

7. Kildare Dobbs (1923–2013), Canadian travel writer also known for his short stories.

8. Norman Snider (b. 1945), Canadian author and screenwriter for films including *Body Parts* and *Casino Jack*.

9. Robert Weaver (1921–2008) worked at the CBC as a producer and broadcaster, and used his shows to promote Canadian writers and writing. He was also the founder of the literary journal *Tamarack Review*.

10. Fats Waller (Thomas Wright Waller, 1904–1943) was an American jazz pianist and composer. Nellie Lutcher (1912–2007) was an American jazz singer.

11. Lorne Pierce (1890–1961) was editor-in-chief at Ryerson Press, much appreciated for his promotion and publication of Canadian writers.

12. Jack McClelland (1922–2004), president of Canadian publishing house McClelland and Stewart.

13. P.K. ("Pekay") Page (1916–2010) was a Canadian writer and poet, and an artist under the name P.K. Irwin.

14. Joyce Marshall (1913–2005), translator of Quebec authors, among whom was Gabrielle Roy; she was also an editor, an essayist, and a literary reviewer.

15. *The Double Hook*, a novel by Sheila Watson was published in 1959.

16. Joe Fiorito (b. 1948), newspaper columnist and novelist. While there is no park Toronto named for Souster, there is a commemorative plaque at the Souster Steps of Willard Gardens Parkette, a small park near Souster's residence.

17. E.J. (Edwin John) Pratt (1882–1964), academic and award-winning poet known for his poetical volume retelling the story of the Jesuits in seventeenth-century Canada, *Brébeuf and His Brethren* (1940).

18. Born in Prussia and raised in Germany, Frederick Philip Grove (1879–1948) was an award-winning novelist whose works often focused on the prairies.

19. Chinua Achebe (1930–2013), renowned Nigerian academic, poet, and writer.

20. George Elliott Clarke (b. 1960), Canadian playwright and poet, became Canada's Parliamentary Poet Laureate in January 2016.

INDEX